141437 – SPAD OF COL. JOHNSON – SECOND PURSUIT GROUP

Wooden Crates & Gallant Pilots

by

Stuart E. Elliott

DORRANCE & COMPANY
Philadelphia

Permission to reprint "Whom the Gods Love" in Chapter 26 granted by the *Ladies Home Journal.*
ISBN 0-8059-1911-2
Library of Congress Catalog Card Number: 73-85342
Printed in the United States of America

To the Order of Daedalians,
and to the Order of World
War One Overseas Flyers.

CONTENTS

FOREWORD

Wooden Crates and Gallant Pilots, by Stuart E. Elliott, presents a highly interesting, personalized picture of the life of an aviator during World War I, from the time he started his training, to the Armistice on November 11, 1918, when he was a fighter pilot on the front in France.

We have had several glamorized compilations of events in the combat careers of the great air aces of that period, with blow-by-blow descriptions of the deeds of those heroes, but this has been the first story to appear that tells of the humor, the pathos, the tragedies and some of the frustrations in the daily lives of these early flyers of World War I.

When the United States declared war on Germany on April 6, 1917, the adventurous youth of this country could see only one branch that appealed to them. A mixture of patriotism, the lure and challenge of the unknown, and perhaps some of the old-fashioned pioneer spirit of their ancestors, all contributed to the urge to take part in what, in those early days, was looked upon as the great adventure. They had heard that the physical and educational requirements were stringent, that the casualties in training were high, and that, if they eventually reached the front, the odds were decidedly against living more than a few weeks at best. With the glorious optimism of youth, and the unshakable belief that Americans are innately smarter than other people, they easily dismissed these stories, and decided they would not repeat the mistakes of the French and the British. They were bound to be better shots and better flyers than the Germans, so what was there to worry about. It was war, and certainly there would be casualties, but each one said to himself, "It won't be me." They hurried to the nearest examining board, submitted their college degrees as evidence of their educational and intellectual qualifications, passed their physical tests, signed on the dotted line as privates in the Signal Enlisted Reserve Corps, and started the first phase of their training in what was then called Ground School. There had been some talk of their having the status of a cadet—a sort of hybrid rating between master sergeant and second lieutenant—but nobody asked any questions. They just wanted to get going.

Here for the first time they came into official contact with regular officers of the army they had just become a part of. Coming from the best colleges in the country, most of them superbly conditioned athletes, bubbling over with real patriotism, and burning with a desire to get to the front and help win the "War For Democracy," they rather expected to be welcomed into the fold. The idea of discipline had not bothered them. They had anticipated that part of it. Of course there would be discipline on the ground and in the air, obedience to orders, respect for superiors, and all the other qualifications to be expected from members of a real military organization.

To their shocked surprise however, the first words of their commanding officer seemed to show a curious resentment that they were to become officers during the next four or five months. They were reminded that *he* had spent four years at the military academy, and that it was practically impossible in four months to make them into officers that would be a credit to the uniform, but he and his staff would do their damnedest. In the meantime, they were not to forget, that while they might call themselves cadets, they were actually privates in the army, and would be treated as such. They got the impression that their commander would like to keep them as privates for the duration of the war, and that maybe he hoped for excuses not to graduate them to the next stage, which would be the flying training they were really after.

A few weeks after joining, the local tailors had fitted some of them with uniforms that were made of much better cloth than the government-issue stuff. Furthermore, these uniforms fitted, which greatly distinguished them from the mismated garments the army supply sergeants had given them. The "cadets" admired their new soldierly appearance in the glass, and decided that at the next inspection even the commandant would be pleased. Once again their hopes were dashed. It was not enough that the accident of war had so interfered with orderly processes of the army, that they were being made officers far too quickly, but here they were insulting his rank, by wearing uniforms of the same cloth as his own. He did not say what would happen if he ever saw them wearing them again, but they noticed during the next few weeks that the cadence of the endless close-order drills was considerably stepped up, and inspections were much more frequent, than before they had incurred their commander's displeasure.

In a way it was probably good for them. They deeply resented such treatment, but decided they could take anything the army dished out. They were going to become aviators and shoot down Germans, and no one was going to stop them. The indignities that followed them in flying school did not seem so serious, after their initiation during the first six weeks of ground school.

A really serious consequence, however, was the implanting in the minds of these budding aviators a deep conviction, that all regular army officers, especially the "Kiwis" or nonflyers, were a sadistic bunch of narrow-minded, pompous tyrants, who deep down inside wished that the airplane had never been invented. It did not fit into the bible called Army Regulations, and it was needlessly complicating the ancient and honorable profession of arms.

While these impressions should not have applied, except to a small and rather stupid minority, they nevertheless persisted during the war, and they were retained by the majority of those who returned to civil life after the conflict was over. Nor can all the fault for this attitude be charged to the cadets. They and their branch were looked upon as interlopers in the business of warfare. No wonder that they resented being told with unnecessary frequency "to be soldiers first and aviators afterwards." It is even understandable that one of their improvised wartime songs assigned to General Pershing the remark, "They ain't worth a damn for soldiers, so put them in the Flying Corps."

The cadets were good sports, however. No matter how much they disliked conditions encountered, there was no bitterness involved. They might gripe among themselves, but they philosophically accepted all rules, regulations and wartime restrictions placed upon them, in the manner of good soldiers since the beginning of time, ignoring or evading them when they could get away with it, and learning to live fairly contentedly after all.

The author's pictures of the preliminary flying training in the United States, and the advanced training in France, prior to being sent to the front, are particularly vivid. The book will be of interest to early flyers of World War I days, but the Air Force veterans of World War II will recognize many of the old mistakes that were repeated in the 1940s. For the generations since World War II, there is still the charm of a well-written, factual narrative by an author who knows what he is writing about. It is his story, and he was there.

George C. Kenney
General, USAF Ret.

Ret.

Chapter 1
BACKGROUND

At this stage, 1972, of our nation's history, the United States Air Force is unquestionably our country's and the entire free, noncommunist world's first line of defense against its powerful enemies, although progress in missiles, satellites, and atomic submarines may eventually change the picture. Whatever the future, the United States Air Force, not only a major cause of Allied victory in World War II, and the chief deterrent to a general Communist attack thereafter, is still the right bower of Christian civilization, and of a way of life for the average man far better than ever before. Nevertheless, this great air force, immensely vast and complex, highly technical and scientific, of huge political potential, enormously expensive, and far flung over the globe, is only a few years over sixty-some years old, if one accepts the year 1907 as its birth year.

For all effective purposes, the real birth year of our air arm was a good ten years later, not until 1917, after we had declared war on Kaiser William II's empire of Germany. Up until then, our military aviation had been no more than a tiny section of the Army Signal Corps, with a handful of commissioned pilots, a few hundred mechanics and enlisted men, and a very few, primitive for even those days, rickety airplanes, for which there was generally scanty gasoline available. In addition to being puny and neglected, this embryo of an air force was generally regarded as a freakish frill by most army officers, and early pilots were looked on as so many eccentrics, who had somehow managed to get through West Point and were thereby in the family, but who were just the same *nuts*, who might as well crack up and break their necks in those "ha-ha" flying machines, since they undoubtedly lacked what it took to become real, serious officers, future colonels, even possible generals. To most West Point graduates and our regular army officers, military aviation ranked about one jump ahead of ballet as a military function, and even after the war started, it took months of great growth and expansion, before the army took aviation seriously. Even then some of the older officers never got over a *set opinion* that flying was for the birds, and that pilots were a lot of unweaned brats who should be handed a rifle, stuck in the trenches, given severe discipline, and "Now, no more nonsense, you men!"

Fortunately, in spite of army prejudice, Congress and the American public took our aviation seriously, even enthusiastically, and with that blessing and the all-important appropriations, our aviation grew in one year and a few months from babyhood to young manhood, from a little regarded experiment to a force that contributed a considerable share to the Allied victory in World War I. It is concerning that period of our air force that this book is written.

To be understood, this book is not primarily about great air aces, with detailed stories of their air battles and victories, their total scores and records, the knowledge of which is so important to the public. All that has been written in many books and articles, although most of the authors, with exceptions of Elliott White Springs, William Bishop, Charles Codman and some others, never flew combat in that war, and have only second-hand information. Many such authors not only fail to grasp the atmosphere and total picture of those days, but they also tend to gross exaggeration and distortion. In a vague way, the public knows the score of the great aces in World War I, just like it knows the homerun record of Babe Ruth, the winning races of Man of War or Citation, the grand slam of Bobby Jones, and such. The public, always fascinated by figures, as if they alone were the key to truth, knows a lot of records, but they know little of the life and training of a major leaguer, of the life on the racing track's backstretch, or the years of preparation needed, and the frustrations and politics that play so large a part in important sporting activities. In the same way, they know little of the background story of our military aviation, nor how it first was developed. This book tries to tell a part of that story by recounting the experiences of a more or less typical trainee and combat pilot during the period 1917-1919, describing the early training methods and flying fields, recounting combat methods, organization, front-line tactics and routine of pursuit squadrons,

"When a pilot had to wear boots and spurs, and to know how to present arms with a sword."

and describing the appearance and characteristics of various planes then in use, whether Jenny, Niewport, Spad, Camel, Breguet, Farman, Caudron, Voisin, Salmson, Liberty and others of those early models, all of which I flew on some duty or other.

Through many incidents, some trivial, some of more moment, some somber, some gay, this is an attempt to recapture the general atmosphere of America's World War I aviation as it really was, and not as the sensational exaggeration of some fiction writers, nor as some of the glossed over and deceiving official documentaries, released for propaganda purposes. Being a first-hand account, much of this has to be personal reminiscence, but all written here could well be the story of any contemporary combat pilot, for the setting and background, as well as the forces governing our lives, were much the same for all of us. All of a war is not necessarily found in official documents and the papers of important personages, and the personal diary of some private who fought under General Grant or General Lee might bring out interesting aspects of the Civil War not found in any serious history. This work attempts such an account, through the recollections of a run-of-the-mill, *flying lieut* of that era, who at least saw and experienced quite a bit.

In summary, military flying was then a very individual business as compared with today's flying, much as individualistic action in the Trojan War compare with modern army tactics. The flyer was then free while flying, in the sense that the old-time cowboy was free on the range from close supervision. Today's pilot has some Big Brother always breathing over his shoulder, and he is never away from the voice of superior authority. This suits modern conditions, but a Daniel Boone could never have stood being a modern pilot. There would have been much too much regulation, and he would have found too *damn many people in the flying contraption, anyhow.* However, a Daniel Boone type might have accepted flying conditions in those long past years, when planes were crates, engines as uncertain as a mule's behavior, and an airborne flyer was free as a bird to choose his flight route and level, and like an old-time sea captain he was master of his vessel, even if once again on the ground, he might have to wear boots and spurs, and know how to present arms with a sword.

Chapter 2

WAR DECLARED

On April 6, 1917, the sovereign United States of America in full Congress assembled, having a fairly respectable navy, a small army containing not one organized, trained and equipped division, and just about the merest fetus of an air force, declared war on Germany. At this date, over two and one half years after the start of World War I, and long after Germany, England, and France had developed large and powerful air forces, we the richest nation in the world, the nation whose native sons, the Wright brothers, had first made motored flight a reality, had but one puny section of its Army Signal Corps for military aviation, which section had about 48 officers, and around 1300 enlisted men. This Signal Corps section had possibly two hundred obsolete and unarmed airplanes, a very few small flying fields, which were not much more than converted cow pastures, and thirty-five more or less trained military aviators. Of these pilots only six had any advanced training, and not one had any experience with guns or airplane bombing. In spite of the increasing daily lesson from the news in Europe, the War Department had done the absolute minimum to build up military aviation, but it had spent much of the taxpayers' money on numerous cavalry regiments.

At this time a graduate of Harvard University, I was studying at the Massachusetts Institute of Technology, and having a struggle with one subject in particular. This was thermodynamics often referred to as *thermogoddamics* by the students, and the approaching rigorous final examination loomed before me, very much like the prospects of a tumbrel ride to the guillotine in the thoughts of an old-regime aristocrat.

Going to war seemed a lesser evil than that examination, but not war as a private fighting on foot. I thought it over. There was a good chance of being admitted to the Officers' Training Camp at Plattsburgh, New York, but that meant a probable assignment to the infantry. There was also a welcome-back to Troop B of the

National Guard Cavalry of Massachusetts, where I had previously attained the high dignity of being a corporal, before terminating an enlistment. However, the cavalry, highly enjoyable and good for the body as that most gentlemanly outfit had been during many summer encampments and field maneuvers, seemed to have become an anachronism in this new age of airplanes, machine guns, tanks and barbed wire. There was also the navy for consideration, but it seemed to promise less action in this war than the army. Besides, although I had been raised with boats and salt water since childhood, I had given up wearing sailor suits at the age of eight, and for a grown man they seemed silly. There remained aviation.

Unlike many who had been talking about it, I had had no burning urge to fly. Several years previous, in 1911 I think, I had seen an Englishman named Claude Graham-White fly something like a chickencoop over Boston Harbor and around Boston Light. Soon after he had married a famous musical comedy star, generally known as the Pink Pajama Girl, and had vanished into the blue, probably around London. Since then I had seen no airplanes either in flight or on the ground and, except that it was regarded as very dangerous, I knew nothing about aviation.

However, for some time, I had been aware of a lot of talk about military flying. Friends who had been serving as drivers with the American Ambulance Service in France, came back with tales of air combats they had witnessed at the front, and of famous flyers they had met, members of the American Escadrille Lafayette. Some of the latter I knew, for I had attended prep school with Victor Chapman, and I had been acquainted with Norman Prince, Elliot Cowdin and several others of that brilliant and heroic group. By now over half the original Lafayette had been killed in action, but other Harvard or Tech friends had taken some military flying training. Among these early birds had been my cousin, Quentin Roosevelt, who with some twenty others had just completed primary flying training at the army's field at Mineola, Long Island.

Here seemingly was the solution, if the choice lay between war and that dreaded examination. The infantry, the *poor bloody infantry* as the British referred to it, meant mud and bunions, the cavalry was on its way to join the legendary Elephant Corps of

"had given up sailor suits at the age of eight, and for a grown man they seemed silly."

ancient Carthage and the vanished, spear-armed impis of the Zulus, the navy was for those who like tin boats and kiddie suits, but the flyer was the fair-haired, plumed knight of modern warfare. Flying was something very new, very mysterious, and very exciting. It was an esoteric art that combined sport and war, such as formerly did the cavalry. Now overnight, flying became the thing to do, the *dernier cri*, the military service most *veddy veddy swell* of all who considered themselves dashing young bloods of spirit and fashion. That was the atmosphere, and since few I knew had inferiority complexes or had ever heard of that later much overused expression, it suddenly seemed that half my friends were planning to get into aviation.

On looking into it, the path to military aviation did not seem to be wide open. With a very few exceptions one had to have a college degree, and one had to pass a special and very rigorous physical examination. It also occurred to me that one might well do with a little influence, or at least an acquaintanceship with some officer on the selection board, if one were to be chosen for training in the early cadres, from among the thousands of equally qualified candidates. As in all things, democracies, monarchies, or even getting past the Pearly Gates probably, whom one knew seemed most important; so, recalling an old family friend, who was more or less a human key to much in Washington, I was able to get a short interview with Major General George Squier, the brilliant electrical engineer and chief of the Signal Corps, under which branch came military aviation.

General Squier was kind, but he was a very busy man, and I sensed he was pretty bored with interruptions by the sons of friends of congressmen or other important personages, who wanted to fly and knew nothing about it. Taking his advice but not expecting to hear anything for months, I sent in my application. Within a very few days, while staying at the New York Harvard Club, I was notified by the War Department to repair to Boston, and there to enlist without delay in the Aviation Signal Corps, U.S. Army. Then, provided I passed the routine test, I was to report to the Navy Yard, Portland, Maine, for the special physical examination for pilot candidates.

With a whoop I crammed my dirty shirts and belongings into an old portmanteau, told Dan the elevator man, who knew every member's name on sight, that I was off to the wars, ordered drinks and told some dozen friends at the bar. Then I had my car brought from the garage, and was soon rolling up Fifth Avenue, headed for the Bronx and the south end of the old Boston Post Road, on a night drive to Bean Town. The daytime bustle and traffic had dwindled, the great street was quiet and all but deserted, and at that time there were no traffic lights to delay. Soon I was passing the little square, from across which gleamed the lights and glitter of the then hotel of all hotels in America, the Plaza. It was there then just as now, and so is General Sherman with Victory leading his horse, but there is no longer the vast Vanderbilt mansion, a French chateau with its entrance drive, its port-cochère, and its own little park right in the fashionable heart of Manhattan. Like in *Gone with the Wind*, this war would bring about great changes, and the social and economic broom was being fashioned that would ultimately sweep out most of the old and truly elegant way of life from America and Europe.

In the spring of 1917, motoring from New York to Boston was not the easy four- to five-hour run that it is today. There were no parkways, freeways, nor eight-lane, strip-divided toll roads. Seven to eight hours between New York's Fifty-Ninth Street and Boston's Copley Square was good going, for the environs of cities and larger towns had miles of cobblestoned streets that were crowded with horse-drawn drays and slow, ponderous wagons, and bisected with trolley tracks that often gave little room for a car to squeeze between the trolley cars and the curb.

As to the Boston Post Road, most of that venerable highway, then the shortest and principal link between the two cities, was not much better than in the days of the stagecoach. True, it was paved, but it was narrow with no bypasses around the towns, and the roadway was filled with sharp curves, right-angle turns, detours, frost pittings, and holes and bumps in the macadam that were hard on tires and could ruin a pair of springs in a day's run. As to tire, they were more expensive than today, and five thousand miles was a lot to get out of the best tires, under the best of road conditions. On that night's journey, my not too new set of tires, including two old spares, suffered three blowouts, and several punctures. There was even one more, but that was to my bank balance.

My car, the pride and joy of my life, was a secondhand 1913

National, an open roadster with two bucket seats, a brass, deep honking French horn operated by a rubber squeezer, and one of the first lefthand drives in America. It had a big four-cylinder engine that could hurtle it eighty miles an hour on a long straightaway, and it had an electrical starter, one of the earliest ever manufactured. As to the starter, it could and did work intermittently, but there was also a hand crank that always worked, come rain or shine, or frost or gloom of night, come even hell or high water, provided one had patience, control of temper, know-how, cunning, courage, caution, a squirtcan of gas to prime the pet cocks of the cylinders, and above all plenty of muscle and unlimited endurance. I had the latter, having developed them through many years of cranking small but very perverse, make and break, marine auxiliary motors, while becalmed in Vineyard Sound and Nantucket waters. Despite starting troubles, my car was faster and more powerful than most cars of those days, and it was rakish and poetically disreputable looking, like a fast, rake-masted pirate schooner of the early nineteenth century. It was no sober, hard-working married man's car with conforming respectability written over it, but one for adventure and excitement, a bus that made one feel like a mixture of Lord Byron and D'Artagnon. It was a car for a rebel, a questioner of customs and authority, and in some ways it was symbolic of the way of thinking of most World War I military aviators, a dreadful group of heretics in the eyes of most of the old and holy regular army.

My tires were not new; I drove as fast as the road allowed; and punctures and blowouts arrived at regular intervals after passing New London. After the third mishap, with no more spares, and with no place open to make repairs nor purchase a new one at that late hour, I had to proceed on one bare steel rim. Finally, around midnight, somewhere on a completely deserted Hope Valley Road in the most Godforsaken part of Rhode Island, I was reduced to four naked rims and a speed of fifteen miles an hour. Being a good seventy miles from the cultural Hub of the universe, I stopped to sleep by the roadside, under a high bank on which was situated a long-abandoned country mansion. This was now a home for flitting bats and hooting owls, where broken panes reflected the gibbous moonlight, and ancient doors and decrepit shutters creaked and groaned as they swung in the occasional night breezes. It was a most Charles Addamsish setting and a proper place for a black thing to peer from, but today it is the location of a neon-lighted bar and motel, and the only bad spirits are its martinis. However, between my stopping and sunrise, not one headlight gleamed along the highway, although the route was the most direct between two big cities.

At six the next morning, I was off again, creeping along on four steel rims that sounded like grindstones on the hard road's surface, when somewhere off Greenwich I saw a farmer leaning over a fence rail, and inquired of him where and when I might buy some tires and tubes. Further talk revealed to him that I was on my way to enlist in the army and to become a flyer, and on learning this my tall, lean friend showed much interest, and he volunteered to take me to a friend, who would open up shop on our arrival, and supply any want for my car. This he did, and more, for he vouched for my character and financial responsibility, so that the country garage keeper took my check, and supplied me with new tires. As such were large and most expensive, even as tires cost in those days, this garage keeper may have seemed overtrusting concerning a complete stranger. However Frank, the farmer, had vouched for me, and the garageman said, "Frank's never mistook about a man."

Reequipped, I drove Frank back to his farm, and met his entire family, which consisted to two grown sons, both as tall and rawboned as their father. It was now about seven-thirty, and Frank suggested I might like some breakfast. Hungry, I agreed, and one of the lanky sons disappeared into the kitchen. Presently he called us in, where we found chairs set at the bare boards of a rough table.

Breakfast was no namby-pamby, orange juice, soft-boiled eggs, toast and coffee abortion, fit for only a modern, soft and diet-conscious generation, but a morning meal for pioneer heroes able to whip their weight in wildcats, or those minutemen who made the lobsterbacks of King George run all the way from Concord to Boston. It consisted of four very hard boiled eggs apiece, an eight-ounce tumbler filled to the brim with straight bourbon whiskey, and a bottle of beer for a chaser. This, said Frank, was their regular breakfast, and it was the best one he knew to set a man up, and give him strength and energy for a good morning of spring ploughing.

I lingered over the last egg and potent drop, while Frank hitched up his team of powerful Missouris for the morning's work. "You don't have to go Harvard to know how to fly a couple of mules," he said to me with a wink, for I had told in conversation that a would-be military flyer was supposed to have a college education. We then said goodbye and good luck, and I left this scene of true hospitality, feeling like a balloon that was about to tear from its moorings. On the remaining ride to Boston, it sometimes seemed that the car had taken off from the road and was flying. I finally arrived safe and sober, but to this day I remain highly impressed with that kind of Rhode Island farm breakfast.

In the latter half of May 1917, almost seven weeks after we had declared war but had done little or no fighting, I enlisted at Boston. In the scrubby little recruiting office somewhere off Scollay Square, another candidate and I took the oath, and the regular army physical test. This latter included weight, with a certain required maximum and minimum according to a man's inches. My companion, who was tall but rather on the slender side, seemed somewhat worried. "I'm afraid I'm a bit underweight," he whispered.

The sergeant had left the waiting room, and there were no witnesses. "A pint's a pound the world around." I indicated the water cooler. Hastily my friend gulped down ten glasses.

All might have gone well, except that a short pompous major burst in, bustled across the floor with that walk of an adjutant on parade, demanded to see the doctor, and was admitted to the inner sanctum. A half-hour passed, then three-quarters. My friend looked uncomfortable, muttered and fidgeted. Finally after an ages-long additional ten minutes, the steatopygic major strutted out, and the medical lieutenant waved us in. We entered, my friend wearing a distressed expression.

There were more minutes while we were stripped, weighed, thumped, measured, and otherwise examined. Finally the doctor indicated the usual little bottles. My friend groaned. "That little pint!" His face was pallid, and he seemed on the verge of dancing the Charleston, although that dance had not yet been invented.

No doubt the doctor had known of similar weight-adding tricks. "It's on the left," he said drily. When my friend returned, the doctor and the sergeant were laughing.

Despite apprehensions, we both passed the physical, but the sergeant, although gruffly friendly, professed he could not make out our use to the army. "I've sworn in hundreds of ordinary recruits, and I've sent them on to the fort to learn their left foot from their right, but you two are different." He tapped his teeth with a pencil, and regarded us quizzically. "What are you, anyhow? Regular recruits, who may become good, dumjohn soldiers, the backbone of our country's defense? Not from your orders. You're new specimens. You're a pair of college pine-apples, who are going to become aviators. So it's the birds and the bees, and the likes of you who will be cluttering up the free air of heaven, and that's it. Well, boys, I wish you luck. But God save the United States Army!"

That sergeant, I soon found out, just about summed up most of the old, regular army's opinion of the new branch of the service, except that he was less disdainful than many. We soon found out that most old soldiers regarded aviation as a crackpot frill, a waste of the army's time and money.

The army, as usual having less money and poorer facilities than the more politically favored navy, had neither the trained personnel nor the establishment to give the *new-fangled* tests for flying fitness, so the Portland Navy Yard had set up the operation. There, the new aviation physical tests, except that they lacked the many modern electrical measuring devices, all with their flashing and blinking lights, were basically much like today's examinations for pilot candidates. They included depth perception, balance, speed of reactions, and quickness of recovery after having been jerked around and spun in a device that was supposed to simulate a plane doing acrobatics. The eye and ear tests, which included the peculiar, to us, injection of belladonna, were as rigorous as today's, but to us they seemed amazing.

The need for perfect vision was obvious, but why, we wondered, was there such insistence on perfect hearing. What difference did acute ears make to a flyer? In those open-plane cockpits with wide-open engine, one could not hear oneself screaming. This aviation physical, so routine and taken for granted today, seemed to us somewhat inexplicable and a bit *nutty*, some sort of a jolly game for the doctors, but perhaps quite in keeping with all the deep mysteries of flying.

Chapter 3

THE MAKING OF A PILOT

In the latter part of May 1917, having readily passed the elaborate tests for flying training, I was admitted to the School of Military Aeronautics, at the Massachusetts Institute of Technology. This preliminary ground school, one of eight that had been very rapidly organized and set up since our declaration of war, was situated in the west wing of the institute's huge, sprawling, and semiclassic-looking building, that overlooked the Charles River Basin from the Cambridge side, and I was a member of its initial cadre of twenty-five pilot candidates.

Among former friends in this first cadre, were two destined to fame; Hamilton Coolidge and Douglas Campbell, the latter the son of a famed astronomer, who was then the head of the Lick Observatory, and later president of the University of California. Both Ham Coolidge, a gentleman of character and innate nobility if anyone is to be so described, and Doug Campbell had been Harvard first string football men, in those now incredible days, when Harvard was actually a terror to most football opponents, and both were destined to be listed among our famous and earliest aces. As I recall it, Doug Campbell became the very first American-trained pilot to become an ace, even before Eddie Rickenbacker. This feat possibly spoiled his chances of ending up our ace of aces, for soon after shooting down his sixth German plane, he was sent back to the United States to be exhibited, to help promote the sale of Liberty Bonds, and to serve as a battlewise instructor.

Among others whom I clearly recall, were Robert Moore, who survived a lacerating burst of enemy machine-gun bullets to become a very big hotel-chain tycoon, and Gustave Kissel, William Sterns, James Miller, William Ely, Bartlett Bacon and Edward Bates. There was also John Mitchell, not the same John Mitchell who flew with Rickenbacker to become a squadron commander and a prominent ace, but the tall, ruggedly handsome, possibly either cousin or younger brother of famed General William Mitchell, a very fine fellow, unfortunately killed too early in a crash in France. There were others too and famous, but of them later.

On our arrival at ground school, we were one by one summoned to the commandant's office for a special looking over and interview by the Director of the United States Schools of Military Aeronautics. This proved to be a very formal audience, and if conducted with the intention to impress the flying candidate with the gravity of his path ahead, and also the sanctity of his higher superiors, in my case it did.

Our supreme director, as well as organizer of all army aviation ground schools, was Lieutenant Colonel Hiram Bingham, Yale professor, archeologist-explorer, author and, after the war, United States senator from Connecticut. Colonel Bingham was a very tall, slim, handsome and distinguished-looking, but outwardly chilly officer, who seemed to gaze down on us from such Olympian heights of rank (in World War I, a lieutenant colonel was a rare and impressive rank in aviation) and intellectual preeminence, that most of us felt overwhelmed in his presence. Few big wheels escape being nicknamed by those under them, and our chief was soon referred to as Holy Hiram, or the Living Presence of God by the more irreverent cadets. However, save for periodic and awe-inspiring inspections, and a few very dignified addresses and admonitions, we saw little of our director.

We did, however, frequently encounter our school's immediate commanding officer. This junior pope was a guaranteed, gold-plated, whip-snapping, fire-breathing West Point shave-tail with the temporary rank of captain, who seemed to have religious convictions as to the original sin inherent in ex-civilian reservists, and especially semidisciplined, militarily uncouth young graduates of mere civilian universities. With this very severe young captain, who was no older than most of us, the shortest way with any Harvard, Yale, or like whippersnappers, was to give them very short rope, and plenty of squads right, and lectures on military courtesy.

All this was to be expected, but we were also to be always addressed in a very stern manner, to be jerked up short for the most minute deviation in conduct, bearing, or regulations, and to be duly reminded that we were *NOW IN THE ARMY!;* that we

"a genuine gold plated,
fire breathing,
West Point shavetail —"

ranked well below any private second class of the rear rank, even *yardbird* of the *REGULAR ARMY;* and above all that compared to that Brahmin of military Brahmins, a certified graduate of the holy institute at West Point, we were just nothing, and no better than a bunch of peasants out of Upper-Lower Slobovia, had those extremely oafish nitwits of Al Capp's famed satirical comic strip been then invented.

Many months later, I again encountered this Captain Benjamin W. Mills, and found him surprisingly mellowed and much broadened, and a first-class officer, who took good care of all under his command, but I left his office after a first interview with the impression that I had encountered an alligator-snapping turtle, and that his strong, white, West Point teeth held torn fragments from the seat of my breeches. On entering his lair, I had not forgotten to salute, to report in a military manner, to stand at attention and say, "Sir!", and I had not been reported for any infraction. However I was I, another typical recent civilian, a benighted being reared outside the true and glorious traditions of the Holy Regular Army, and this chewing out was for the salvation of my soul, or as the legendary, marine top sergeant said, as he lined up and methodically walloped each newly arrived recruit on the jaw, "This, punk, is just for nothin'!"

Today's aspirants for a pilot's rating and a commission are designated cadets, and occupy some kind of temporary bastard status between an enlisted man and an officer. We did not. Officially we were ordinary buck privates of the Aviation Section, Signal, Enlisted Reserve Corps, and as such we drew thirty dollars a month, which pay rate had, not long before, been raised from fifteen dollars. For that matter, ordinary carpenters, many no more than wood-butchers, were now said to be getting four dollars and more a day. War, as usual, was ushering in inflation.

Unlike today, when so many buck privates are legitimate fathers, there were then no allowances for dependents, even if we had any, which in most cases was most unlikely. In 1917 and before, the lower grades of enlisted men were assumed to be single men, and very probably born out of wedlock, and even the West Point shave-tails, those second lieutenants, who actually drew the munificent stipend of one-hundred-and-twenty-five dollars a month, had to get official permission from their commanding officer to get married, which was seldom granted unless the girl had money, or there were the most urgent of reasons. As for the great majority of regular army enlisted men, they were regarded as rolling stones or ne'er-do-wells, who were in the army to avoid the pains of life's responsibilities.

In those days, second lieutenants and privates were bachelors, and since those grades did most of the fighting and dying it made good sense, as wives and children are a brake on combat daring. Today, things are greatly changed, and many a modern post resembles a snug landscaped community of happy homes, swarming with housewives, babies, tiny future master-sergeants and other little monsters, and manned by young, but often too fat and well fed, settled-down-looking, married warriors.

We had eight weeks of training at ground school, which was divided into two terms, the first of three weeks, the second of five. The first term was largely given over to intensive military training, infantry drill, regulations, military courtesy, the customs of the service, the Articles of War, and all the other pillars of the army, hoary with tradition, and as little subject to change as the laws of the Medes and the Persians. We also learned how to take apart and reassemble the Lewis machine gun, this to be accomplished within a very few minutes, while we duly named each of its myriad parts with an exactitude that allowed of no mistakes. In addition, we had plenty of excellent physical conditioning.

Our physical instructor was a Mr. Frank Kanaly, the gym instructor at MIT, who had acquired a considerable reputation in conditioning athletes. He was a tall rangy man with an odd, high, piping, almost falsetto voice, but he was master of his business. It is the solemn consensus of all who have ever attended service schools that, next to the dreary readings of the articles of war, and the deadly dull lectures on military courtesy, calisthenics is the bore of the first water. Here it was not, for unlike the usual poopadoop ex-boys-camp counselor, our instructor conducted all the exercises with so much rhythm and timing, that we got some pleasure, and much benefit from doing them. After eight weeks of doing this, we left ground school glowing like polished apples, and in wonderful condition. As one student said, "It's funny to be put into such fine shape, so you'll be fit to be killed. Makes one feel like a turkey before Thanksgiving."

At the end of the first three weeks, we were given a weekend pass. Taking along Johnny Mitchell and Doug Campbell, I visited a relative who had a beautiful country place on Cape Cod. Her daughter bred show dogs, and maintained a small dairy farm as a hobby. In due course we visited the kennels and wire enclosures, all filled with yapping terriers, and then inspected the cow barns, where a prize Jersey bull was the main attraction.

The bull had a dubious reputation, and was considered too dangerous to graze in open pasture. During the day he was confined to a small yard, whose walls were a five-foot, stout board fence. There, he pawed the ground, rolled his eyes, and snorted.

We lingered to admire, when suddenly Doug Campbell vaulted the fence, skipped across the twenty feet, not six inches from the bull's nose, and leaped the other side. Not liking the idea but feeling that a host must follow suit, I did the same, although I could almost feel a pair of sharp horns puncturing my posterior. The bull, if really aroused, could have charged and gone through that fence like Joe Louis's fist through a paper bag, but he seemed too amazed to make a move. "Crazy birdmen!" he may well have snorted. Regardless of that, with Doug Campbell in such a mood, I was glad my cousin's farm did not contain a pit of lions.

For the second five weeks, instead of Captain Mills and his sergeants, our instructors were mostly civilians and professors connected with the institute. We still had plenty of drill. This drill, the old infantry, close order drill, was ever so much more intricate and precise than today's column of threes. It had to be well and snappily done too, or there was the devil to pay, and we did not present the appearance of a *baggy-arsed* Coxey's army on parade, that has occasionally been so painfully evident with some parading units of today's air force. Most of our classes were conducted by civilian experts, under a president of the academic board. This president, an able college professor and administrator, acted as something like a dean for us students, and he was the one to consult in time of trouble, although our commandant was in charge of general supervision, especially the military side of it.

Our classes in the last five weeks included theory of flight, types of airplanes, principles and care of engines, guns and bombs, rigging and repairing, map reading, and a cleverly designed simulation of aerial, artillery spotting, where small lights blinked on and off a huge floor map, while we sat in a high gallery interpreting their exact location. This course was a major worry to us, since it was tied in with another course in wireless telegraphy, where we had to acquire a minimum skill in sending twenty words a minute, and receiving eight, if we were to graduate.

By constant practice in our spare time, most of us squeaked through, and we were able to send and receive messages concerning the simulated artillery firing, to the satisfaction of our instructor. That nightmare over, most of us gradually forgot the International Code, as very few of us ever had occasion to send or receive a wireless message during all of our subsequent flying careers. There were a few exceptions who, lacking flying aptitude, became aerial observers, but the great majority of us who graduated from advanced flying schools became fighter, bomber, or photo-reconnaissance pilots, and never handled wireless.

Besides the above courses, we had lectures on rudimentary meteorology, then almost a total mystery to the average man, although today almost any intelligent schoolboy knows all about air masses, cold fronts, dew points, temperature inversions, and the reading of weather maps. We also had classes on aerial navigation, which were little more than map reading, boxing and the use of the magnetic compass, the laying off of a flight course, the use of rivers, railroads, and other guides and landmarks, and some elementary dead reckoning and rough methods of estimating ground speed and drift. It was all very primitive; little was known about icing, thunderhead turbulences, down-drafts on hillsides, fog and other weather hazards, and except for compass and map, there were no instructions on instruments and aids to navigation, since for airplanes they were either not yet invented, or not in general use.

At school we ate in one of the the institute's cafeterias, and slept in steel double-deckers in a vast engineering laboratory. This enormous hall contained all manner of performance-measuring mechanisms and testing of materials devices, and among these were some huge empty tanks. One of these, whose uncovered top could be reached from an elevated catwalk, was diametrically braced from rim to rim by two narrow crossed girders. These, like a mountain to climb, soon presented us with a challenge. This was to walk one of these I-beams from the near side of the tank to the far side, and then to return.

During our physical tests for flying fitness, we had been required to walk an undeviating path along a narrow line, but it was chalked on a floor, and not sixteen feet up and over a yawning pit, with a steel floor at the bottom. Across this pit was a good fourteen feet and the girders were not over two inches wide. To me, to walk this girder and return seemed a feat for a tightrope artist, for someone like that Frenchman Blondin, who had crossed Niagara Falls on a rope, carrying a friend, who must have been a supremely trustful specimen of sucker, on his back. At that, Blondin had a balancing pole and plenty of experience, and we had none. Like climbing Mount Everest, to cross this tank was a challenge, but after several approaches to the brink, most of us thought better of it, and gave up. There was one exception.

Robert Moore, with hardly a preliminary glance, walked across and back. He not only walked, he sauntered in a casual manner, as if he were strolling in the park. Many years later, I sat with Robert Moore in the Happy Valley Bar of the Palace Hotel in San Francisco, just after the famous old hostelry had been acquired by Moore and his associates of the Sheraton Corporation. During the course of some pleasant drinks, he told me a little of the founding and the amazing growth of his company, how they had started with little capital, and how through a combination of good timing as to buying, pyramiding, and good luck, they had built up their hotel chain, and had finally reached a reasonably safe financial shore. "We had many a ticklish moment getting established," Moore said to me.

That could hardly have been otherwise during the phenomenal expansion of the enterprise, but I recalled the tank-crossing by a young flying candidate, and it occurred to me that he was also well qualified to walk an equally nerve-testing financial tightrope. In ground school, Bobby Moore, just out of Harvard, may have been twenty-one, but he then looked about sixteen and almost girlish. He did not look the popular conception of a steely, falcon-eyed aviator, and he could never have modeled for one of those *real men* cigarette ads, but he had nerves of iron, and right then I knew he would make a good combat flyer which he became in France.

The ground school worked us hard, and exacted a high standard of performance in classes and examinations during the eight weeks, but we all studied very hard, sweated out the tests, and few failed to graduate. Then at the end of the course, final marks were computed, and the sheep were separated from the goats. The ten or so sheep, including Campbell, Coolidge, Moore, Kissel, Ely and others, received orders for immediate transportation to France for flying training, while the rest of us, the goats, the lower division on the scholastic totem pole, were to get our preliminary flying training in the U.S.A. As it turned out, we probably got the better of the deal, although at the time it appeared otherwise.

On July 12, 1917, I received Special Order No. 61, from Headquarters Northeastern Department. This read:

> The following named privates first class [on graduation, we had been promoted from the status of plain bucks] will proceed to Mineola, Long Island, so as to arrive there July 14, and will report to the commandant, United States Aviation School for duty:
>
> S. E. Elliott in charge
>
> * * * * * * * * *
>
> BY COMMAND OF BRIGADIER GENERAL EDWARDS

This General Edwards was the same Major General Clarence Edwards who commanded the 26th, or Yankee Division, during its battles in France. After the war he became somewhat of a controversial figure, and the hero of several New England military politicians, their newspapers and followers, who did not like General Pershing's opinion of the abilities of several of the division's high ranking officers, most of whom had strong political connections in Boston.

Well, I was no better than one of the lower division goats, but for one day I was the head goat, so to speak. Among my charges, an unabashed member of our dumber group, was one, who many years later was to become rich, famous, and admired in his artistic profession and business, and another who was destined to become a famous four-star general. For one whole day, I was responsible for their safe and prompt arrival, and for their good conduct en route. *Sic transit gloria mundi!*

Chapter 4

BIRDMEN, HOLES IN THE AIR, AND OTHER ABSURDITIES

The United States Army Aviation Field at Mineola, Long Island, later part of Roosevelt Field, then presented a high, yellow board fence, that partly enclosed a considerable acreage of former cow pasture. Of this grassland, some fifty to one hundred acres were reasonably level turf, but a large part was rolling meadow, where confused, soloing students sometimes made high bounding, forced landings, that fortunately seldom caused personal injuries, except to the arteries and ulcers of the instructors. The rest of the post consisted of a few white one-storied barracks, a small headquarters with a flagpole, a water tank, guardhouse, a few warehouses, and about a half-dozen, portable, dirt floored, wooden framed, wind ballooning, canvas hangars that housed a motley collection of not very new Jennys (Curtis JN-4s), and a few somewhat beat-up-looking LWFs. Inside these hangars was a smell compounded of dust, musty sun-baked canvas, oil, and the strong but not unpleasant odor of *dope*, a kind of varnish then used on the canvas fabric of the planes, but outside there were no signs of any control tower, signalling, blinker light devices, nor of any flagman to direct aerial traffic. However for landing and takeoff guidance, there was a movable T, and a wind sock.

This was the post. There was no glittering PX, filled with everything from wristwatches to ladies' foundation garments, although one could purchase tobacco and a few necessities from out of the quartermaster sergeant's locker, provided you could persuade that venerable warrior to rise from his long service posterior. Neither was there any post movie theater, nor library, swimming pool, tennis court, gymnasium, USO, information and education office, branch bank, commissary supermarket, parking lot, noncoms' casino, man-proofed WAC barracks, stenographers' snack bar, de luxe officers' club, ladies' powder room, and post diaper service, all of which are found so essential on many air force base today. There was not even a men's room, only open air, cold-water faucets, a bench with a few tin basins, some yellow dog soap for a soldier's ablutions, and a nearby ten-holer, of early Ozark architecture.

As for the enlisted men's mess hall, it was an open shed adjoining a cook shack, where we placed our messkits on rough tables, and sat at long benches. Concerning the grub, the mess sergeant, rightfully or not, was thought to be building a fortune, the cook was suspected of being a direct descendant of the Borgias, and the assistant cook had no chin, a head pointed like a three-inch shell, answered to the name of Zip, and only spoke the grunt language. The food, slapped and slopped into our messkits, was greasy and terrible, hardly tempting to a buzzard. Today's service food is often dull and tasteless from uninspired cooking, but it is not close to the offal, which it was for a time at Mineola, nor does today's soldier have to clean his messkit in only one tub of hot but filthy water.

For the rest, it was in keeping. For us enlisted men, there were no hot showers, nor any other creature comforts. There was cold water, dog soap, and few cheap mirrors affixed to posts, that returned a strange, cockeyed reflection. In those days, no one could say that the American enlisted man was a pampered being. He was treated strictly as a soldier, and no private dared talk back even to a lance corporal. Even a private first-class held a respectful position above recruits and buck privates. From generals down to the lowest noncom there was a strictly recognized hierarchy, and any promotion in rank meant something more than a pay boost. There was no talk of democracy in the army. For better or worse, that was invented later.

Besides us student flyers and a handful of officers, there were a Signal Corps housekeeping unit, and a section of aviation-mechanics. The latter were a good, well-trained, hard-working gang, more educated and intelligent than the average soldier, but the others were mostly old regulars and a pretty hard lot, although good enough soldiers. These regulars of the old army, few of whom had gone beyond the sixth grade, looked on us college graduates as freaks, but they were friendly and tolerated us, since we also policed the grounds and stood guard duty,

"the cook was suspected
of being a direct descendent
of the Borgias".

which afforded them considerable relief from those dull tasks. Unlike many modern posts, there was no local, junior replica of the Pentagon, complete with female civilians, rows on rows of filing cabinets, and a horde of desk officers. The adjutant, the top sergeant, and the company clerk did all the needed paper pushing.

At Mineola among those who had come down from ground school, was a short, thickset, somewhat older student flyer, who had a crew haircut, a scarred cheek like a Heidelberg student corps duelist, was a graduate of MIT, and had joined the air corps after experiencing some years of surveying and railroad engineering in Quebec. He was a very calm, sensible fellow who, off duty, was apt to be found sitting and contemplatively smoking a rather distinguished-looking pipe. One afternoon he told me that this pipe had been presented to him by his boss, as a mark of gratitude and esteem, for not having pressed attentions on the latter's attractive young wife, while the husband was absent on a business trip to Montreal.

This virtuous aviator's name was Private First Class George C. Kenney, and the last time that I met him was at the Hamilton Field Officers' Mess. This was a later war, and ex-private Kenney was wearing the four stars of a full general, and carrying the added prestige of having been General of the Army Douglas MacArthur's chief of aviation. Although he shook my hand and recognized an old-timer, he was surrounded by an awestruck welcoming committee of local colonels, and mere buck generals, so we did not discuss pipes, for I was only an old grounded retread, like many officers who had been First War flyers.

Among the regular officers at Mineola there was, for a short time while I was there, Colonel Kilner, a very fine man and one of the army's most experienced pilots, who had been one of a handful of young officers to take up flying, in the really early days, about the time of the first flights of that great builder of our air force, General Arnold. One also remembers First Lieutenant June Salmon, a recent Princeton graduate, who had taken his primary flying training in pre-ground school days, along with Quentin Roosevelt. Another officer was Lieutenant Victor Page, who was a distinguished aeronautical engineer, and the author of *Aero Engines*, a textbook we studied. Whatever Mineola lacked from the point of view of today's fancy trimmings, it did have some inspiring and very superior officers.

There was also Sergeant Vine, who was a veteran, regular army top sergeant, able, and very loyal to all the hallowed military traditions, and who knew his paper work, and all the regulations and intricacies of army administration from A to Z, so exactly and minutely, that we flyers, who seldom learned more about paper work than signing the payroll, looked upon him with awe and amazement. We saw a great deal of Sergeant Vine, since he was assigned to us for our administration, and for our immediate supervision in all duties except flying.

The sergeant was a scrupulous and fair man, but he was a stickler for regulations and performance, and he stood for no ex-civilian slackness. One hot weekend when I had a date, and all our crowd had gone on pass to New York City, I spent all of Saturday afternoon, and most of Sunday, washing a total of seventy-two barrack windows, because my cot had not been made up with the correct, regulation, square corners. One learned a lot about the meaning of military duty under Sergeant Vine, the hard way but never forgotten. In spite of that, or perhaps because of it, we liked him.

One thing more about the sergeant, perhaps typical of the best of the old, regular army's professional soldiers. Some time after I had gone to France, the sergeant was shipped overseas. Off the Irish coast, his transport, the *Tuscania* I think, was torpedoed and sunk. Among the survivors was the sergeant, bringing his squadron's records and papers with him, in the abandonment of the ship. It was commonly said that Sergeant Vine was picked up swimming in the icy ocean, with the unit's payroll safely in his teeth. This tale may have been just a good story, but it typified his reputation and character, and he could have done it.

Among the other students at Mineola whose names and personalities one recalls, were Frank Patterson of the Dayton (Ohio) National Cash Register clan, Eckley Markle of the hard coal regions of Pennsylvania, whom I had years before known at a small boys' boarding school in Massachusetts, Joe Estil, George Crawford, Harold Amory, and an Eli Yale named Roberts, whose first name now escapes me. There was also a slender, quick-thinking fellow, who years later became famous as the explorer-maker of such documentary films as *Grass*, and the producer of the fantasy, *King Kong*, and other well-known motion pictures. His name was Merian Cooper.

During the summer of 1917 at Mineola, most of the flying instructors were civilians, with perhaps a pilot or so on loan from the Royal Flying Corps, later the Royal Air Force, since our own army had a mere handful of qualified aviators. One instructor was a big, husky, red-freckled fellow named Jenkins, who looked like a genial farmer and was a fine teacher, and another was a handsome, very dashing Latin type individual named Bert Acosta. Bert, who looked like a natural for Hollywood's idea of an international set, playboy-wolf, and who after the war made one of the very first, nonstop trans-Atlantic flights, in company with Bernt Balchen and Admiral Byrd, was a brilliant flyer, but sometimes a bit of a wild man, both on the ground and in the air.

However, Bert, in his most daring mood, was never as wild as a certain British pilot, who had been assigned to the school as an instructor. One day some congressman, or other VIP and his wife visited the field, and as they had never seen a plane in flight, the word was given that Lieutenant X should take off, circle the field, and make a few spirals and figure-eights for exhibition.

The *leftenant* was bored, and the *leftenant* was somewhat drunk, for he had done his instructing stint for this Saturday, and he was all set for a jolly weekend in the city. However orders were orders, and if they wanted a *bally* show for the visiting *blighter*, he was ready. On this, the lieutenant took up a Jenny, circled the field about thirty feet above ground, spun his landing wheels on a hangar top, banked vertically around the flagpole, with his lower wing tip all but trenching a furrow in turf, zoomed over headquarters missing the stove pipe by a hair, buzzed the onlooking visitors, and so frightened the VIP's wife, that the headquarters clerk, an unpleasant, cynical fellow, swore that she left a big puddle where she had been standing.

Then on the next turn of the field, the Jenny's engine did the not unexpected of those days. It *conked*, and the crate crashed with a horrible sound of rending tin and splintering spruce, but as the dust settled and the field's *Tin Lizzie* of an ambulance came with a shaking rattle to life, out of the debris stepped Lieutenant X, without a scratch or button missing, and as nonchalantly as if strolling down piccadilly. On this, the *leftenant* disappeared for almost a week, to some place he alone knew of.

Then to our surprise he came back, was instructing again, and all seemed to be forgiven and forgotten. We never did know the secret of this, except that good instructors were scarce and hard to replace. However some of the post wiseacres shook their heads, and surmised that Lieutenant X was either a secret by-blow of good King George, or of the British prime minister.

At Mineola, most flying lessons were given in Curtis JN-4s, the famous Jennys of those early days. These wire, canvas and spruce biplanes had a span of around forty-four feet, two cockpits, each with a dual control of the wheel, Despurdessin type, and each plane was powered with a Curtis OX-5 Model, 90 HP V-8 engine. This motor was the lightweight aluminum engineering marvel of its day, but it was one that was not unlikely to fracture and toss out a piston rod, cylinder head, crankshaft or other guts at any moment, to the accompanying damage to the wings, and to the nerves of the pilot, and it roared and rattled like a thousand tin cans filled with bolts and nuts, when wide open. There was a two-bladed, wooden propeller, a cat's cradle of lift and other wires and, at low altitudes, the top speed of the plane could not have been much over seventy miles an hour. The Long Island Railroad tracks paralleled close to our field, and we often raced the commuter trains. If there was but a moderate head wind, the snorting engine would beat us.

Flying instruction was pretty simple, as there were few of today's complicated collection of panel instruments, to depress and bewilder the beginner. There was an engine tachometer, an altimeter, gas and oil gauges, an ammeter and little else. There may have been a compass on some planes, but we never looked at them. One simply climbed into the front cockpit, adjusted the belt, rested one's hands on the dual wheel, and tried to get the feel of the controls as the instructor took off, circled the field and landed.

The instructor sat in back, with a club nice and handy in case some pupil became panicky and froze on the controls, and when he wanted to say something, he just throttled down, put the crate into a glide, and bellowed. Generally the pupil had only the vaguest idea of what he was saying, except that it did not concern the beautiful view, and it was not complimentary.

Like most trainees of those days, I had scarcely even seen a plane before coming to Mineola, and my first flight was an utterly confusing experience. We taxied out to the center of the cow pasture, headed upwind, and then took off as soon as Jenkins saw that the coast was clear. Then at about one thousand feet, we flew around the field and the neighboring territory.

Very gingerly I held the controls to follow Jenkins's actions, but the wind tore at my goggles, engine oil, opaque like a film of vaseline, blotted out all view through the tiny windshield, the roar of the engine and the propeller deafened me, and all seemed nightmarish and terrible. Once, Jenkins throttled down, yelled something and pointed. It may have been the field, the town, a train, anything, but I recognized nothing. I had no idea where I was, except up in the air, figuratively as well as literally speaking. We went through a low bank of clouds, a blinding and to me terrifying five seconds, and then Jenkins banked at ninety degrees, throttled, dipped and swooped, and finally glided in for a landing. I climbed out shaken, and really recognizing the field again, for the first time since taking off.

"Well," said Jenkins, "How did you like it?"

"Fine!" I lied, for the whole world seemed heaving.

"Good! And now you've had your first half hour of instruction; that is, on dual," said Jenkins, giving me a searching look.

"My *first* half hour?" I said.

"You first half hour. Get it?" said Jenkins. "I'm repeating your first half hour of dual instruction, because you've got to learn fast. The army and your Uncle Sam have no time to waste on slow learners. Inside of six hours of dual, you must be ready for solo. That's five and a half more hours with me, or some other instructor. After six hours, up you go alone, or else you'll be eliminated. Think you can make the grade?"

"Yes," I lied again; a colossal lie, for my heart had sunk, and I thought it impossible to meet this requirement. It would take me one hundred hours to be ready for solo, if I ever were ready, I thought at this moment. Well, my war would probably be foot-slog-slog with the infantry or, at best, bouncing an aching bottom on the hard seat of an artillery caisson, and acting as valet for a picket line of restive, powerful, noncostive horses and mules. Just then, another instruction plane landed nearby, and a student clambered out of it. He was eventually to become a good front-line flyer, but now his countenance was pallid and green, and he suddenly leaned over in that pitiable manner seen on shipboard. Somehow his misery made me feel a trifle better.

Nevertheless, nothing was as bad as that first flight; familiarity with being airborne gradually built confidence, and I was ready for my first solo after five hours of dual instruction. This solo was a dubious success, and somewhat of a loss to the taxpayers. I took off, circled the field and landed; took off, circled, and landed; took off, circled, and made a third perfect landing, except that it was thirty feet above the terrain. Down pancaked the Jenny; up it bounced higher than a telegraph pole; down it pancaked again, and this time to stay down, for the landing gear splintered and crumpled, and the Jenny rested on her belly, her outstretched lower wings hugging the grass, like a cowering bird.

Booted and long-legged Lieutenant Y, who was in charge of this day's flying, now came grimly striding over. Gloomily I stood by the wreckage, visioning a hollow square of soldiers, the drums beating the rogue's roll, the ripping off of my insignia by a purple-faced commandant, the awful dismissal from the air corps, the pointing fingers of shame at my bowed back, the distress of my family, and the future—the artillery picket line, with its long elevation of switching tails, and nervous, steel-shod feet and hind legs. There I would be, holding a pitchfork instead of the controls of an airplane.

"You!" yelled Lieutenant Y. "Get right into that other ship over there, and take off at once. Next time you pancake, give her the gun right off, and go around again. As for this wreck, we'll leave her right here for the rest of the day—as the number-one horrible example."

I had no more mishaps, and all our group, except two who were eliminated for lack of aptitude, were able to solo within the six hour limit. Today, many students are able to solo after much less dual instruction, but almost all of today's students have previously experienced many passenger hours in the air, and they are at home in that element. For we who had never flown before coming to Mineola, it took time just to get accustomed to being airborne, and to regard our surroundings calmly and comprehensively in those now bygone quivering, rattling open planes, which at first seemed so tricky and uncertain. Even in those days, it was noticed that some air mechanics who had experienced many hours as passengers in airplanes, seemed to absorb both confidence and the piloting touch from such duties. Such mechanics, if qualified and accepted for pilot training, were not infrequently able to solo after two to three hours of dual instruction.

By the early summer of 1917, daredevil flyers had looped the loop, but few in America seemed to know much about other acrobatic stunts, and everyone seemed fearful of a spinning nose dive, or tailspin. Our cadre had not been long at Mineola, when Captain H. Taylor, a very popular officer in general charge of flying, fell into a spin, and crashed between the field and the old Garden City Hotel, killing himself and seriously injuring a student to whom he was giving a lesson in making close spirals.

We all saw the plane go down, heard the horrible crunch of the crash, and shuddered, for this was not only violent death, to which we were not yet hardened, but it was so mysterious, and therefore all the more terrifying. This was an ever lurking death that menaced all flyers, one that might develop out of any steep spiral or turn, if the plane's nose dropped a little too much. Once in the grip of the deadly spin, a crash was the only ending. This was the story told us, for no one seemed to understand the aerodynamics involved in a spin, or to know the answer, and the few lucky survivors just told of their trying to overcome the spin, and how the controls seemed to be acting in a vacuum, and gave no reactions to the frantic manipulations of the pilot.

Then one day, a pilot (one forgets his name, but he is one of the unsung heroes of the air force) fell into a bad spin, from about three thousand feet above the field. We all saw him coming down and down, while he kept desperately cutting, then gunning his engine, in a vain attempt to escape from it. He seemed doomed, when suddenly at around five hundred feet the spin ceased, he pulled out of the dive, circled the field and landed.

"What did you do? How did you get out of it?" we said to him.

"I tried everything. Nothing worked. I was dead sure it was curtains."

"What then?"

"I think I just let go of the controls, shut my eyes, and called on

God. He must have got me out of it. At least the spin stopped, and I just had room to pull out of the straight dive."

We now knew the answer to most spins. This was to retard the throttle, and put the controls in neutral position, but never to fight the spin with rudder or ailerons, as this only intensified it. None of this procedure was mentioned in our theory-of-flight booklet. It was only discovered by accident, and in the nick of time for our group. No doubt, British and French flyers had for some time known how to escape from a spin, for European aviation was much more advanced than in America at this time. True or not, this was the way we learned to lesson of the deadly spin at Mineola.

At this time, the U.S. Army had three ratings for military pilots. Those who had passed advanced flying tests and had had more flying experience were rated *Military Aviators*, while less experienced pilots were rated as *Junior Military Aviators*. Both of these ratings, which carried with them pay increases of seventy-five percent and fifty-percent respectively, were normally reserved for regular army officers, who were generally West Pointers. For reserve officer pilots, a still lower rating, *Reserve Military Aviator*, was established, and this carried the much smaller increase of only twenty-five percent over the officer's base pay.

Prior to our declaration of war, these distinctions, with their corresponding bonuses, had had some validity, since regular army pilots did, as a rule, have more flying experience than the occasionally flying, reserve officers. However, not many months after we had declared war, these ratings became more and more arbitrary and unjust, because the active RMAs were soon, as individuals, doing much more flying than most of the regular army pilots, and at the war's end the RMAs had become well over ninety percent of our trained, combat flying personnel. During the war, for that matter, the RMAs did most of the dying, and they formed almost the entire list of America's World War I aces.

Regardless of the indisputable fact that the RMAs developed into the most veteran pilots, that they were the most effective flying force of the AEF, and that they were the right arm of the air corps, if not its soul as well, not one RMA ever received any more than the standard twenty-five percent bonus, even if the individual was flying (which many did) twenty to thirty or even more, two-and-a-half-hour combat missions a month, while during this same period, MAs and JMAs were receiving triple and double such premiums for a minimum of a four hours per month of flying, generally on nice days in safe rear areas.

Some MAs and JMAs flew combat and flew well, but they were a handful, and this pay inequality added fuel to other causes for resentment on the part of RMAs. For a time in France, some RMAs growled that it was a West Pointer's war but a reserve officers' fight, which was not really fair, because most regular army pilots wanted and eagerly sought combat assignments, but were denied it, since their superior rank and their far greater organizing and administrative experience were needed elsewhere. Although some high ranking officers tried to correct this bonus injustice, it remained, and this was commonly attributed to the unsympathetic attitude of the Army General Staff, who seemed suspicious, if not jealous, of the American public's great interest and enthusiasm for the air corps. On the part of most of us reserve pilots, we were not out for money; we merely resented the discrimination. Had all bonuses been reduced to our twenty-five percent level, we would have been as satisfied as the nation's taxpayers. However, in the bureaucratic mind, that would have been something to shake the pillars of government. To actually reduce the emolument of a civilian or military government servant for the benefit of those rats, the taxpayers, then as today—"My dear sir. It is unthinkable!"

After about five or six hours of solo flying, most of us took our RMA tests. These consisted in a barograph-checked altitude climb to a minimum of twelve thousand feet, which was a long and tedious climb in those primitive Jennys, followed by certain maneuvers to show air proficiency, such as making figure-eights around pylons, and then doing a series of right and then left, tight, vertical spirals, with motor throttled. These over, the candidate had to cut his switch at a minimum atltitude of one thousand feet, and land, dead stick, to within one hundred feet of a designated mark. The final test was a cross-country flight to a distant location, a landing at that spot, a takeoff, and a return to the field.

My test flight was to the region around Westhampton, some sixty-odd miles to the east of Mineola. There I had to land, stop the engine, register in a book, crank up without any help, take off and return. It was a breezy summer day, with white-caps on the sea, and little fleecy clouds that resembled flocks of sheep. From my altitutde of five thousand feet, I could view the surf on the outer beaches of Great South Bay, the inlet at Fire Island, the distant towers of Manhattan, and recognize Islip, Sayville, Bayport, and similar pesky little Long Island villages as they passed under the scalloped trailing edge of my lower wing. Far below, white puffing railroad trains seemed to crawl, roads ran like fine ribbons through fields and woods, the earth was a green and brown checkerboard, and tiny white sails dotted the great bay.

All this scene, so commonplace and familiar to the general public today, was then new, strange, and thrilling to my eyes, as the unknown and beautiful shores of America must have appeared to the eyes of an imaginative early sixteenth-century sailor. The wings quivered, the motor roared, and I sang at the top of my lungs. I thought of Daedalus and Icarus, of Sinbad the Sailor lashed to the leg of a soaring roc, of Bellerophon on Pegasus, and all the ancient myths of flight. I was tremendously thrilled by my first cross-country flight, back in those days when any sort of flight was a rare experience.

Where I landed was a genuine cow pasture, complete with browsing cows. There were daisies, buttercups, lush grass and shade trees, in a thirty-acre clearing that was moderately level, and there was a welcoming committee of farmer-landowners, local dignitaries, Long Island yokels, wives and children, and at least a dozen dogs that raced about barking with excitement. I cut the switch, got out, and was soon shaking hands with several dozen people, who seemed to regard me as if I were man from Mars. Refreshments were offered—cake, coffee, and lemonade—and there was not only the army's official register to sign, which was most ceremoniously brought to me by the owner of the field, but there were personal autographs to inscribe, requested posings for snapshots, while a little girl handed me a bouquet of wild flowers.

For those farmers in those far-off days, my airplane landing was something new, exciting, and amazing, in a minor way like Lindbergh's Paris arrival ten years later. I then cranked the propeller, and in due course took off, while the little crowd cheered and waved goodbye. A pilot, any young punk of a pilot, was a somebody in America, in the early summer of 1917. The newspapers wrote of us as "America's own intrepid birdmen," and a ten-hour greenhorn, flying in a Jenny, was almost in the same class as an astronaut in this era.

On my return flight, I ran into more excitement and a new experience. This was only a thundershower, which I could have detoured, but I knew nothing of the dangers from this kind of weather, and flew right into it. Fortunately it was a mild one, and it did not contain one of those terrible upper air tornadoes, which heavy thunderheads may conceal, but it did give me a terrific buffeting and, to my amazement and consternation, I was carried upwards like a balloon to almost sixteen thousand feet, which must have been close to an altitude record for a jenny. There was more buffeting, some sudden terrific drops, and the rain speared horizontally through the yellow varnished struts, like flashing javelins of water. I fought and struggled with the controls, and was thoroughly frightened, but the crate came through into sunshine, and I finally landed safely back at Mineola.

After we had completed our tests and were rated RMAs, we used to fly all over Long Island, and occasionally even over New York City, which was very foolish with those unreliable engines. Such flights occurred because there were no prescribed flight plans, giving course and altitude as today, and no one checked closely as to where we flew, provided we returned safely. In 1917 at Mineola, flying was still an informally conducted activity and, once a pilot got off the ground, he was completely cut off from further orders, and pretty free of all regulations. Aviation was then no business, for the public looked on us as romantic daredevils, the average, nonflying, regular army officer disdained us as unmilitary screwballs, and the usual newspaper or magazine article spread the greatest misinformation about flying.

There was no limit to the absurdities that many reporters wrote in their columns. They loved that term, *birdmen*, as if we ate seeds and grew feathers, and one writer solemnly stated that flying was so tricky an undertaking, that a pilot hardly dared sneeze while aloft, lest the shaking of his diaphragm throw his *aeroplane into a death-dive*. Besides this rubbish, there was a tremendous amount of nonsense written about air bumps, which writers termed *holes in the air*, and which they described as mysterious and awful vacuums in the atmosphere, and whenever a plane crashed for some unexplained reason, a hole in the air was generally mentioned. Of course, rational people knew that nature abhors a vacuum, and that the only holes were in the heads of the reporters, but the general public seemed fascinated with the conception of an atmosphere that resembled a Swiss cheese, and the myth persisted.

I used to fly over Oyster Bay, and watch the sloops and knockabouts in the local regattas. At this time, Ex-President Theodore Roosevelt was spending the summer at his home, Sagamore Hill, on the hooklike peninsula across the bay from the village. My father, up to his death a mining and civil engineer, had been a first cousin and an intimate boyhood friend of TR, and hearing that I was at Mineola, Teddy asked me over to spend the weekend at his house, where I had once previously visited for two weeks, as a small boy of eight.

Sagamore Hill, in 1955 presented to our nation and dedicated as a national shrine by President Eisenhower, was and is a moderate-sized, rambling old structure, with high-peaked, shingled roofs, many gables, wide encircling porches, roofed carriage entrances, and that general look of post-Civil War, American-Victorian, or perhaps quasi-Queen Anne architecture. It was the typical summer home of many a well-to-do family at the turn of the century, although it was rather contemptuously dismissed in his book, by Count Witte, the Russian plenipotentiary at the Russo-Japanese Treaty of Portsmouth, as the summer house of a "burgher of small means."

The old manse probably did seem most insignificant to the great and brilliant Russian nobleman, who may well have owned a hundred-room palace with a grand central staircase, of carved, green malachite, but it nevertheless had an atmosphere of distinction, and the charm of a real family home that had been lived in for a long time. The living room and dining room were filled with the relics of lions, leopards, rhinos, bears, elephants, and other big beasts, all victims of the *Bwana Tumbo* of the African gun bearers, and a visitor had to step with caution to avoid putting his foot into some gaping maw on a rug, and perhaps kicking out a big fang. In fact, there must have been dental bills for repairs to bears and lions, on several occasions.

However, in spite of all the ferocious, reproving or disgruntled heads on the walls and floors, the frequent arrivals of distinguished callers, and the gentle, hospitable charm of Cousin Edith's (Mrs. Roosevelt) presence, TR's personality overwhelmed everything. He would stand on the floor, with a grin like a big Cheshire cat, while his body seemed to exude an inaudible but mysteriously felt hum, as if he were some sort of psychic dynamo. One could feel this personal magnetism like an electric charge, as a manifestation of enormous physical and mental vitality. I have never met anyone who seemed to ooze such presence and life force. As he talked and gesticulated, ate, paced the floor, sat his saddle horse or did anything, there seemed to be an aura about him.

Besides the glowering animals, the rooms contained many curious objects given to him by all manner of people. Many of these were from various kings and other rulers whose nations he had visited on a grand tour of Europe, after returning from his celebrated African hunt. Among these were signed photographs and other mementos, presented by Kaiser William II of Germany. Naturally at this time in 1917, we Americans thought very ill of Germans. There were current all sorts of utterly believed, atrocity tales, such as German troops goose-stepping through conquered towns, with Belgian babies impaled on their bayonets, and of French women with their hands and breasts cut off, as punishment for having harbored escaped prisoners. To us, a German was a *boche*, a Hun, a demon about as popular as a cobra, and a being, coarse and less well mannered than a hog. It was gravely stated by many traveled people, that arrogant bestiality was ingrained in the German character, and that there had never been such a thing as a German gentleman. No, not ever!

"Cousin Theodore," I said, "did you ever meet a German whom you considered to be a real gentleman?"

The former president was sitting on the porch in a rocking chair, which he had been vigorously rocking. He now began to rock it so terrifically, that he and the chair began a rapid forward creep across the bare boards of the porch.

"Stuart, I may have met one, possibly even two Prussians who seemed on the surface to be gentlemen." TR squeezed the arm of the chair, and bared his celebrated teeth. "But I am absolutely certain I never met a Prussian lady." Like many traveled Americans, he drew a sharp distinction between the ultramilitaristic Prussians, and the milder Germans from states like Bavaria, Wurtemberg, and Baden, who were considered more civilized people.

The ex-president was a most tremendous reader of almost everything of interest in science, history, travel, and diverse subjects including poetry and art. He was an all-around educated man, and the antithesis of so many Ph.D.'s met today, who seem to know little outside their own specialty. I was mentioning some impressions of wonderful scenes observed in flying,and how the sea often looked like a carpet of blue silk crepe from a plane.

"You flyers can look through the eyes of eagles," said our former president. "It's like that fragment of Tennyson's that goes,

> The wrinkled sea beneath him crawls;
> He watches from his mountain walls,
> And like a thunderbolt, he falls.

"The sea seems to crawl, all right," I said. "But that business of falling like a thunderbolt? It's not quite for me. I want to come down gently, and safe."

"Over here, yes," he said. "Take no unnecessary chances. But when you go overseas, and fly over the lines, fall like a thunderbolt on those Germans. Hit them hip and thigh, Stuart. Hip and thigh!"

It was a pleasant weekend, with horseback rides through wooded lanes, swims from the shore of the estate, and long talks with the great TR, and his charmingly sympathetic wife, Cousin Edith. Teddy had recently come back from an extremely hazardous exploration trip in the Amazon Basin, where he had followed the course of an almost unknown river, then called the River of Doubt, but since renamed El Rio Teodoro Roosevelt, by the Brazilian government. He had come back with health much impaired from hardship and jungle fevers. Now in spite of that, and his close to sixty years, he looked extraordinarily vigorous and well. A little over a year later, he was dead.

Although our cadred of student pilots were all rated Reserve Military aviators, we were still no more than privates first class, and our monthly pay was no more than thirty-six dollars, regardless of how many hours we might fly. This small pay did not bother us so much, but something else made us burn. This was the attitude of a considerable section of the general public around New York towards uniformed, enlisted men. Even at this late date, this was about the same as before our declaration of war. It was very unfavorable.

In August 1917 and a good four months after we had declared war, the enlisted man was still subject to being considered a roughneck and a bum, a being unfit for respectable company, and not to be admitted to the better hotels, restaurants and other resorts. In addition to this bias, there was an enormous social gulf, far greater than today's between the commissioned officer and the enlisted man. This caste cleavage, which was almost Hinduesque in its rigidity, was so pronounced, that an old college pal, whom one well might have, in some prewar football victory celebration, drunk under the table and lugged to bed, would suddenly become a sort of holy Brahmin, upon whose very shadow his old friends must not tread, because this ninety-day wonder had become an officer, and by act of Congress, officially a gentleman, whereas we, his former old cronies, who mentally, physically and morally were quite superior to this prickmouse, were still PFCs and on the wrong side of the tracks.

This was pretty general, for regardless of his background, education, or even courtly manners and cultured way of speaking, any enlisted man was apt to find himself to be somewhat of a second-class citizen, with a social status not very much above that of a Negro's, and in 1917 the Negro was not a black man, but North as well as Deep South he was a *nigger*, without much more consideration than a Pariah in India. All this might have been not quite universally so, but it was the general rule until the draft got well underway, and it gradually came to be recognized that the enlisted man was, after all, the cross-section of the nation.

Dress greatly accentuated the gulf between officers and men. The military Brahmin wore a totally different uniform of fine material, well tailored, with polished boots, a trim and expensive Stetson campaign hat, black and gold threaded hat cord, a Sam Browne belt (this, only overseas), and smart insignia. Provided an officer kept his figure, he looked like a proper soldier, and since he rode horseback or hiked, instead of riding around and broadening his posterior in a jeep, he was apt to keep fit, trim and slender.

The enlisted man who wished to look sharp, started with one big strike against him. In canvas leggings, breeches, shirt, and a rather floppy campaign hat, he might pass a fairly satisfactory scrutiny, but his regulation blouse was cut with a high, choking, Prussian style collar, and the rest was along lines that tended to minimize his shoulders, and to accentuate his situpon. This was especially noticeable from his rear, where the outcurving lines of the seams gave a semi-corsetted appearance to the waist, from which they flared out into the skirts of the blouse, almost like the tutu of a ballet dancer.

A good tailor could modify this cut, and give a trimmer and less bumpkinlike garment, but few enlisted men could afford good tailors, and they had to be content with the regulation hand-me-downs of the supply sergeant. Some of these supply sergeants were good, conscientious men, who tried to fit the uniform to the man and not vice-versa, but others were sadistic sonsabitches *of the purest ray serene*, who seemed to delight in giving some big, innocent recruit the looks of a man in a ten-year-old's suit, while his pint-sized buddy was handed one of the biggest sizes, and had to go on duty as if enveloped in a tent.

As to the enlisted men's overcoats, they had originally been of very good material, but with the coming of war, the huge expansion of the army, and the almost inevitable fast-buck uniform contractors, many of the new issues were of such coarsely finished and fuzzy-looking cloth, that jokers referred to their overcoats with a "Sure thing. Nice camel-hair coat. Just skinned off the outside of a camel!" With these sartorial handicaps, even if he had the physique of a Greek god, it was hard for the enlisted man to look like a smart soldier.

Being enlisted men, we wore what the supply sergeant had

flipped us over his counter, and although up for commissions and rated as pilots, we wore no distinguishing insignia. One hot Saturday afternoon, four of us rode to Rockaway Beach, in Frank Patterson's big open Packard. There, we entered a rather pretentious restaurant, and ordered a broiled lobster dinner. The waiter, giving us a strange look, took our orders, but did not return to our table. We sat and sat, but waiters avoided our eyes, and none would come near us.

After about a half hour, it dawned on us, that the boss had passed the word to freeze us. We were enlisted scum and, as such, persons to be discouraged, even if we were clean, sober, and quiet. As we realized this, our gorges rose, and we were on the verge of picking up chairs and tables, and taking the place apart. However, we realized that this might endanger our being commissioned, and suddenly the absurdity of the situation made us laugh.

Here were four of us, everyone a graduate of a famous old university, and used to the best of everything. Either Frank Patterson's or Eckley Markle's family could have bought out the rococo establishment, lock, stock, and barrel, as easily as the average man could buy a ham sandwich, and the other two of us came from substantial backgrounds. We were all accustomed to good society, and to attending the best balls in Boston, New York, Tuxedo and elsewhere, but because we wore the enlisted man's uniform of the Army of the United States of America, we were eyed like skid row characters, and by a pompous little man, who was completely outside the world we had come from.

However, everybody was not like that. In contrast to the Rockaway Beach lobster palace, was the attitude of the Waldorf. The old Waldorf Hotel was then at Thirty-Fourth and Fifth Avenue, and the same four of us went there, having passes for the weekend. The management was very cordial and, although they knew none of us from any other Joe Doughboy, they immediately showed us to a fine two-room corner suite, for which they charged us the nominal sum of one dollar apiece. That sort of thing made a big impression on us, and created lasting good will for the hotel. It was the difference in the attitude of real people towards the enlisted man, and the fearful lesser breed of unsure bonifaces.

Chapter 5

TEXAS, AND OVERSEAS

Mineola having given us about all it could in flying training, in early September our group was ordered down to Kelly Field, Texas, for advanced instruction. As befitting our status as low-caste, enlisted Sudras, we did not rate Pullmans, but rode the entire way by day coach, in one of those hot, cindery wooden relics of the Grover Cleveland era, part of a slow train that jerked, rattled, and stopped for hours on sidings, during the four days of the journey.

In September 1917, Kelly Field consisted of about six canvas hangars, a small headquarters, a few shacklike barracks and such, and a collection of squad tents, in which we were quartered. Cleared of its sagebrush and cactus, the landing field was no more than a flat piece of desert, which was furnace-hot by midday, freezing cold by midnight, and always dusty. It was especially locally famed as a breeder of the *Texas*, as the frequent dust whirls were called. Some of these were quite spiteful and powerful whirlwinds, almost midget tornados, and no sooner would we be eating our midday beans (the chow was mostly beans, monkey meat, and goldfish—all cooked the army way and awful) in our stifling and musty tents, when the *Texas*, several hundred feet high, thirty feet thick, and black like factory smoke, might come roaring and waltzing into our midst, and down would go tent, poles, canvas, beans, coffee, and us, in the smothering dust of those perverse little twisters.

The flying contraptions at Kelly Field, in its dawn age, were not impressive, as they consisted of about a dozen more or less ramshackled Jennys and LWFs, which seemed to fly in a somewhat punch-drunk manner, and for which there was never a sufficient supply of gas. However, we were much impressed by the daring of a certain major, whose name I, unfortunately, cannot recall, who was in the habit of taking off in an LWF, and looping the loop in the moonlight. Except for the fact that an LWF, a plane very much like a Jenny (save that it had a monocoque fuselage and a bit more dihedral angle to the wings) had a reputation for sometimes shedding a wing for no great reason, flying in the moonlight was probably pleasanter and safer than flying through the heat bumps of the Texas daytime. However, there were no lights to mark the field, nor any lights on the planes, and any night flying was still quite an outstanding performance. Neither in those days nor for a good year later, were there any parachutes for pilots.

At Kelly I met another RMA, a small dark-haired youth, who off duty liked to explore the bush south of the field, to poke around its scrub forests of cactus and mesquite, and to observe the denizens, such as any chance encountered rattlesnake. One afternoon I went with him, and just missed stepping on a thick, torpidly crawling specimen. My friend picked up a rock, and casually dropped it on the vicious head.

"I like the bush," he said. "It's interesting to study nature. The cactus, the lizards, the tarantulas, the snakes! They're interesting to wander among, and to observe their habits."

"Pardon me! I'm not too keen about studying these snakes," I said. "They seem to quite numerous, and we have no antivenom with us."

"Oh, you'll get used to them. Besides, I've read articles by authorities, about them. It's rare that they bite anyone."

"I'm not so sure that these snakes read those same articles," I said. "Besides, it's rare that two damn fools like us give them a good opportunity to bite. Let's get going, before these worms get annoyed with us. We're no Saint Patricks."

My friend, who was a nice fellow, and very serious and sane in all other respects, was named Harold George. I never saw him after leaving Kelly Field, but someone of the same name became, in World War II, an air force major general.

We never flew even once, in all the weeks we were at Kelly Field, although we had been shipped down here at the taxpayers' expense for advanced training. Kelly Field was not ready. It had no visible instructors, no operating program of instruction, no respectable planes, and mighty little gasoline, but whoever was scheduling the training program from Washington seemed unaware of this. A long-distance telephone call might have avoided our needless trip, but in World War I as in World War

II, and most probably the Civil War and the Revolution, that would not have been our army. So we drilled at Kelly Field—"Right forward, fours right. Haww! Pla-TOON, on left into line. Haww!" and all the rest of it. We drilled most of the day in the heat and the dust, defying the sunstroke, and slowly growing scaly and meager like lizards, and that done, we sat around listening—listening to lectures on military courtesy.

Those lectures! "You men should consider it a rare privilege, not just a duty, to salute." Listening to the everlasting, droning readings of the Articles of War—" . . . shall suffer death, or what penalty the court shall decide"—listening to lectures on camp sanitation, and how to construct a military gent's room for an overnight bivouac; to customs of the service, protocol and such, and even how the base commandant's own true, lawful dragon could lay down the social law to all the subordinate officers' balls and chains, who had better mind their steps, or else! Listening to lectures on all possible subjects, except flying, that could frantically be devised to keep us occupied, and to threaten us with stenographer's spread. These awful lectures finally over, we rose from our aching bottoms, and then sat around listening to latrine rumors in the stuffy tents, stood in line for beans, and growled about the kiwis (nonflying officers) and the regular army.

For diversion in the evenings, we would go into San Antonio, seven or eight of us packed into the ramshackled Ford tinlizzies that gave taxi service. These rides were thrills and chills, since the owner-driver, who was usually a long, lanky, one-gallused character out of *The Grapes of Wrath*, was always in a tearing hurry to complete as many paying round trips as possible. One night, while we were careening, loaded full, throttle wide open, rattlety-bang-bump over the badly pitted, truck-worn highway, an enormous meteor, rumbling like a freight train, arched over the sky, lighting up the heavens with a strange greenish glow. This so distracted our driver that he veered into a ditch, and the car turned over. Luckily, no one was much hurt, although one flyer swore that he had been catapulted through the air, and had only avoided a nearby telegraph pole by banking with his outspread arms, and using his feet as a rudder.

In San Antonio, to our eastern eyes still somewhat of a roaring, Wild West town, there were the hotels St. Anthony, and the old, charming, Spanish type Menger, and there were innumerable soldiers on pass, from about seventy thousand troops of all branches in the area. There was a lot of pay being spent, and there were thousands of girls to collect a good share of it. These wantons had come from throughout the Great Plains and the Mississippi Basin regions to practice their ancient profession, and many seemed no older than fourteen, and were often most innocent looking.

This was amazing to us, for we had always pictured tarts as hardened women, and not as baby-faced schoolgirls. This might have been once generally true, but war was beginning to spread sex and prostitution all over the nation, and making many a formerly staid city resemble an old-fashioned gold rush town, and soldiers were commonly saying that San Antonio was filled with very nice girls, who only slept with friends, but who of course had no enemies.

Besides the gold-digging harlots and the carefree soldiery, San Antonio seemed to abound in saloons that were decorated with extremely long cow horns on the walls, and with glass-enclosed, realistically preserved habitants of the state, including coiled rattlesnakes and hairy tarantulas, to greet the visitor's startled eyes from many nooks and corners. Amidst these settings of delirium tremens, there would invariably be two or three, tall, elderly men, who drank with dignity, wore ten-gallon hats, and who seemed to be in oil or cattle.

Often one of these ex-shefiffs, U.S. marshalls, Texas Rangers, cattle barons, whatever his career had been, would graciously invite us to a drink, and then, nine times out of ten, the words would come, even as they have been uttered from the days of the Alamo, and are solemnly reaffirmed at this time.

"Son," the impressive old Lone Star would raise his straight bourbon, and gravely speak. "Let us drink to Texas, that great, great state!" We would drink, and then conversation would tend to prove that Sam Houston and his incredible followers had discovered the fourth dimension, before Einstein was born. The four dimensions were length, breadth, thickness, and Texas, and this last was the greatest dimension in the universe. We agreed that was so, and after four or five more, mighty toasts to Texas, to Sam Houston, to Davy Crockett, to the Yellow Rose and the other

"To Texas! That great great state!"

beautiful women of Texas and, in consideration of us foreigners, one to President Wilson, even the faces of the tarantulas seemed a bit genial.

After a good three weeks of costing the taxpayers no mean sum, and accomplishing nothing in flying, we were ordered back to Mineola: four more days of day coach, cinders, hotdogs, soda pop, and stomach cramps for us intrepid birdmen, who had never gotten higher off the ground of Texas than the mezzanine at the Hotel St. Anthony. Then on arrival, we were suddenly discharged as enlisted men, and immediately commissioned and sworn in as first lieutenants in the Aviation Section, Signal Reserve Corps.

Proudly I donned my officer's uniform, ordered long before and fashioned by the then most fashionable and expensive New York tailor. It had the regulation high Prussian style military collar, whose inner lining was fitted with brass collar buttons, for attaching the regulation white hard-boiled throat-choking neckpiece, which was a must for formal occasions, and it had a Sam Browne belt with shoulder straps and a hook from which to dangle a shining sword, and a pair of wide flaring breeches, designed for horseback riding. With this went a very smart Stetson campaign hat, costing all of a golden eagle, expensive, high, riding boots, and a pair of shiny brass spurs. The riding boots had to be dazzingly polished, laceless, to fit like a lady's glove around shinbone and manly calf, and to be always the *goddamnedest* struggle to put on and take off.

Concerning the knightly spurs, we as members of the Signal Corps, whose officers were supposed to be mounted, were in theory to wear them on all occasions with the possible exception of flying, although the regulations made no provision for that. We did wear them on a few formal occasions, "to prick the gas tank, and get more flying speed," as we explained to perplexed civilians. Following the prescribed military etiquette of those days, I once wore them at a very formal affair, where the ladies had long evening gowns, and high ranking officers threw piercing looks at subalterns. Waltzing with prickers on both heels was chivalry in full flower, but always mighty close to being in trouble. The revered old army theory for this business, which threatened to change a ball into a literal *shindig*, was that we, as mounted officers, were supposed to be ever ready to mount our trusty steeds, and to gallop off on a moment's notice, like the Duke of Wellington's officers from the Brussels ball, on the eve of Waterloo. If for us the tocsin had sounded, and it had been, "Arm! Arm! it is—it is—the cannon's opening roar!" I don't know what we would have done. We had no horses. I think we would have had to spring to the saddle, behind the nearest mounted policeman. Then, "Trot, gallop, charge! The Air Corps is coming!"

Our Sam Browne belts had a hook and gear to hang a sword and, for us too, swords would have been *de rigueur* on reviews and formal occasions. Fortunately, the metal was needed for more modern weapons, and no swords were available. Otherwise, we might have had to take off from the field, brandishing flashing sabers and shouting, "Forward! Gallant, six hundred Jennys!"

We had a few more weeks of some flying, but much more of gallivanting about New York City, where we could cut a dash in our fine new uniforms, by squiring some debutante or other candy puss, to a tea dance at the Plaza, or taking some other beautifully dressed young lady to the Crystal Room of the old, now gone and much lamented Ritz. Like the Plaza, this last was a real abode of true glamor, even though it was suspected of being a listening post for several German spies. This was probably true, for in all wars we Americans, relaxing, were gullible about spies, and were notorious for talking too freely.

We might also go to some hectic restaurant like Bustanoby's, or Bust Anybody as many called it, or to Murray's that featured the world's first revolving dance floor, or to Jack's, famed for its scrambled eggs in the wee hours, and for its way of bouncing drunks with a flying wedge of waiters, or even to the old Haymarket, where the waiters had to be still tougher.

Naturally, we did not take our current Junior Leaguer, or other very nice girl of that month, to the dine and dance dumps of that era, for in 1917, the ghost of Queen Victoria (from accounts a type of Mrs. Grundy with a crown on her head), still lingered, and no really proper young New York girl was supposed to dine with a beau, in even such a famed and genteel place as Louie Sherry's, unless it was a party with a chaperone.

I once made the suggestions, and got the ruling from the mother of a very attractive cousin. Tea at the Plaza was very nice, but no unchaperoned dining, theaters, or other engagements after six o'clock in the evening. That was only for chorus girls, and young female persons not in good society. Such was the social law and the custom, and not to be broken lightly, although one year and six months of war was to bring about many changes, and the decade of the twenties a full-scale revolution. In 1917, no proper young girls painted their nails, nor used lipstick, and a bar was a male sanctuary, free from the chatter of women. Just the same, and despite such handicaps, most girls had no special trouble getting their men, and a really smart New York miss, without a vestige of today's warpaint, could look like an angel in crisp silver and gold on the top of a wax candle lit Christmas tree.

My heart was doing a series of loop the loops, and then one evening I attended a gala first-night performance of Chu Chin Chow, as the guest of a beautiful and most fashionable young lady and her family. The star was Florence Reed, and it was a very special night, with high ranking officers in uniform, gentlemen in white tie and tails, and all the ladies in their best evening gowns. There must have been many celebrated persons present, for the producer made a curtain speech, in which he kept referring to "this most distinguished audience." During an intermission, I told my *faire ladye* that I expected to go overseas before long, but that perhaps I might run into her, as a Red Cross worker, somewhere in France.

"I'm now pretty busy with the Red Cross, and I'd love to go overseas," she said to me. "But there's little hope, for they told us at headquarters, that no girl would be sent overseas, unless she was thirty-five, or very plain."

"I see. Plain fare for the troops. Plain food and plain women, so not to spoil us," I said and felt depressed, because she did not then qualify for overseas by a Swedish mile which is twelve of ours. Back again in camp in the very early morning, I ran into orders, confusion, and hasty packing, and inside one hour we were entraining for the docks, and then herded on board a transport. We hung around incommunicado for two days, while we sweated blood but could get no word through to friends, families, nor sweethearts. Then we sailed on October 27, 1917, on a clear but most bitterly cold, early morning.

I stood on deck, with a knifelike wind piercing my heavy officer's coat, and watched the passing Statue of Liberty, and the receding Manhattan skyline. Stark and functional like a series of high Haman's gallows, they stood out, a silhouetted frieze against the coldest looking, gun-barrel blue, glinting sky, and somehow beautiful beyond description. I now felt that I was severing all roots, that nothing I had been in the past meant a thing anymore, and that I was embarking on an unknown sea, an adventure of the soul. My heartsank. It seemed that something like a curtain of iron was being rung down with a clang, on my former pleasant and familiar world.

Chapter 6

ENGLAND AND THE BATTLE OF LIVERPOOL

Our transport was a Cunarder, the SS *Manchuria*, of around sixteen thousand tons register, and with a cruising speed of around sixteen knots. The ship's captain, the officers, the crew and the stewards were all as British as roast beef and Yorkshire pudding, and everything was clean, well run, and in shipshape order. This I recall with pleasure, as in vivid contrast to a miserable eleven days on a U.S. Liberty ship in World War II, where our ten-knot vessel was a stifling slum, its food unspeakable, a good part of its machinery in haywire condition, and its misnamed captain, a merchant marine species of milquetoast, apparently afraid and unable to extract discipline and proper performance of duties from his foul-mouthed, filthy, and utterly incompetent crew of goons. That Liberty ship, whose navy gun crew was at sword's points with the merchant personnel, and whose real name we readily transformed to the SS *Gruesome*, was like some foul county jail afloat, but our *Manchuria*, considering it was wartime, still ran like a gentlemanly Cunarder.

In her hold *Manchuria* carried some assorted munitions, but she was not heavily laden, nor were her passengers crowded, the great majority being some two hundred and fifty recently commissioned pilots, and flying cadets. We were four in a stateroom, instead of being packed, five deep like sardines in a Black Hole of Calcutta of a hold, and instead of a greasy frankfurter and a half-cooked potato being slapped on one's messkit, by a grouchy and hairy-chested ape in a dirty undershirt, we dined on clean linen with gleaming silver and glass, and were served by correct stewards, who were cheerful and solicitous, but never familiar.

In that ocean were many submarines; it was a dangerous voyage and we were rather casual and boisterous young Americans, much less reticent in speech and reserved in manner than the average graduate of Harrow and Oxford, but with our stewards it was still carry on in the tradition of the line, meaning duty and decorum. It was still all pip-pip, and remember your Cunard training. That was the general atmosphere. In comparison with all other military transport voyaging which I endured in two wars, this first troop crossing was very genteel.

Among the recently commissioned RMAs and flying cadets on the *Manchuria* whose names I can recall, were George Crawford, the brothers Guyon and Estes Armstrong, James Osgood, Joe Estill, Reed Chambers (destined to become a leading ace) William (Hank) Stovall another ace-to-be, Bradley Gaylord, Tom Ring, George Fisher, and St. Clair Street, years later a distinguished air force general. There was also Hugh Fontaine, one of our more eminent crapshooters, who was to fly with Eddie Rickenbacker and, many years later, to become nationally famous to all good horseplayers, as the trainer of the racehorse Needles, the winner of the 1956 Kentucky Derby. Well, even then, he had a certain mint julep look about him.

We enjoyed a fine weather, three-day run to Halifax, Nova Scotia, with no escort and little fear of enemy submarines, since they were then, but quite mistakenly, not believed to cruise so near our shores. On board, Estes Armstrong, one of the several Memphis boys in our contingent of flyers, played and replayed the "Missouri Waltz" on his guitar, while elsewhere at the same time an obscure artillery captain named Harry S. Truman, may have been playing it on some piano.

Music, even the music of southern Democrats was all right, but the main diversion was black jack. Many of the Memphis gang were adept at this game, and they played it rough and for keeps. I once sat in with a group of these southern gen'lemen, and found out that both liberal arts at Harvard, and advanced mathematics at MIT had taught me nothing about the supreme importance of holding the bank. After an all-night session in a smoke-filled stateroom, I staggered out for an icy breath of fresh salt air, minus a month's pay, and convinced that the Memphis brand of black jack was like its namesake up in a dark alley.

Landlocked Halifax harbor was sparkling and beautiful, but Boreas was blowing a stiff breeze, and it was as cold as the ever frozen marsh Cocytus, even its innermost circlet, the Judecca, in

Dante's bottommost pit of Hell. Being cold enough to freeze solid the most precious possessions of the proverbial brass monkey, it would have seemed madness to enter the waters, but we had a hero.

On board was a handsome, curly-haired, jolly-looking cadet from San Francisco, named Tevis. Willie, as he was known all over the ship, worried no more about submarines than the rest of us, but his mama had read all about the great increase in sinkings, and she wanted no child of hers doing a "*Down Went* McGinty to the Bottom of the Sea," a popular song she may well have heard in her girlhood. Somewhere, she had found and purchased a new invention, a patented, guaranteed, nonsinkable suit, which she insisted that Willie bring on the ship, where its fame was soon known. Since we were not given shore leave and there was little excitement, a hue and cry arose that the unsinkable suit be given a trial run, and like *Barkis*, Willie was willing.

The suit was made of thick rubber, and it was lined with thick, warm, insulating material. It contained air compartments, that could be inflated with a bicycle pump, and it had a large waterproof pocket that contained victuals, guaranteed to sustain life while bobbing the billows. Most important, there was a whistle, attached by a chain to the suit, so that the castaway could sound a blast, and summon friendly shipping.

This suit, which enveloped the entire body, save the hands and head (for which latter was provided a smart patented rubber hat), weighed a great deal, and it was all but impossible to don without considerable assistance. For this, many volunteers were available, and there was also the friendly cooperation of the ship's captain, and the services of the gruff but amiable old sea dog of a boatswain, who rigged up a launching apparatus.

With considerable difficulty, probably much like a medieval knight getting into a complete suit of tournament armor, Cadet-private Tevis became enveloped in his monstrous garment, upon which his squires adjusted the fastenings, and made all ready. At last, his smart, patented rubber *chapeau* tied under his chin, whistle in place, patented unsinkable doughnuts in waterproof pocket, our seagoing man of rubber was ready for launching. Resembling the Michelin Man, he smilingly posed for pictures, but he was barely able to walk a step in his whale-suit.

But now the faithful squires have used the bicycle pump to blow him and the suit up to vast proportions, a boom has been swung from the ship's clifflike sides, and a donkey engine has begun an infernal clatter. A noose drops and is adjusted under the hero's arms, the boatswain signals the donkeyman, and amidst intense silence, the entire ship's company watches the daring descent into the icy, white-capped waters. Cadet-flyer Tevis is in, but the patented suit is truly unsinkable, and he bobs around like a bottle, while he duly opens his pocket, eats his perhaps not so unsinkable doughnut, and then graciously blows on his whistle.

This gives out a peep like a dejected Monomoy sandpiper, and a great, grey herring gull, no doubt thinking this object a new, whistling, channel buoy, makes a close pass as if to settle on its summit. However, the *Manchuria's* skipper acknowledges the whistle, and answers with a great blast from the foghorn, we cheer and shout, and the frightened gull wheels away, and does not do what gulls may do on whistling buoys. Then again the veteran Cunard donkeyman goes into action, and dripping but smiling, the intrepid tester of the one and only patented, guaranteed, nonsinkable suit in the entire U.S. Army, is hoisted safe on deck into the arms of his admirers. It was a good show, the best of the entire crossing.

After three days at Halifax, our convoy being all assembled for the crossing, the great log boom, with its dangling steel antisubmarine nets, was swung open by the guard tugs, and we steamed into the open sea. There in company with about a dozen more vessel, that ranged from good-sized liners to small tramps, and led by the *Victoria*, an old British cruiser, we began the long, zigzagging voyage over the wintry North Atlantic, that dark, stormy, and dreaded Western Ocean of the early navigators. When we departed Halifax, the town and its harbor were still in the grip of intense cold. Not very long after, a great ball of flaming gas and heat rose from a rammed ammunition ship, a locomotive was said to have been hurled from one side to the other of the wreck-strewn harbor, city blocks were leveled, and over two thousand of Halifax's citizens perished in the blast and fires of the immense explosion.

Since our speed was limited to about eight knots, by the needs

"a peep like a frightened Monomoy sandpiper."

of the small freighters, it was a long and rough crossing, with little to do except take one's turn on watch against enemy submarines, although spotting a periscope in those huge, foam-flecked seas was highly improbable. Our rather lightly laden *Manchuria* rode dry like a duck, but huge seas could be seen sweeping the other vessels, all but swallowing the smaller cargo boats, and the sight of the old *Victoria*, rolling, wallowing, and burying her forward gun turret under cascading tons of water, somehow made me think of once seeing a determined old lady, her wind-tortured umbrella ready to turn inside out, bravely trying to cross Park Avenue in a vicious northeaster. Finally off the north coast of Ireland, we were met by four British destroyers, and were safely escorted through the North Channel, and the tiny but amazingly rough Irish Sea, into Liverpool harbor.

In Liverpool, where we remained only a few hours before entraining, I happened on an American sailor off some destroyer, whom I had known at college. Because of his rugged build, his familiarity (since a Buzzards Bay boyhood) with small boat handling, and perhaps also his great sense of humor, he had been made a boatswain's mate.

We greeted each other jocularly, with a "Fawncy meeting you here, old chap!" as supposedly befitting an encounter in *deah old England*, and in the course of conversation, I casually asked him if he had seen any action.

"Well, officially no, but so to speak in a way, I might say yes," he said and put down the cup of strong tea that the railroad canteen ladies had given him." I've not yet helped sink a sub, but I was in the Battle of Liverpool. In fact, I was at the opening of that great battle."

"The Battle of Liverpool?" I said.

"There were four of us in a pub," said Bo'sun Ben, taking a hitch in his bell-bottomed trousers, and buttoning his pea jacket against the damp chill of a Liverpool late afternoon. "We were in there having a couple of wee drappies, and feeling no pain, when in walks a couple of Limeys from some ship or other. They ordered a couple of '*awf and 'awfs*, and then one looked around, lifted his mug and said, 'And 'ere's to 'Is Mawjesty, Gor' bless him. Come on you, Yanks. A drink to 'Is Mawjesty.' "

"Well, did you?"

"We did. Why not? We had nothing against the King of England. We even kind of thought well of him, but then——"

"Yes. What then?"

"Oh, more damn Limeys came in, and one said, 'Oh, 'ere's to the British Nyvee, which rules the wyves, and protects the freedom of the seas. Ho, you Yanks: J'ine us in a drink to the glorious British Nyvee."

"You did?"

"Oh sure. Why not? Though we sure had mental reservations about that ruling the wyves bunk, what with the German subs raising the hell they were doing."

"Right!"

"Right. Also, it was beginning to get a little tiresome, and one of us, a pretty high-strung fellow, muttered to me, 'Look. Here comes another one of these Royal Nyvee swabs, and I'm getting sick of it. If that bastard just dares to lift his beer!"

"Which I suppose he did?"

"Sure. Another one of those, *'Is Mawjesty* toasts, and you, Yanks, join us."

"Well?"

"Well, what? It was beginning to interfere with our own conversation, and my friend just said, 'Look here, Limey. We've drunk three times to your king, and okay. But enough's enough, and I am getting mighty bored. So I say to you, and all the swabs in the British Nyvee, you go tell 'Is Mawjesty to take a long, running jump at the moon, and leave us in peace.' Then the hassel started, but good!"

"I can guess."

"Well," said Ben, "the barmaid was yelling bloody murder and police, so we moved into the street. Then some more of ours joined in, and some of theirs, and more and more as the word got round, until half of both fleets were in the rumpus, with fists, bricks, bottles, sticks, and plenty energy."

"Sounds rough. Who won?"

"The shore patrols, with the police, the fire department, a half-battalion of some British regiment, plus a company of our gyrenes finally won. That is, only after we sailors got tired. That was the battle. Good clean fun, with no one getting killed, either."

A locomotive now slid in from the shadowy outer yards, crept up, and backed gently into the two projecting end bumpers of a string of dingy-looking railway carriages. There was no ram-you-damn-you, grinding jerk on making this coupling, such as back in the U.S.A., and the gentle, springy reaction seemed odd to the American troops on the platform. Then the engine, to our eyes funny-looking, since it had no cowcatcher, and not much of a cab, gave out a birdlike peep, and the troops burst into laughter, since it seemed so absurd compared to the musical, deep whistles of our American locomotives. However, it was time to take leave of Ben. The guard locked the doors, the little engine gave another peep, and we were gliding out into the city's dark and depressing outskirts.

The compartment, in the third-class carriage, was lit by one dim blue bulb, and the windows were covered with black cloth, for on any reasonably clear night, the Gothas and other Hun bombers might fly overhead. Inside our troop train, the air was damp and cold, as well as bitter and stale from untold thousands of previously smoked Woodbines and other cheap *gaspers*, and this was mixed with the rancid odors left by muddy, oiled boots, sweaty uniforms, unwashed bodies just out of the trenches, and all the spittle, filth, and general unclean abominations that go with war. This was new to us, and very depressing. It was a long and gloomy ride until, cold, cramped, and famished, we saw the gray dawn of a foggy morning, and detrained at Southampton.

Here, our temporary location was a nearby rest camp, cold, muddy, utterly cheerless, and composed of unfloored tents. Walking from this to town on pass, the rain fell in a fine, misty drizzle, but the white, puddly road, the tall, stark trees, the high thick hedges, and whole countryside, dreary though it was, nevertheless seemed to give out a strange spell, and to present a mystic and eerie beauty, like something seen in a surrealistic landscape painting, or in a dream. Along our route, we met few people or vehicles that seemed of the common, workaday world, but as if fit inhabitants of this enchanted land, we encountered many women, walking alone or two by two, and all were dressed in complete black. Most of these seemed young or fairly so, and tall and slender, with pale, unsmiling, haunted faces, and they appeared to drift past rather than walk, like in some Danteesque vision of saddened ghosts eternally wandering in Limbo, on the edge of the abyss of Hell.

The seaport was a bit more cheerful than the highway and its ghostly widows, and we entered a small restaurant. The waitress, naively part and pretty, like so many of the British working girls, said there were *chops and chips.* These came, along with the inevitable pot of tea, the lone chop apiece being about the size of a fifty cent piece, and the fried potatoes a few spoonfuls. That was the entire meal, and nothing further was allowed to be served a single person, under wartime regulations. We left still famished, and as hungry as bears. America, the land of heaping meals, lay three thousand miles away across a stormy ocean, and one too, infested with submarines. We then realized that England was tightly, uncomfortably, and rigidly honestly rationed, because England was only one jump ahead of famine in November 1917.

Chapter 7

CROSSING THE CHANNEL

After a dreary, monotonous, ever drizzling week at Southampton, we received orders and, about eight in the evening of another gloomy day, we tramped down a sodden quay, to embark for a channel crossing. Our boat was a sidewheeler, a venerable antique with a high funnel stack, a walking beam, and huge paddle boxes that seemed to have been resurrected from some marine museum to be pressed into war service, along with the retired Colonel Blimps and other relics of a bygone time, but the fog was so thick that we could barely see fifty feet along the deck of our vessel and, for all we visualized, we might as well have just embarked on the ghostly Flying Dutchman. To cross the narrow, crowded seas in the midst of this pea souper, seemed madness, but a British steward said, "This is fine, sir. Jerry's subs will not 'ave 'awf a chance, sir."

Perhaps he was right, but we were only an hour out after leaving Spithead, when there came, even through the impenetrable fog, a great red flash from our starboard, which was shortly followed by the heavy, muffled boom of a great explosion. What ship was hit, whether by mine or torpedo, and who might now be struggling in the swirling, icy tides of the channel, we never did know, but suddenly our dimly heard, unseen destroyer escorts blinked signals as they ranged alongside in the darkness, giving out odd, whup-whupping whistles. At this, our own very ancient engines rumbled into greater life, the paddles raced and churned, strained steam pipes hissed and wheezed, and we fled through a sea of dark green grease, which seemed only a bit scummier than the night air around us.

Landing at Le Havre, France, in the morning, we marched uphill to another British rest camp, where I saw something that confirmed Bosun Ben's tale of British touchiness about anything that reflected on their institution of royalty. In our camp, there was an officers' lounge equipped with an old piano, and gathered around were a mixed group of British and American officers, who sang and drank while an American lieutenant played the battered instrument. All seemed very jolly, and filled with the old, *blood is thicker than water* and *hands across the sea* sentiments, the usual general alcoholic friendliness, when the pianist suddenly began that ancient, ribald ballad:

> Oh, the minstrels sing of an English King,
> Of many years ago,
> Who ruled his land with an iron hand,
> Tho his mind was weak and low.

During this and the subsequent bawdy verses, the Americans sang with gusto, but the British became strangely silent. It was clear from their frozen expressions that they did not approve of a song reflecting on British royalty, even if it was about an imaginary king who never existed. Under their cool stares, the song finally petered out, and there was a painful silence. Then the drawling voice of a tall British captain addressed the assembly. "Very clever that, Yanks," he said. "But now, you chaps! How about giving us a jolly song about your president?"

Our two day stop in camp was dull, and having met a couple of congenial captains, one a South African, the other a kilted member of the Canadian Princess Pat's Regiment, two of us were glad to accept their invitation to sample the nightlife of the seaport. Le Havre did not offer much excitement and, after sampling several beers in the rather dark and dingy wartime cafes and bistros, our kiltie friend suggested that an inspection tour of a certain off-limits district might be in order.

In a few minutes we had walked some blocks of muddy streets, when our further progress was blocked by a fence of boards and barbed wire. This barricade had a gate, but it was locked with a padlock and chain, and up and down before this marched a young British sentry, his bayonet gleaming at the end of his rifle. Under the dim street light, he recognized us for officers, and he stamped to a ringing halt, faced us, and saluted by presenting rifle.

"Sentry!" Our towering and impressive-looking kiltie captain addressed the private. "These off limits, here. I assume that they do not apply to officially inspecting officers?"

"Sir! My orders are to admit inspecting officers."

"Good then. And now, my man! We two, and these two American medical officers have the duty of inspecting the establishment of Madame X. I'll trouble you to open that gate."

"Sir." The sentry unlocked and swung open the gate. "It is but a short distance, and my orders are to escort all inspecting officers to their destination. This way, sir."

In a column of twos and keeping step, we were escorted by our armed guard to the notorious portal, where our extremely correct private ran up the steps, rang a jangling bell, ran down, and again presented arms to us, as the door opened, and a light streamed on the stoop.

Within, it was frowzy, filled with stale air, and far from tempting, most of the ladies being short, common-looking, and one hundred and forty pounds on the hoof, but it was amusing to open a couple of bottles of warm, cheap champagne, and to hear the views of Madame concerning *la guerre*, which was *affreuse, terrible, épouvantable, et si triste, messieurs.*

We *medical officers*, having now inspected and ascertained the current frightful social conditions existing in Le Havre, took our leave, and we were again met at the barrier by our enlisted friend, who once more presented arms, and wished us a cheerful and civil goodnight. This sentry was smart in appearance, having all that air of military chic that is so noticeable in many British regiments, and his was the British military way of handling any situation, always with military punctilio, and due respect for superiors on all occasions. Jim, my American friend, and I, on talking over this night's adventure, got a great laugh over being so formally saluted under the dubious circumstances, but our British friends took it all quite for granted, and saw nothing particularly humorous about it.

Chapter 8

ARRIVAL IN PARIS

Receiving orders, we entrained at Le Havre for Paris, where we reported to USAF headquarters at 45 Avenue Montaign. There to our delight, we were told to report on the following morning, but that we were at liberty in the interim. That meant that Paris was our dish for that afternoon and evening, and until ten the following morning. This was a happy break.

During the summer of 1913, I had spent a gay and happy six weeks in Paris, and now, except that the streets and the hotels were filled with soldiers, in all sorts of differing and often colorful Allied uniforms, the city seemed much the same and just as gay, and apparently with none of the general gloom and sadness that we had encountered during our brief stay in England. For one thing, with the exception of bread and sugar, there was plenty to eat in the way of meat and vegetables, plenty to drink in various wines and liquors, and plenty of attractive young women all over the town, and all of this was a most pleasant change from our previous days of drabness. In addition, all the old and famous shops, hotels, restaurants, including the most hectic night spots, were going full blast with the dampers wide open. Wartime or not, Paris seemed in business as usual.

The city was still smart, beautiful and exciting. British soldiers might sing of going on leave to *Blighty*, but a lot of their officers seemed to go to Paris, and the French capital was referred to as *Paname*, Panama, the fabled city of Eldorado, by all the front-line French soldiers, who dreamed and schemed of getting a *permis* to visit the city while on leave. To be sure, France was seriously wounded, perhaps almost bled white, as some said, but the nation's heart was still very hopeful—were not the Americans starting to come over—and Paris was the heart of the nation.

My pilot companions and I made full use of our short liberty, dining at the former, much smaller, ancient Tour D'Argent, taking in the Folies Bergeres, and taking rooms at the Hotel

Crillon on the Place de la Concorde, then as now famed for its atmosphere of luxury. In those days its bar, then on the ground floor and not in a cellar, was a principal meeting place for all American aviators lucky enough to get to Paris. There I met some old friends of the American Ambulance, and of the Lafayette Escadrille, but our stay was brief, for in the morning we received orders to report to the 3rd Aviation Instruction Center, for advanced flying training.

During the seven months since we had declared war, the United States Army had established three aviation instruction centers in France. The first, an experiment organized near Paris, was soon deactivated, perhaps because it was too near the city and its distractions. The 2nd Aviation Instruction Center was formed by taking over an old French airdrome and primary flying school, across the Loire River at Tours. Here, many of our cadet flyers, both those who had led their ground school classes in the U.S.A. and, as a supposed reward, had been immediately shipped overseas, and those recruited in France from the American Ambulance, received their first flying training. I do not think that their primary training was as good as ours, received on Jennys at Mineola, and for a good reason.

At Tours, the instructors were French, the methods were French and very good, but the planes were, even for those days, very primitive Caudrons. These were very slow flying *chicken-coops*, powered with sixty horsepower, radial Anzani engines, and they were not too far advanced in design beyond the powered box kites of the Wrights' earlier models. True, these flying machines were tractors and not pushers, and they had landing wheels, instead of the skids of Kitty Hawk days, but they had nacelles instead of fuselages, twin rudders but no ailerons. Lacking the latter, banking and maintaining lateral stability, was done by warping the wings, which took no inconsiderable muscular effort on the *manche-a-bâlai*, the broomstick, as the French called that control. The air speed was slow, and the landing speed was very gentle, like a leisurely pelican settling down on Pyramid Lake, and in case of a forced landing on almost any sort of terrain, there was so much under the pilot in the form of wooden undercarriage and struts, to crumble and so cushion the shock, that there was a minimum danger to the pilot, unless he was pierced by a splinter, which was rare. Incidentally, it was one of these same Caudron models, that Vedrines, a French pilot, landed on the roof of a Paris department store, in the spring of 1919. For that matter, more than one was landed on treetops during the training at Tours, with little or no injury to the student flyers.

These model Caudrons were about as safe and foolproof as a plane then could be, but they were wearisome wagons on a windy day, as I found out on ferrying one from Orly Field to Tours. This one one-hundred-and-thirty-mile flight took over two hours, during which I was forced to exert great effort on the stick, to warp the wings and avoid being turned upside down in the turbulent breeze. The entire flight was a battle, with a wind that attacked like a wrestler, and my arms ached for days afterwards.

Although I did not attend the school at Tours, I heard many strange tales from friends, who had taken their primary training there. During 1917, there were a good many old regular army officers who were temporarily promoted to field grades, and then transferred from other branches, to be given commands in our brand new but fast growing air force. Some of these proved excellent men, but others made little attempt to qualify as pilots, or even to learn anything about this new arm of our service.

A majority of these little military Bourbons, who could never forget their old *squads right* way of thinking, and would never learn the barest rudiments of the air, had been transferred from the obsolescent cavalry. The first thing that some did, on taking command of a flying field, was to order a stable and hitching post for their horse. One of these brass-bound jockeys, on the first inspection of his command, because the roar of the engines that were being warmed up on the flight line frightened his horse cried angrily, "Hey there! Stop those damn pinwheels. Don't you see they're scaring my horse!" as his charger pranced and snorted, to the open-mouthed stares of dumfounded and amazed students, instructors, and mechanics.

Tours had something similar, for a time, in the way of a commanding officer. This old centaur, who may well have ridden hell for leather to saber down redskins in the days of Geronimo and Cochise, had never heard that airplanes could be laterally controlled through warping the wings. Hearing that student flyers criticized the Caudrons because they warped their wings, he gave strict orders that all idle planes be kept in the hangars and out of the sun, "which might warp their wings." Naturally such ignorant commanders did not gain the respect of the flyers, and when such misfits, as sometimes happened, sought to use their power in petty and tyrannical ways, to cover up their lack of knowledge about the air, morale suffered greatly, and even a feeling of near mutinous hatred might be engendered.

No doubt from lack of sufficient flying officers of age and experience in administration, a good many old-timers had to be transferred from the ground branches to the air corps. Some were superior types, who studied and made good in the end, but too many were mere blustering odd crocks, perhaps transferred for the good of some regiment as a hidden reason, who never made the least attempt to understand the new arm of the service, and such gave their bewildered and dismayed cadet charges the impression that their commanding officer considered proficiency in close order drill vastly more important than good formation flying.

The Third Aviation Instruction Center was established for advanced training a few miles northwest of the old historic town of Issoudun. This location was right in the heart of France, being about twenty miles northeast of Chateauroux, and about seventy miles due south of the famous city of Orleans, the site of Joan of Arc's most famous victory. Not too far distant were Gievres and Romorantin, two of our largest supply depots. It was to the school at Issoudun that we were now ordered to report, after our brief glimpse of Paris.

Issoudun had been picked for an advanced flying training center for various reasons. One hundred and thirty miles south of Paris, on the main government-owned railroad line to the cities of the south of France, it was not too far from the aviation factories, and the new plane assembling airdromes, such as Villacoublay, where we obtained the Caudrons, Niewports, and other models used in training. At the same time, it was far enough from the stabilized front lines to, most probably, insure the center from any danger of a night bombing raid. It seemed hardly likely that the German would risk their ninety-mile-an-hour Gothas and

Friedrickshavens on a three-hundred-mile round trip within our lines, for less than a major objective.

Probably the main reason for the selection of Issoudun, was that the countryside was very level and, since the soil was rather poor, the farms had need be large, with only a few and widely separated villages and farmhouses. This gave plenty of extensive, wide open space for flying fields and probable forced landings, as well as the least disruption to the agriculture of the country. One drawback that may have been overlooked in picking the site, was the nature of the ground, being mostly clay and shaly rock, that was so impervious to water that it was either mud or ice crusts, a great part of the year. Mainly it was mud, "God's mud hole," as we got to call it, and General Pershing named it the worst mud hole in all France, a superlative from an undoubted expert on military terrain conditions.

Issoudun consisted of a main camp of three flying fields and, within a radius of a half-dozen miles, were six or more satellite fields for successive stages of training, so that the entire center covered about fifty square miles of land. Within this domain remained Ronze, Lizeray, St. Valentine, Menetreols, Pody, Voeu, and such hamlets with their adjacent farms and cabbage patches, all separated by acres and acres of next to nothing, so that it recalled a sort of small-scale South Dakota. Through here, the few male peasant inhabitants toiled and grubbed in their fields, with scarcely an upward glance at our planes, even when we flew, hedgehopping, not thirty feet above their heads, which we frequently did in those golden days of great freedom from so many of today's flying regulations. However, if the majority of the *Jacques Bonhommes* ignored us, their good wives could see a twenty-franc note a hundred yards off, while it was still inside a pilot's leather jacket, and they were more than glad to fix us up a tasty dish of fried potatoes, an omelet, fresh bread and a big bowl of hot chocolate, at any time on short notice. Such simple meals, but well cooked, proved lifesavers when we felt we could no longer face the horrors awaiting us devised by fiendish cooks in our messhalls.

In November 1917, there had been much rain in this part of France, and our first view of the main camp was more than usually depressing. This first glimpse was a big sign saying,

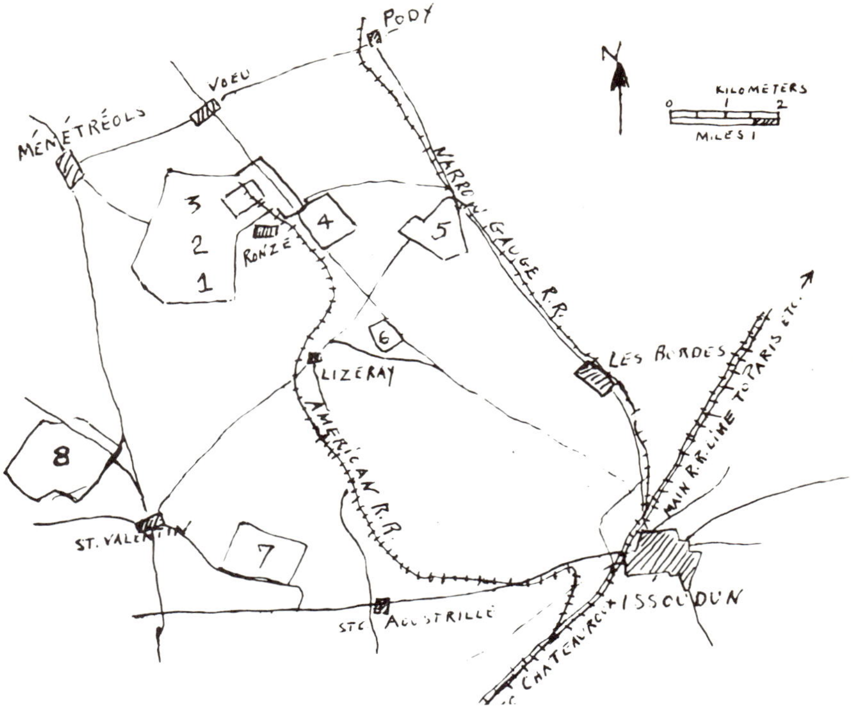

3RD AVIATION INSTRUCTION CENTER
WITH
NUMBERED FIELDS

"Police, Prison, and Labor Officer." Within the main gate stretched a wide, slimy street, footpaths of muddy planks and duckboards, and rows of long, one-storied, tarpaper shacks, that seemed to rest on the mud, like barges stranded by low tide in an estuary. A short ride, and we were scrambling over the hard tailboards of the White trucks that had brought us from the railroad station. Trundling our baggage, we officers (or rather, what the enlisted men distinguished as not quite real officers, to be feared and perhaps suspected, but *flying lieuts* and a breed apart), entered our barracks, a warren of closely spaced double-deck bunks, broken by a few wider openings, which contained benches, and a huge old-fashioned pot-bellied stove.

Toilet facilities were of the crudest, and the latrine, a gruesome tent housing a trench and a rail, was across and down the street a stretch, a frantic dash on raw rainy nights, when suffering from the common complaint caused by bad water. In France outside of Paris, water was strictly something to run under bridges, it was never safe and, in spite of the doctor and his ill-smelling, chlorinated water bags, it was hard to avoid getting the cramps, frequently.

Next to our quarters, the one for us *flying lieuts*, was the famed Barrack 4. This housed the still-out-of-luck cadet who should have long before received their commissions and the accompanying pay, but had not, due to the usual delays and confusion. Many of these cadets were former ambulance drivers, who had taken their primary at Tours, and others were U.S. ground school graduates, the upper half of their classes, who had been among the first to be shipped overseas for flying training. Now, they were still cadet-private in many cases, while we, the lower ranking, ground school graduates, were officers, and officially gentlemen by act of Congress. This was hardly justice, but it was the army and to be expected, and in all life too for that matter, although the direful Day of Judgement may correct a lot of that—I hope! As for the cadets, they lived like us, in something like an old-time, French-Canadian lumberjacks' air tight bunkhouse, and *snororium*.

We never gave a thought to the frightful social conditions of our barracks, just so long as the stoves were fired red hot on the wet, cold, raw nights, and that the windows were opened to a minimum. Every now and then, some medico would accompany the O.D. on his nightly rounds, and give horrified orders that windows be flung open, and the night air of France allowed to circulate. This was done, but no sooner had he departed, than the windows were banged down, the drafts of the stoves opened, and once more a guttural snoring, nightmare muttering, carbon dioxided peace would settle on our home, whose atmosphere could be cut with a knife.

Heat was life and during the terrible winter of 1917-1918, it was hard to ever feel warm and dry at Issoudun. The nights were always raw and cold, the days were half the time rainy, snowy, or misty, and the fields, unless frozen and at times covered with a hard pack of snow, were apt to be ankle deep in a mire of unbelievably sticky mud, that both bogged down the landing wheels of planes, and collected in huge gobs of goo on one's boots. Often, we slept in our fur-lined flying suits, a bad practice as any polar explorer knows, and this often resulted in a very severe cold, and sometimes pneumonia. It was, all in all, a horrid winter, but somehow we managed to get in a lot of flying.

At Issoudun, our old Mineola gang ran into most of our friends of ground school days, who had crossed in July for their primary training at Tours. A handful of these had had the luck to receive immediate training and their commissions, but most had to wait months for training assignments, and they were still cadets. Among the more fortunate ones were Hamilton Coolidge and Douglas Campbell, both especially brilliant flyers, and among the first to graduate in advanced training at Issoudun.

We naturally made many new friends and acquaintances, both from those who had first trained at Tours, or from other primary fields in the U.S. In our barrack was a fiery southerner, Frank "Monk" Hunter, destined to become an ace and, in World War II, a major-general. There was also St. Clair Street, another future general, who was to become distinguished in later years. Also among the many at Issoudun, who became distinguished in later life, was Gilbert Winant.

Gil Winant was a tall, loose-limbed, very reticent Princeton graduate, with a definite Abraham Lincoln look about him, whose character was unusually noble and sensitive. As a pintsized second former at prep school, I had known Gil when he was captain of the crew, and unofficially the head boy of the school. In those days, certain old prep schools were just emerging from a long established, but medieval era of hazing and schoolboy savageries, when so-called fresh new kids were, on certain traditional *Bloody Sundays*, lashed with switches, cocked up with tennis balls, or even perhaps green apples, and those considered to be especially chesty specimens might have their heads pushed under the ice of the wintry brooks, to teach them school customs and proper respect for *old boys*.

Gil Winant did not stand for this, and his influence greatly modified the old barbaric institution, which the masters had not been able to eradicate. Gil was a rather heavy-handed pilot, a trifle slow on his reflexes and given to rough and bouncy landings, but he proved an ideal officer who as commander of the 8th Observation Squadron, was greatly admired by his officers and men. Later in life, he became governor of New Hampshire, and later, ambassador to England.

Among the most famous graduates of Issoudun, in fact the very first pilot to graduate from that advanced flying school, was Eddie Rickenbacker, our first great ace of aces. *Rick*, who had been a top notch racing driver, was a bit older and much more mature than the general run of the eighteen to twenty-four-year-old student flyers, and he knew a great deal more than almost any individual on the base, about engines and mechanics. Shortly after finishing training, he acted as engineer officer, and it was his invention that made flying at all feasible during the long rainy season. This was a pair of small mud guards, which prevented the landing wheels from throwing mud and rocks at the propellers. Our eight-foot, two-bladed props were made from laminated strips of wood, and previous to Eddie's mudguards, they were being constantly shattered on takeoffs and taxiing, causing great delays in training, as well as additional expense.

For various reasons, one's memory retains vivid pictures of certain incidents and individuals, even after scores of years, and I can easily see the Rick of those far-off Issoudun days, as he strode on long legs along the flight lines, his eyes in his aquiline face noting everything. All men can be said to resemble some animal or other, such as a horse, a terrier, a goat, and even a pig. Rick made one think of the secretary bird, that species of African great bird of prey with the long legs of a crane, who is known to pounce on poisonous serpents, even mambas and spitting cobras, to destroy them. Rick looked the part, and over the front lines, he certainly had those characteristics.

As one of the earliest graduates of Issoudun, Douglas Campbell acted as assistant training officer, and another early graduate was Quentin Roosevelt.Quentin, full of vitality like his father, had various jobs wished on him, from post quartermaster to transportation officer, and for a time he was in charge of flying at Field 7, better known as Valentine Field from the nearby hamlet, where formation was first practiced by the students.

From those Issoudun days, I retain two sharp memories of

Quentin. One concerns his floppy campaign hat, which seemed about two sizes too small for his high domed head. Somehow he kept this on with a chin strap, but it perched on top of his head like a comedian spoofing Herbert Hoover, or Beatrice Lillie representing Britannia, and the rest of his uniform seemed much too tight for his robust body. As a graduate with full-fledged officer status, and not just another student flyer, he would sometimes inspect us and call the roll, at one of those drizzly and grizzly reveilles which now and then were inflicted on us, when something had not quite gone right, and the mood at headquarters was repulsive.

These crack of dawn assemblies, ordered on some theory that "these flying prima donnas have got to be reminded that they are soldiers first, and flyers afterwards, by God, sir!" were just one of many small irritations that we student pilots had to endure, under the policy of the General Staff, that was rather ignorant of the problems and possibilities of the new air arm, and not too sympathetic to aviation in general. They angered us by their sometimes utter futility, effecting nothing except to lower morale. They only proved that a fur-lined flying suit could conceal a pair of pajamas, as we stood blear-eyed and ankle-deep in the mud, and realized that the everlasting, driving rain meant another frustrating day of nonflying. At some of these lineups, Quentin would call the roll a bit apologetically, since he too was a flyer, and not a headquarters kiwi all puffed up with smug zeal and ostentatious efficiency, but he perspired and breathed hard, and his uniform, too tight for his frame, seemed ready to pop its buttons.

The other sharp recollection goes back to flying a Niewport fifteen meter, at about five thousand feet above Chateauroux. Returning from a high altitude flight, and peacefully enjoying the panorama below, I was suddenly aware that a shadow had cut off my sunshine, and that a pair of wheels was dangling about six feet above my head. I dove, swerved from danger, and then climbed to get a good look at the intruder.

In another Niewport was a pilot, capped with an undersized campaign hat, held on by a chin strap. Quentin! He had never seen me, while gliding down from a higher altitude. When I told him about it, saying that he might have given me an unusually crude army haircut with his propeller, he apologized but pointed out that danger at the front lines, came from above and behind, and that I might consider this a good lesson for always keeping a sharp watch, above and to the rear, when flying. He was right, even if he had not seen me, but we were both lucky.

As to not seeing, Quentin was a fine fellow, and he proved to be a very brave air fighter, but his eyesight was not quite up to the minimum standard for a military flyer. This defect had been waived by some examining board, because of other outstanding qualities, and perhaps because he was the son of the great TR, but it was common talk that he did not see as sharply as a war flyer should, and this may well have been a cause of his death in action.

The main camp at Issoudun contained headquarters, hospitals, warehouses, bakeries, repair shops, portable hangars filled with training planes, mess halls, barracks, and other accommodations for several hundred student flyers, and several thousand men. These enlisted men, usually officered by nonflyers at the beginning, made up numerous supply, engineering, transportation and other nontactical units and squadrons. This main camp, of three flying fields, was also the terminus of an amazing railroad, and it contained one real godsend, the Red Cross canteen, which in the eyes of us students should have received a special presidential citation, for keeping morale from crumbling during the darkest weeks of the winter of 1917. It was the only spot of cheer and comfort in a camp that was often little more than a sea of mud and depression.

Adjoining this main camp, was a stockade and a prison for captured Germans and Austrians. This was then administered and guarded by the French, but we had some arrangement to use a number of the prisoners for dreary chores, such as digging trenches, and kitchen police. These Heinies were often ingenious in fashioning various little articles, cigarette lighters, models of planes and such, out of scraps of material, which they were always anxious to peddle for cigarettes, candy bars, and soap. This could be done through proper channels, but we preferred to haggle with them through the wire. Then the French commandant rightly objected to this, since any spy in American uniform could have thus smuggled in wire cutters or weapons, and he gave strict orders to his guards, mostly middle-aged or too old for the front lines, to stop this traffic.

Not long after, I was passing not far from the prisoners' stockade, when I noticed a small group of student flyers bargaining with a couple of Germans, through the wire. Recognizing friends, I was about to join them, when there suddenly came screams and curses, and an elderly bearded Frenchman, in a uniform with incredibly baggy red trousers, came around a corner. He came a-running, holding a rifle with its three-foot long, old-fashioned, triangular fluted bayonet extended well ahead of him, and this point aimed dead center at the stern counters of the "intrepid birdmen," who took one good look, and ran away with all possible speed. Among these heroes were two future aces, and one future general.

As for the Germans, they seemed a much relieved and fairly happy lot, who sang and gave little impromptu concerts with a remarkable orchestra that they had fashioned out of cigar boxes and other scraps, into flutes, fiddles, guitars and other instruments. Although there was considerable muttering that they had a fine chance to poison us, they caused no trouble in their kitchen duties.

Our own special railroad was something indeed to gape at and wonder. Nine miles long to connect our camp with the main French line at Issoudun's railroad yards, it had been hastily built with the labor of enlisted men and flying cadets, in the hard way of crowbar, pick, shovel, and muscle, since bulldozers were not yet even a dream on an engineer's drawing board. Called the American Railroad, it was something like from the cartoons of Rube Goldberg or Al Capp, a regular "Dogpatch Line."

The great American Railroad, built by the blood, sweat, and curses of the "flying carpenters," as the luckless cadets referred to themselves, had just about no cut nor fill, and practically no roadbed. Tracks and ties just meandered over the mostly level, but in places slightly rolling farmlands, like a wagon trail over pioneer prairie. The curves had no banking, and the line's profile resembled a measuring worm's over several stretches, but it somehow functioned, delivered equipment and supplies, and even transported passengers.

Naturally over such a track and roadbed, speed was at a

minimum, and the evening train to town, with its single third-class carriage, coupled on the tail end of a string of small, French type, four-wheel gondola cars, and the usual and famed *hommes quarantes, chevaux huits* (forty men, eight horses) boxcars, was known as the Creeping Princess, or the Tape Worm. Most fantastic was the engine, which seemed to have been requisitioned from the antiquarian collection in the Louvre.

La Locomotive du Chemin de Fer Americain had all but no cab, no cowcatcher, a skinny, brass-bound boiler, one pair of huge driving wheels, and a tall smokestack, that was topped with a high spiked, brass crown. As the big drivers revolved, the cylinders swiveled up and down with the rise and fall of the connecting rods, the contraption huffed and puffed, and I was reminded of a woodcut picture of a train in one of the earliest editions of a Jules Verne novel. This was the same model engine that had drawn Phileas Fogg over part of his famous round-the-world journey.

During the war, France was hard put to replace destroyed rolling stock, and all the most ancient engines and cars were rounded up from forgotten yards, and put to work hauling troops and supplies. Our engine was a collector's piece, one of the most ancient models dug out of some locomotive cemetry, but it was a locomotive nevertheless, and covetous eyes regarded it. One night it disappeared from the Issoudun siding, and was never seen again. It had silently vanished onto the main line, probably snitched by some desperate French transportation officer, for his own vital duties.

This loss was replaced with some other relic of the 1840s, and the Creeping Princess resumed its evening run, at a speed seldom over fifteen miles per hour. Once or so while on the return trip from Issoudun, the engineer, gay and brave from cognac, might open up the throttle to twenty miles an hour, sometimes jumping the track, and scattering cars and contents along the right of way. These wrecks caused no serious injuries that I heard of, but one morning blood was found on the wheels, and search revealed a body removed of its head. Some soldier, some reports say a cadet, walking back to camp along the track, had felt sleepy, and had lain down with a rail for his pillow. That was the grim deduction.

Chapter 9

FRENCH INSTRUCTORS, UNIFORMS AND PECULIARITIES

After we had been a few days at Issoudun, the steady rain, whose falling drops could damage a revolving propeller, let up, and we began our training. The first stage meant walking over to Field 1, to practice on the *rouleurs*. These rollers or as sometimes called, *Penguins*, were old Morane monoplanes, equipped with forty-horsepower rotary engines, whose wings had been somewhat bobbed and whose ailerons had been removed, so that they could run over the ground like frightened jackrabbits, but could not fly. Their purpose was to teach pilots who were not familiar with rotary-engine planes how to control and run a straight course in a Niewport, while taxiing and taking off.

The Issoudun training Niewports were powered with 80 to 120 horsepower, Le Rhone rotary engines, which revolved during flying speed at about 1200 revolutions per minute. These planes had relatively small rudders, and their left lower wings had a greater angle of incidence than the lower rights, to compensate for the engine's torque, which at flying speed was considerable. These small rudders were delicately effective on the short-fuselaged Niewports, when airborne and at air speeds of from 90 to 115 miles per hour, but on the ground at lower speeds, the rudder had to be used very vigorously to control the plane, and to keep it rolling in a straight line.

On the ground, the left wing dragged, and unless the pilot was alert, and instantly ready to apply hard right rudder as a check, the Niewport had a habit of suddenly making a violent turn to the left, which the French called a *cheval de bois*, a wooden merry-go-round horse, and this generally ended in a burst landing tire, a crumpled wing tip, or even a nose-over and a broken propeller, plus the extra expense and time lost for replacements. This tendency towards a left ground loop was still worse when the ground had undulations, which was commonly the case on most fields in those days, and if there was ice or a light blanket of snow, it took a kind of sixth sense coming from experience, and lightning action to anticipate and check a bad, complete face-about ground loop. It was to teach this control that the penguins were invented.

A group of us gathered around, while the French instructor explained the *manettes* controlling the engine. The rotary engines of those times had one manette, a small lever that regulated the flow of gasoline into the carburetor, and a larger manette, the actual throttle, that regulated the flow of mixed air and gas into the inlet valve. The trick was to manipulate them both while flying, all the time making constant small adjustments to keep the motor running smoothly. This took a delicate sense of touch, and a few students were never able to make a complete success of it. It took what our French instructor called, "de la finesse, mes lieutenants. Ah! La finesse comme avec une belle dame á Paris! Comprenez?"

We nodded and took our turns practicing with the penguin, or ostrich. My turn came, and left hand on the tricky manettes, with tail down, I did the required taxi run down the field, where a soldier turned me around, and I taxied back. So far, this was satisfactory, for I had gone at fair speed, and had managed to keep fairly straight. The next stop was to run down against the slight wind, raising the tail and opening full throttle, but to guard against *un cheval de bois* and overshooting the field. This was to be like a takeoff run without leaving the ground, for the penguins were not supposed to be able to leave the ground, even while running at close to sixty miles an hour.

This was usually the case, but there was danger that a sudden gust might cause them to leap fifty or even three hundred feet, a good ten to thirty feet above the ground, like a frightened chicken who had spotted the farmer and his axe. This sometimes happened, and ended with a broken landing gear and a splintered propeller from a bad ground loop. Fortunately this did not happen to me, but charging down the field, with the tail parallel to the ground and the nose level, was quite different from taking off in a Jenny, where the nose was somewhat elevated and the tail depressed. The JN-4s were very much easier to control on takeoffs than the small Niewports, and it took considerable practice on the penguin for some students to fully master the trick. I was among the slower learners, whereas most of my group caught on with a few runs. Most of these clever ones were part of the so-called Memphis gang, who had come over on the *Manchuria*, after completing their primary training at Chanute Field. They eyed me with proper scorn, and I heard one mutter something about damn Yankees and Mineola flyers. They were really a fine bunch, who developed several aces, but they were still slightly unreconstructed rebels, quite self-conscious about the Civil War, and one or two even painted the Stars and Bars of the Confederate flag on their planes, while serving with combat squadrons.

Graduating from the rouleurs, we walked to Field 2, where we were given dual instruction on a Niewport, 23-meter model, whose total wing surface was about 256 square feet, and a good deal less than the Jenny, whose wings covered somewhere around five hundred. The other Niewport models, used as training progressed, were still smaller, having only 18 and 15 meters of wing surface. There was even a 13-meter, the Baby Niewport, but it never proved successful. The 15-meter Niewport had been the best French fighter plane on the front, although by this time it had been replaced for combat by the Spad and later Niewport models.

The Niewport 23 had an 80-horsepower Le Rhone rotary engine, and it had a consequent tendency to stall very suddenly and go into a dangerous spin, or *vrille* as the French called it, if one climbed a little too steeply, or made a sharp turn in the wrong manner. Due to the torque of its spinning engine, there was a strong tendency for the nose to drop on a steeply banked right turn, and an opposite climbing effect on a left turn. Uncorrected, either could easily cause a spin, and the pilot had to use a differing technique with his rudder and elevator, according to the turn's direction. All this was much trickier than with the Jenny, equipped with a V-8 engine, where there was no engine torque and little difference in turns, and one had just to nose down slightly on turning, to insure safe flying speed.

It was not too easy to transfer from the stable Jenny to the delicate, unstable Niewport, but it was much easier for us than for the pilots who had taken their primary training on the primitive Caudrons at Tours. The latter, with their warping wings took some muscle to control, but they were slow and almost foolproof. The Niewports could be controlled with thumb and forefinger, and the delicate touch of a lady's lilystem wrist, but they were fast for those days, and very treacherous both in the air and on the ground, and many unwary students were killed flying them.

Although I had not shone on the penguins and, in the eyes of the Memphis gang, had appeared somewhat like the half-trained Union army must have looked to Beauregarde's rebel horde after the first Battle of Bull Run, I finally mastered the trick of the takeoff run, and did not have much trouble in getting the feel of the Niewport 23. With an instructor in the back cockpit, another Frenchman full of insistence on *de la finesse*, *toujours la finesse*, I made three takeoffs and landings, without driving the French lieutenant completely insane. In fact he said, "*Tres bon! Vous avez le vrai toucher, fort mais doux, ce qui est égelement bon pour l'avion et pour l'amour, mon lieutenant*." Having thus been assured that I had the genuine touch, strong but gentle, which was good both for flying and love, by an undoubted authority, I was told to report, at once, to Field 3, for solo flying on a Niewport 23.

As I got into my plane for my first solo, I was vaguely aware that there seemed to be a rather good-sized crowd, including many important officers of the school, gathered under a small clump of tall trees, and gazing in my direction. Among them I could make out Capitaine Pelissier, the chief of our French instructors, who seemed engaged in conversation with Lieutenant-Colonel Kilner, Issoudun's commandant, and with Major Carl Spatz, who was in general charge of flying training. Mildly wondering what it was all about, I climbed into the rear cockpit, adjusted safety belt and goggles, and gave the mechanic the signals of *Coupe*! and then *Contact*! as the latter turned over the propeller, gave it a hard downward swing, and the engine came to life.

Taxiing downwind preliminary to the takeoff run back, I glimpsed a great many more people joining the crowd, and all gazing at my plane. Giving little thought to this, I swung around, waited for the all-clear, then roared down the uneven and somewhat pebble-strewn field for the takeoff. Once off the ground, I flew a most conservative *tour de piste*, circling the field and treating the controls as if they contained dynamite, and managed to make a fair landing. I did two more of these, following instructions, then taxied to the flight line and cut the motor. Then to my surprise, I heard a cheer, and a small group of pilots ran up.

"Good work! Great!" One of the first ones reached for my hand, and shook it. He was one of the Memphis gang, Hank Stovall, a future flight commander and ace, and a very fine fellow, although another unreconstructed rebel, and one with a plantation and *niggahs in ole Miss.*

This mystery was soon explained. I had been an experiment, a guinea pig, an answer to an argument between the American command and the French instructors. The French schedule of instruction had always called for several hours of dual, before soloing the Niewport. We now contended that American pilots who had had primary training on Jennys were much further advanced and better prepared than those who had trained on and had only flown Caudrons. We said that an American Jenny-trained flyer should be able to solo a Niewport after two or three dual landings.

To all this, the French were very dubious, and were strongly of the opinion that undue haste would only result in increased fatalities, for that had been their experience. We insisted that JN-4 training made a very great difference and, like arranging a horse race, a test was agreed on to settle the argument. One thing remained: to pick a victim.

How I happened to be picked, I have never known, but it was probably because I happened to be the nearest Jenny graduate handy, that I was no less expandable than a hundred others, and that I had no close relatives in Congress who might raise howls to Heaven if my demise were untimely. Apparently, almost everyone knew this was to be a test except me, and it was a mighty good thing that I had taken off, thinking it all normal routine, and having no inkling that I was to be the answer, in good health on earth, or perspiring very freely in some pilots' section of Purgatory, to an argument on training policy, and perhaps a few bets. However although I had survived this hurdle, and had justified the Jenny above the Caudron, the demon experimenters were not finished. I was told to report immediately to Field 4, for solo on an 18-meter Niewport.

Field 4, somewhat over a mile distant, was in the charge of a French lieutenant, a weatherbeaten, most hardbitten-looking, veteran pilot, in the drab, mustardish-brown uniform of some French-Colonial regiment. He looked amazed on reading the note I handed him, but he shrugged his shoulders, muttered something that ended in *fou* (as if everything in this war were not crazy!), spat and said "*Merde*!" and made a few more remarks that did not sound too complimentary to an Ally. He then indicated a nearby 18-meter.

"*Regardez-la!*" he growled. "Montez-vous in zat avion. The manettes, the moteur, zey are like the vingt-trois meetair, mais this avion is much more difficile, more treecky to fly. Take off that way, ovaire zoze trees. *Prenez garde!* Do not hit them. Do not keel yourself and damage that avion. We need zat avion for ozair peelots."

All this, as the French say, might have given one to think, but now assuming that this French instructor was unaware that an American ex-Jenny flyer was a very superior pilot, I took off and was immediately confronted with a missing motor. It was too late to cut and land within the field, and close ahead loomed the tall trees that bordered the highway. Somehow I staggered over them, my landing wheels brushing the treetops, and managed to fly a low, wobbling, poopetty-cylinder turn around the field, to finally just make it with a dead stick landing. I was very lucky, for the whole short flight had been a hairline from stalling and crashing.

"*Sâcre nom d'un nom d'un nom!*" The instructor came striding up with a scream. "I will not be *responsable* to eediots for a murdaire. *Moi, Je ne suis pas assassin!* Vous, you are not prepared to fly ze 18-meetaire. *Non, parbleu non! Sâcre nom de Dieu, non!* You leeve to perhaps someday keel yourself ovaire zee front lines. Not here!

The next day I was back soloing the safer and more stable 23-meter, and I did not return to the 18-meter, until I had had several more hours of experience. The 18-meter, powered with the same motor as the 23-meter, flew and landed faster because of its lesser wing surface, and for some reason in its design, it had the greatest record at Issoudun for stalling and spinning with little warning, and it proved more dangerous to student pilots, than the still smaller and quite faster, 15-meter Niewport. A great many students were killed at Issoudun, on all training models and from numerous causes, but the greatest percentage of fatalities, for the number of hours flown occurred on the 18-meter, at least while I was there. The 18-meter stage of instruction seemed one of the greatest pitfalls, and it came to be dreaded by many students. It took many a life, and I had been lucky.

After this experiment, no more students were sent to the 18-meter until they had had ample time with the 23-meter. Headquarters had learned this lesson. However, they were right in one respect. The JN-4 was a much better preparation for advanced flying than the Caudron. Later, it was discovered that the British Avro was a still better primary trainer. Our cadets who had trained in England on Avros were among the quickest to master advanced flying.

While I was at Issoudun, our instructors were all French pilots who had experienced many hours of flying over the lines. At this time, French flyers were not, in a strict sense, a separate body of men in one service, all members of an air corps. In a way, France did not exactly have an air corps. Primarily, the French flyer was an officer, warrant officer (adjutant) or noncommissioned officer, belonging to the infantry, artillery, cavalry, or other ground forces, who had been merely detached and detailed for aviation duty. He might fly as a pilot or as a gunner-observer, but he always retained his status in his original branch of the ground forces.

He also retained the uniform of his branch, and such uniforms, especially the dress uniforms, varied a great deal in appearance, especially as to color. Out of his flying clothes, the average French pilot was apt to wear his dress uniform. Consequently, our instructors often presented a most striking, colorful medley of horizon blues, black tunics, red breeches, mustard hues, sky blues, red kepis, blue kepis, brown kepis and others, so that compared to us Americans, all in our unmitigated olive drab or pumpkin pie brown, the French resembled scarlet tanagers, Baltimore orioles, blue birds of happiness, and other fine feathered creatures of song and beauty, amidst a flock of sadly drab sparrows. Always trim, and some very handsome and tall, with their black boots shining like patent leather, their red breeches, black tunics, yellow gloves, gold banded kepis, everything smartly immaculate, and always so gallant, even to bowing from the waist and kissing the hands of ladies, the French pilots were a sensation with our nurses and the ladies of the Red Cross, whereas we Americans, even the graduates of our most illustrious universities, and the scions of our most ancient families—meaning three generations of substantial mediocrities in the hometown papers—must have looked like so many yokels.

Among these Frenchmen, Le Capitaine Pelissier, the chief instructor, was the eldest and most distinguished. Always immaculate, and ever so polite to ladies, officers, enlisted men, no matter who people were, he looked every inch an officer and a gentleman, and he commanded universal respect. Most other names one forgets, but there was a tall and athletic curly-haired blue-eyed Norman lieutenant, who could handle a 15-meter Niewport as a virtuoso handles a violin. On occasion he would give an exhibition, not of ordinary stunting, but of flying very low and waltzing the plane, by making it rise and fall in graceful arcs, as if to the strains of the "Blue Danube." Falling off one wing, from not over one hundred feet above the ground, he would skim over a hangar top, to rise just before his wheels touched the earth. This sort of flying took the most delicate use of controls and throttle, and the finest sense of depth, touch, and timing. It involved a near tangential skimming of obstacles, and the utmost precision. The slightest error of judgement would have caused a crash, but this never happened.

Another French pilot and good instructor seemed to have just stepped out of the covers of *La Vie Parisienne*. Tall, slim, with a small moustache, a John Barrymore profile and sleek black hair, he appeared the living model for the gay lieutenants escorting very sexy and pretty Parisian coquettes, which drawings made that magazine so very popular. He was the popular image of the military wolf in Paris, but the French-Colonial pilot, a hard-boiled and rougher type, did not approve of him.

"Lui, il est un *sale maquereau*," he remarked of him on one occasion. This reference to a mackerel implied, in the French argot, a pander or a man kept by a woman, and it all could have been no more than the envious sneer of the rural roughneck at the big city smoothie. On the other hand, *le lieutenant* in question may well have had some rich and fashionable countess for a *bonne amie*, as he looked the part to perfection. Another good instructor was Lieutenant Blumenthal, or Bloomy as he was known to all of us. He was said to come from an extremely rich family of French bankers, and he had been everywhere. He was interesting to talk to, and very popular.

We had not been very long at Issoudun, when we were authorized to wear wings, and all pilots hastened to obtain them. These original, first World War pilots' wings were not metal pins, but were handsomely and colorfully woven with gold and silver threads, and they had to be sewn on. The central shield was not a dull, vertically banded surface as today's, but was studded with thirteen silver stars against a background of dark blue. During the First World War, and for a considerable time after, only pilots, observers, and balloonists had any special flight insignia in our armed services, although after a few months of war, everyone in the air corps wore the collar insignia of propeller and tiny wings that finally replaced the crossed flags of the parent Signal Corps, for by this time we had grown to a good-sized branch of the army, and were no longer the tiny section of prewar days.

Balloon observers, the neglected and unpublicized so-called gas bag gang, had two embroidered wings centered by a round balloon, and our observers had a single wing for a time, until it was replaced by two, centered by a round disc whose significance was pretty much a mystery. British pilots, members of the then Royal Air Corps, wore the graceful, wide-spreading but drooping wings of the wandering albatross, while we had the wings of the eagle, to my mind a more appropriate bird for combat flyers. As for the British observers, they sported one big wing, with a great round O at its upper end. This emblem was scornfully referred to by all British pilots as the Great Flying Bunghole, when they did not specify some other, rather unmentionable opening.

Perhaps the finest looking of all pilot's insignia was the French, best known as the *brevet militaire*. This was a large and very handsome bronze pin, in the form of two handsome wings surrounded by a laurel wreath, and topped by a star. On passing the primary tests, this insignia was affixed with some ceremony, and its back was stamped with a number, which was registered in the name of the pilot. American pilots who had received their primary training at French fields received these brevets, and they were very proud to wear them, along with our own wings, especially as they were as rare as they were beautiful, and not to be obtained in shop counters.

Today in America, it is easy to buy pilot's wings in any PX, or Broadway hockshop for that matter. Now in our air force, almost everyone wears some sort of wings, if his or her duty calls for regular flying. Except close up, it is hard to distinguish the wings of a pilot, the only real wings actually, from those of an observer, flight nurse, flight engineer, crew chief, flight surgeon, gunner, navigator, or what's your category. This general handing out of wings seems a great deal overdone, much like our Second World War plethora of service ribbons and minor decorations, so often satirically referred to as *salad dressing* by our GIs, who have an unerring eye for anything that savors of even the slightly spurious. Today, the pilot's shield has lost its former stars. They must have blinked out, along with the general cheapening of the insignia.

Chapter 10

BAD WEATHER AND BARRACK LIFE

During a great part of November and December 1917, it either rained or snowed at Issoudun, and the consequent gumbo mud turned the flying fields into quagmires, and the camp and its barracks into a hell hole. For days on end, all flying had to be called off. No flying, horrible weather, depressing surroundings, and little to do except to attend the same old lectures and demonstrations that we had heard so many times in the past, made for disillusionment and discontent. Mutters grew, and there were many and new, pessimistic rumors.

Some mentioned certain names and hinted at spies, others said that, if the rains did not soon let up, the school would be deactivated, and all personnel would be shipped back to Texas. Still others stated that, if *Black Jack* had his way, we would all be transferred to the infantry and sent to the trenches, because he hated the *guts of aviation*, and loathed aviators, since they seemed different from his ideal of real soldiers.

Of course, General Pershing, although he insisted that a man be a soldier first and a flyer afterwards, harbored no such petty feelings, but too many cadets had experienced being under some stupid, transferred officer who knew nothing about aviation, made little attempt to learn, and who seemed to have gone out of his way to inflict little, galling indignities on student flyers, accompanied by some alleged, blustering remark that he "By God! would show these flying Fancy Dans, who thought themselves too good for regulations, what it meant to be in the *YEWNITED STATES ARMEE!*" Whereupon, this specimen would cancel all passes for ten days, because one cadet had a button missing, or someone had failed to salute in the exact, prescribed manner.

In such a case, an extreme martinet who was also a good flyer might have been accepted with a shrug, and the accompanying allusions to female canine ancestry, but such *chicken* coming from a commanding officer who would not even fly as a passenger, made for disgust and resentment, and for a time, until we found out that there were really very many decent and capable nonflying officers in administrative posts, a great many student pilots eyed with suspicion all nonflying officers, or *kiwis* as we called them, and especially so if they came from the old, regular army. Because a few of the most conspicuous misfits had been transferred from the regulars, there was for a time the bitter saying, that there were three kinds of officers: reserve officers, national guard officers, and regular army sonsabitches.

All the above was emotional and unthinking generalization, but at the same time it was symptomatic of a great and growing feeling, that we of the air corps were not just another branch of the army, but that we were a new and separate service, and that we needed oficers with the maximum of new ideas, and with the minimum of the old, traditional, *squads right* mentality to lead us. Vaguely, we realized that the General Staff did not really grasp the problems and possibilities of military aviation. Even then, in the hearts of the long-ago Issoudun cadets, were the seeds of our present, separate Air Force.

On our arrival at Issoudin, Lieutenant Colonel Kilner, an experienced ex-Pancho Villa chasing, Mexican border, veteran flyer, and a very splendid officer, was our commandant, but in direct charge of flying training was a stockily built young major, with red freckles, a bristly reddish moustache, and piercing eyes, that were shrewd but not unkindly. Major Carl Spatz—in World War II, our famous General Spatz—was in those days a fine flyer, and tower of strength to the air corps, but he was a West Pointer and, at first, some cadets were suspicious. His name was German, the headquarter's adjutant, Major Tittle, sounded and was said to be German, and on the staff was another kiwi regular, Captain Weidenbach, who incidentally later changed his name to Willoughby, and became a major general in World War II, as well as chief of intelligence under General of the Army Douglas MacArthur.

They were good men all, but "Spatz, Tittle, and Weidenbach! Three fine Prussians," growled some of the students, and it was only after some time that everyone realized that there was nothing to this about three fine officers, and that Major Spatz was not only a fine officer and a gentleman, but that he was above all a pilot, who thought as an aviator should think, meaning flying first above everything. However in the meantime, it rained and rained, and then rained some more, the mud was foot-deep all over the place, and many planes rotted in the open, for lack of hangar space to house them.

Off duty with little to do, we sat around in our mud-tracked barracks, close to the red hot stoves, or we lay in the rumpled, canvas bottomed bunks that resembled dark caves in the wan light from the small windows, and we listened to the drip and drumming of the rain, and to the endless rumors. Sometimes we sang songs that reflected our prevailing mood of pessimism and frustration:

Officers live on the top of the hill,
We live down here in the muck and the swill;
Oh, I'm so tired of Fra-ance,
Glory how I want to go home!

The above was really the enlisted men's lament, sad like the blues of cotton-picking slaves, but we *flying lieuts* and cadet flyers felt more on the side of the enlisted men than of the side of authority. The latter, West Pointers and their kiwis, were management, and we felt part of underdog labor. We also sang of the misunderstood, nonflying officers:

I don't have to march with the infan-tree,
Ride with the caval-ree,
Shoot with the artil-ree,
I don't have to FLY OVER GERMANEE!
For I am a kiwee-wee.
Oh I am a KIWEE-WEE!
I am a kiwee-wee,
So I don't have to——

The food was, as usual in the army, mistreated by the cooks in the hallowed and traditional way, such as meat cooked to resemble sole leather, vegetables, an endless serving of Brussels sprouts that tasted like knotted dishrags, and hot brown rainwater, or hot black lye, both laughingly called coffee. Breakfast —ugh!—was mostly oatmeal covered with corn syrup, a staple article of our diet, like the Brussels sprouts, which latter were said to have been recommended to us by the British, in a belated revenge for Yorktown. We had a song for all this:

Obadiah
Hadda daughter,
Ran a whorehouse,
For a quarter;
Fed 'em ham,
Fed 'em jam,
Fed 'em anything,
GAWD DAMN!

There were personalities and colorful characters galore, among the student RMAs and cadet flyers in our barracoons. On any Saturday evening, Jay Gude, whose family owned a large, outdoor advertising firm, might don an imitation of a preacher's garb, and produce a side-splitting bawdy sermon for the gang, or he might get out his famous *swinette*, a one-string fiddle made from a broom handle and a cigar box, and bring forth haunting music, to accompany some ballad of ladies fair but frail, or some tale of the old West and long ago. There was also Tom Ring, moustached and small in build, and a bit older than most of us, who called himself the King of Saginaw, because his family owned big lumber interests in that region. The King, although only about five-feet-seven, could speak with the voice of a trumpet if needed and, rushing to the latrine one stormy night, he collided with a barely seen body, close by the trench, in the near Stygian darkness of the dreadful tent.

"I am Colonel So-and-so," said a sharp voice. "You almost pushed me in. Where's your respect for your superior officer?"

"Colonel, my eye!" thundered Tom, thinking it just some cadet. "Why, I'm the King of Saginaw Michigan, and I outrank General Pershing. Make way, base-born private!" However, it was a colonel, and for this social error, the King received a summons.

Others of those December nights in the barracks, were Wacker of Chicago's Wacker Boulevard, Percy Pyne, a blue-blooded scion often mentioned in the New York society columns, but now quite often on the KP list as a cadet, Sumner Sewall, an ace-to-be and, some years later, governor of the state of Maine, Charley Wooley, Bill Conant, Walter Muether, Bill Munn, Joe Estil, Jack Hunter, Jim Osgood, Steve Hopkins, Bert Williams, Zacharias, Jimmie Knowles, and others. There was also Clarkson Potter, known to all as the Baby Bishop, the small but most dignified nephew of a real bishop, and with his best friend, Phil Rhinelander, among the best dressed pilots in the service. In addition, there was Leighton Brewer, years later college professor and author of *Riders of the Sky*, a superb and published, but too little publicized, blank verse saga of the air corps, and there was also Walter Smythe, and Al Cowart, king of the crap shooters, but still more famed as a big medicine man and sex doctor, who could give private advice on all questions.

Prominent was Casgrain, a witty fellow, and the first American-trained pilot to be taken prisoner, during which he spent weary months in a damp dungeon of an ancient castle on some island in the Baltic Sea. Around the stove one might find swart and fiery "Caruso" Vernam, who looked like a fierce Corsican bandit, and who always maintained that he would die in battle, which he did. One more was Bill Smith, *Whispering Bill*, who had lost his voice for no known reason, and could not curse above a whisper, when Rhinelander's dog, of no known breed, left an unspeakable token in his blankets.

There were also many others, many who lived through the war, and just as many who fell, in combat, or in the ever occurring training crashes, but on one especially miserable afternoon, the door of a student barrack was suddenly opened, and a voice rang out, "Attention! General Pershing!"

The dice and cards rested on the brown blankets, as the unwarned, almost unbelieving cadets rose to their feet, disheveled and frowsy from cooped-up stagnation, and the floors of the barrack were littered and tracked with mud from the streets. General Pershing took one, all-surveying look, then spun around and left. At the time, his lips said nothing, but if ever the expression on a human countenance uttered a four-letter word of the deepest disgust, his did. It was then reported, that he had termed Issoudun the worst of France's mud holes.

There were some gleams of light amidst the general gloom of

the camp. To our minds, the brightest beacon was the Red Cross unit, which under the charge of Miss Irene Given-Wilson and her aides, the Misses Brewer, Hussey, and Potter, furnished an officers' club, established a library, and best of all ran a canteen, which gave out real coffee, hot chocolate and other tasty things, as well as the pleasant, cultivated talk of attractive and sympathetic ladies. This was like a spot and a voice from back home, from a longed-for but lost world, and it saved many a pilot's morale, during the worst of that long terrible winter weather, and its depression. There was also Major Brownell of the Medical Corps, the chief of an important ward, but better known as a sort of father confessor and friend of any troubled student or enlisted man who could tell him his story of woe, and feel sure of its prompt consideration at headquarters.

At length, the weather took a turn for the better, the ground froze and hardened, and flying was resumed. In successive stages we soloed, did spirals, practiced dead stick, simulated, forced landings to a mark, learned acrobatics, and made altitude and cross-country flights in the 23, the 18, and the 15 meter Nieuports, each one smaller and faster than its predecessor. In America, we had generally found our way in the air by following the coastline, a river, or some outstanding highway. Here in central France, there was no coast line, few rivers of significance as guides, and far too many similar-appearing roads to readily distinguish from the air. However, there was the railroad, and our French maps gave exact outlines of the towns, the small villages, and the forests, so that each could be readily recognized from above. With these excellent, minutely detailed maps, there was little excuse for getting lost, unless a ground fog developed under one's plane.

These dreaded fogs could often and suddenly form in the wintertime, usually just after the warming morning sun had risen a bit higher over the dank river valleys, and the surrounding, far flung, water soaked fields, and many a student, caught this way with little warning, flew and flew until his gas tank ran dry, and he had to land as best he could through a white darkness, trusting his life to luck and good guessing. This once happened to me, and I spent a most apprehensive half hour, cruising around, watching the gauge drop on a small gas supply, and seeing nothing below except a white blanket, through which the top branches of a few of the taller trees might, here and there, emerge into view. Fortunately, I was able to find, above the fog, a cleared hilltop near the town of Bourges, where I landed with minor damage. Others were less fortunate, and some fatalities resulted.

About the time that I had had some experience flying the 15-meter Niewport, a series of crashes and fatalities that seemed to stem from sabotage, spread fear and suspicion through the school. Wings came off in the air while the planes seemed under no undue strain, and subsequent investigation of a crash might reveal oddly frayed flying wires, missing cotter pins, and turnbuckles so cleverly filed that they might hold in straight flight, but would tear loose under the greater strain of a sharp vertical turn, or the pull up from a steep dive. Again, engines seemed to fail more than normally, even though engine failure was to be expected, but there were now tales of fine sand found in engine oil, of strange leaks in gas tanks, and of tampered with magnetoes and other parts.

One day, a lucky student landed safely, but the whole tail section of his plane came apart, when the ground crew picked it up to wheel it into the hangar. The main bolts were missing, and only the fact that he had made no sharp turn nor pull-up, had prevented a crash. On another occasion, we were receiving ground instruction on the parts, the assembly, and the handling of a Vickers machine gun, and were closely grouped about the table where the gun lay, to watch a demonstration of clearing a jam, when the gun suddenly fired, and drilled a cadet, standing at my elbow, right through his thigh. The gun was not supposed to be loaded, except with dummy cartridges, and investigation cleared the instructing sergeant. However, someone had substituted a real bullet, and talk of spies and saboteurs grew.

One morning I took off in a 15-meter, and was no sooner airborne than I discovered that the pull of my propeller was not through the longitudinal center of my plane, but off center to the left, and so much so that it was impossible to make a right turn. To barely keep a straight course, I had to use hard, right rudder,, and the only way to turn right was to circle clear around to the left. Then in no time, my engine began to vibrate so violently that it seemed ready to jump out of its bed. Fearing this, I cut the switch and landed, as best I could, in the only open space within gliding distance, which happened to be two feet deep with drifted snow. Here, the plane nosed over on its back, damaging the upper wings and breaking the propeller. This was hardly my fault, but the next morning I was summoned and informed that I would no longer be trained for pursuit flying, but would become a bomber pilot.

This was a great blow, for at this time, almost all students wanted to become *chasse* or pursuit pilots, and few wanted bombing or reconnaissance flying. It was all pursuit, ah! From the ranks of the pursuit pilots had come the noble company of Guynemer, of Ball, McCudden, Lufbery, and all the brilliant, knightly heroes of battles in the sky, but who ever heard of any of the bombing pilots, brave and worthy fellows no doubt, but after all only chauffeurs of aerial boxcars, egg dropping flying trucks, and other dull wagons.

This was the general sentiment, and authority knew it, using it like a sword of Damocles over our heads. Yes, they said. Show yourself clever, fast to learn, and adept, and you will fly a fighter, but if you are slow, show poor judgement, or have accidents, you may be relegated to bombing, artillery observation, or photoreconnaissance flying. That was said to be the policy, and many students shuddered. One mistake, and one might be sold down the river to Clermond-Ferrand and its bombing school, a fate worse than death, like the defloration of a virgin in Victorian days, in the feelings of many students. Now arbitrarily and without any hearing as to extenuating circumstances, headquarters had dropped the boom, and I was debased to the status of the flying peasants of the service, a bomber pilot.

Fortunately I had a friend from Harvard days who was in a position to help me. Edwin Post had completed his training, showing such superior aptitude that he had been made a tester, and also one of the assistants in charge of flying training. I spoke to him of the unfairness of the order, and he promised an investigation.

Our rotary engines were affixed to the nose of our Niewports by great lag screws imbedded into the wooden longerons of the fuselage. Each lag screw was a good eighteen inches or more in length, but each lag screw had been filed off to a bare six inches in the plane I had been flying. It was very fortunate that I had quickly cut the switch, for the engine would have soon torn loose from its bed and destroyed the plane, reported the investigating officer. I was now restored to pursuit training, but I was even more fortunate in not being trained as a bomber pilot, since our day-bombing squadrons—America had no night-bombing squadrons on active duty over the enemy lines, that I ever heard of, in World War I—although manned by some of our very best pilots, suffered the heaviest percentage of combat losses, and were almost suicide clubs at one period of the fighting.

Concerning First Lieutenant Edwin Post, he was the son of Mrs. Price Post, the Emily Post of the famous *Book of Etiquette*. Ned Post was tall, slim, good-looking, with dark hair brushed straight back from his pale forehead, a suave, New Yorkish manner, and always well dressed. Now at a certain stage in the life cycle of the average red-blooded American male, such feminine pleasing attributes are regarded with deep suspicion. Such a guy is much too much like a French count, another waist-bending, hand-kissing, smooth-tongued, cookie-pushing, dancing lizard to be trusted. On top of that, there was a story that his gracious mother, on visiting some flying field where he had been stationed, had referred to him as her *Beautiful Black Swan*, before his commanding officer and others. Such a tale was undoubtedly a canard, and an invention of some malicious person, but it was hard to live down, and only Ned's first-rate flying, and other good qualities, made it forgiven.

As to any further sabotage, soon after my experience with the filed-off lag screws, some officers and men were relieved of their duties, and very quietly taken from the school under mysterious circumstances. Nothing was said officially, but there was much talk of secret service men, of the discovery of a nest of spies and saboteurs, and of subsequent court martials, heavy sentences and even executions as a final consequence. We never knew the actual truth about all this, but one prominent major was generally and for many years later, although absolutely mistakenly, believed to have been deeply involved. This major was not involved in any way, but others were, and they were never heard from again. However, from then on, there was no more sabotage reported at Issoudun.

Chapter 11

FURTHER OBSERVATIONS OF ISSOUDUN

At Issoudun, the training of a *chasse* or pursuit pilot was broken into nine stages, each one with its own field and set of instructors, although at a certain stage, target practice with a machine gun from a plane in flight, was given not at Issoudun, but at the French school of Cazeau, situated a few miles south of Arcachon, on the Bay of Biscay. As previously told, the first four stages comprised the penguins, dual instruction on the 23-meter, then solo flying on the 23- and the 18-meter models. This completed, including spirals and cross-country flights, one progressed to Field 5 and flights in 15-meter Niewports, but on models that were still only powered with 80-horsepower engines. At Field 5, we soloed this still faster plane, and had much practice in making right and left, extremely tight, and vertical spirals, or *virages* as the French termed them, which had to be begun at five thousand feet, terminated at three, at which altitude we were to cut the switch, and land dead stick to within seventy-five feet of a mark.

This stage over, we moved on to Field 6, where we were taught general acrobatics, such as getting in and out of a spin, doing falling leafs, making vertical, tail-snap stalls, loops, and we were given constant practice in making controlled wing slips, and in essing, fish-tailing, and the general art of making successful, dead stick landings, over bordering trees, hangars, and other obstacles, onto a small field.

We were also taught how to barrel a plane, and great stress was placed on certain important combat acrobatics, especially the execution of the *renversement*, an improved version of the famed Immelman turn. This was a sharp pull up with a half roll, which properly executed, resulted in a 180-degree change of direction, with little loss of altitude. This was then considered one of the most essential combat maneuvers, in those days of much slower flying, but extremely sensitive and quick turning airplanes, since it was the quickest and surest way to escape from a close, hostile attack from the rear. Using the *renversement*, one suddenly flipped over and ducked under the enemy's wings, in the same fashion that I have seen a small desert bird escape from a huge, pursuing owl. It saved many a fighter's life a split-second before being machine-gun riddled, from a distance of fifty yards or much less to his rear.

Another maneuver was the *chandelle*, which could be used in taking off from a small area bordered by high obstacles, or for suddenly loosing a machine gun burst at an enemy dead above. The *chandelle* (candle), was simply a vertical zoom with a half to full twist, that reminded an observer of one of those tall twist formed candles often seen in Gothic cathedrals. Near the ground, this was a highly dangerous maneuver, for if the near-vertical climb were prolonged an instant too long, or if the engine failed from a choked-off gas supply, which could readily happen in a zoom, a lightning fast stall followed, and the resulting spinning or diving crash was generally fatal. Perhaps because his ears were highly trained and especially sensitive to the slightest warning from a motor, and also because he had unusually fast reflexes to take corrective action against an imminent stall, Eddie Rickenbacker seemed to enjoy these dangerous takeoffs. One bleak, wintry afternoon, with packed snow and areas of glare ice on the field, seeing him make a breathtaking, five hundred foot chandelle out of Valentine Field, made me think of a rocket spiralling straight upwards.

Since the 15-meter Niewport was a one-passenger ship, there could be no dual instruction, so a mockup was erected on Field 6, and we went through all the steps of the stunts on solid ground, before trying them in the air. All this training on the 15-meter was given on Fields 5 and 6, which were only about a mile apart. Students crashed and were killed in learning acrobatics, but Field 4 was also not too far distant, and many of us experienced near collisions, or did collide and crash, when all three fields were operating simultaneously. It was not uncommon to be coming down in a practice spin, to suddenly discover straight below one, some pilot in an 18-meter, so intent on doing tight spirals, that he was quite unaware that he had strayed from his area in the skies, and that he was over the wrong field.

There was a similar hazard on approaching for a landing. These three fields were too closely situated to each other, and there was a great deal of overlapping during practice flights. When I was there during the winter of 1917-18, there were no systematized ground signals, nor much attempt to regulate traffic during landings and takeoffs. It was mainly up to each pilot to look sharp, and use good judgement. Consequently, it was common on gliding in for a landing, having previously looked around and found the approach seemingly clear of all danger, to have a strange plane sail across one's path, coming from apparently nowhere, and flown by some student who had never seen you at all. That this plane missed you by a good hundred feet did not stop you from shuddering. There had already been too many bull's-eyes from these occasions.

Neither today nor in the past, have I ever read any honest, undoctored report by government authority, as to the percentage of fatalities in the course of flying training. Such figures are hidden from the public, or falsely rosy pictures are painted, by misusing statistics, but all of us who went through Issoudun in its early months of operation know very well indeed, that there were many fatalities, both in total number, and in percentage of student hours flown. While I was at Issoudun, from the end of November until the following April, I doubt if there were ever more than three hundred students at one time in attendance, since only a little more than two thousand pilots had graduated from it at its deactivation soon after the Armistice. However, while I was there, there were weeks on end, when a daily average of one fatal crash seemed grim but normal, and on some days, two and even three bad crashes might add their quota to a dreary, barren plot of earth, Field 9 then, but more ironically known as the School for Permanent Ground Jobs, our fast growing cemetery.

If student death in a crash was ever-present during that winter, some of the attendant funerals were as macabre as the most morbid pages in a gloomy Russian novel. The first one I attended, I was one of six pallbearers, for I had been a fairly close friend of the victim. His name is best left out, as too shocking to close relatives, if any still exist, but he was a young Princeton graduate, tall, dark, very intelligent, and very much a gentleman. At Field 7, his engine failed on taking off, and he made the fatal mistake of trying to turn back into the field. He spun into the frozen muck of a small swamp, and although Hungry Lizzie, the name for our Ford ambulances at the fields, hurried up, there was only the usual obscene and horrible caricature of what had just been God's image, to roll into the hiding blankets and cart away.

The skimpy funeral over, a few words uttered over a rough pine box, in a cold and grim shed of a chapel, the six of us loaded the ambulance-hearse, and marched back of it over a road that was deeply rutted by trucks, and ankle-deep in mud and wet snow, to the distant field where rose the wooden crosses. As we gloomily plodded, slipping and sliding in the muck, a fine sleet fell, and an utterly grotesque, hurdy-gurdyish band, in the most ill fitting of GI uniforms, with a God only knows, how and from where collection of battered trumpets, squealing flutes, bull-frog sounding German horns, and a thumping base drum, marched before the wallowing Model-T, while the smell of blood and damp sawdust came from the oozing box in that car just ahead of us.

Arrived at our own Boot Hill, the yellow-tinted, icy-lipped grave was half filled with water, and I slipped on its clayey edge, and fell halfway into its mouth, as we placed the coffin on the beams crossing it. Then, the burial read, and the box lowered into the slime below, we retraced our march, but this time as if to cheer us all up, our band, who had previously ground out the most lugubrious of funeral marches, broke out into "Hail, Hail! The Gang's All Here," and what the hell do we care now? This touch, after all these years, still seems the height of something or other, and it took some time to get over that, and also my slip into the grave, and wondering if that were an omen for the future.

Among the cadets at Issoudun were an inseparable pair, who may be called Eustis and Phillibar in these pages, as suggestive of their real names, which are better left out for a reason. Very close friends, they had come from the same home town, had gone to the same schools, had been together in all things like brothers, but Eustis was small, keen minded, with reflexes like a cat, whereas Phillibar was a Mephistophelean giant, who could have passed for an old-fashioned, wax-moustached villain of the theater. Mutt and Jeff, some called them.

One afternoon late in the day, there was the almost daily, fatal crash, and the rumor was that X, some newly arrived cadet, had been killed in an 18-meter. That same night, the body was to lie in an outlying hangar, then used as a morgue, and this meant that some three of us would be designated by headquarters, as death guards to remain in that hangar, and to keep turn in solitary vigil over the corpse, for the whole of the night. For this grim duty, Eustis was notified to report.

Arriving at midnight for his turn, Eustis found the body completely hidden under blankets, stretched out on a table of rough planks and frames. He sat near it, and tried to while away the long hours in reading by the dim oil light of the guard lantern. Time passed and dragged, the officer of the day, escorted by the corporal of the main guard, paid his brief visit on his after midnight round, and the small hours of the night brought more chill and gloom. Then, Eustis dozed off.

He came to with a start, for a voice had seemingly called him. He looked around and could see no one, but he took the lantern and made a close inspection of the silent, musty hangar, seeing nothing but the dim outlines of planes, the lower beams of the dark shadowed frames that upheld the black cavern of a roof, and hearing nothing but the occasional slight rattle of the canvas walls, as some whispering gust of the night shook them.

Thinking he had been dreaming, Eustis sat down, and he thought he must have nodded, and once more he came to with a start, for again that voice had called him, and a voice that was clear and sounded not far off. Puzzled and vaguely alarmed because it had seemed so real that a voice had called him by his first name, he made another fruitless search of the dim hangar, then opened a flap in the wall, and peered out onto a dark and empty flight line, and a glittering, starry night. From there, and from the distant barracks and other buildings, there came no sounds, except the faint call of some owl or other bird of the night, or the creak of a leafless branch moved by a gust, for the whole camp was deep in sleep.

"This is Eustis. Who is there?" he shouted, but there was no response.

Again he sat, and for a moment closed his eyes, only to reopen them wide, for the voice, a strangely familiar voice too, had for the third time called him by name. This time, he glanced at the table, and a sudden dreadful suspicion came over him, as he took in the form hidden under the blankets. How long it was, how strangely and terribly long! He had met X, and X had been of medium height. This could not be X who lay under that blanket. He now knew who it was, but he must be sure. He approached, hesitated, then swept the blanket aside, and the terribly gashed forehead and smashed face of Phillibar stared up at him.

Very few, if any of us, have ever had similar psychic experiences, even though some human beings, as they tread such valleys of the shadow of death as was Issoudun, seem to become aware of forces not explained by science, and not felt under ordinary living conditions. For some few individuals under prolonged stress, certain perhaps only dormant senses seem to sharpen, and like some insects, who are said to be able to distinguish ultraviolet as a regular color, although it is invisible to our eyes, they may hear and see what we never can.

Issoudun, at least during the winter of 1917-18, was a valley of the shadow, where it was commonplace to share a valued tin of milk with a good friend at breakfast, to see or hear of his crash before noon, and attend his funeral that same day, until we became so accustomed to it, that grief was rarely expressed, death was regarded as a sort of grim, slapstick joke, like being smacked with a lethal custard pie, and the latest victim was often dismissed as just stupid in the air, instead of unfortunate. Outwardly we grew hard and callous, because we had to, or else crack up like a few, who had to be transferred to ground jobs. As for nonfatal injuries, even a broken back came to be regarded as more or less minor. Unless, "that poor dumb bastard, So-and-so, was bumped off," we did not consider his crash of much moment.

Field 9 contained many score graves before I left the school, and much later, sometime after the Armistice, some sort of a monument was erected on it, with the names of 171 crashed pilots engraved thereon. In 1927, only nine years later, I was at Harry's Bar in Paris, and ran into an old friend of flying days. He said that he had been on a motor tour of southern France, and passing through Issoudun, he had made a detour to revisit the old site of the school. All, save traces, was gone, except the monument on what had been the pilots' Boot Hill, and that too was going, for the winters' ice and frosts had cracked and crumbled the stone, and there seemed to be no provision for its maintenance. However, he said, the peasant women from the neighboring hamlets, had brought flowers, and had placed them on the ruined monument, and they had not forgotten those who had lain there, or who might still remain under that earth. Later, it was repaired by the French.

In spite of the atmosphere of almost Beowulfian grimness at Issoudun, where the crash demon seized his daily toll, like a Grendel in Hereot, the mead-hall of the Scyldings, almost everyone was optimistic as to his own chances, and found compensation for dreariness and nervous tension in making flying progress, and in other activities, which might be either part of training, or just social recreation. Among these was trap shooting, which was rightly considered excellent training in hitting a rapidly moving target, that might approach or recede from any angle, such as a plane in flight. Much of this practice was under the supervision of an experienced trap shooter, a cadet named, not inappropriately, Wing, and it was good fun except for a few hopeless dubs, who never seemed to be able to master the art of leading a fast moving target, in order to hit it square. Since a pursuit pilot had to be able to estimate the correct lead for any moving target, instinctively by eye and in a split second, if he were to succeed over the lines, we were all most anxious to make reasonably respectable scores, lest one be transferred to bombing or observation piloting, and such a fate then seemed the equivalent of a thoroughbred being taken out of racing, to pull a milk wagon.

As for social diversions, there was no such thing as a USO, a post movie, or any dances that I can remember, for our First World War was conducted with a bare minimum of enrolled and officially sponsored female contingents and auxiliaries, as compared with our second great conflict, which had cornucopias overflowing with WACs, pretty nurses, Red Cross girls, and even touring movie stars, almost everywhere, except the very front lines. World War I was strictly a man's army as the saying went, and if any *writin' feller* had told us that we were fighting for "Mom's apple pie" or similar blah, we would have given him the old heave-ho in short order. For amusement, we did have football games, where the players, and even the referees, all but got drowned in the mud of the muddiest hole in France, and there were the not too exciting pleasure of Issoudun, the town that is, and some of the local villages.

Issoudun, *la ville*, was the usual small city of the French provinces, complete with the usual smells, small stuffy shops *place* and *hotel de ville*, *gendarmerie*, French style gentlemen's rooms on the sidewalks, and the two usual hotels, which had the two usual names of Hotel de France, and Hotel D'Europe, or perhaps the Hotel Grande. It had also the usual public *bain*, where for one torn and taped together paper franc, or the equivalent in the very peculiar, local money, one could have a tub, a small towel of the thinnest fabric, a sliver of pink soap, and the company of several active roaches.

The bath water, as usual, came out of two faucets, shaped like heads and arching necks of swans, and the water always smelled strongly of the river, and its open air, bankside, do-it-yourself laundry, not far upstream. However, the hot water was really hot, it got the chill of so-called sunny France out of the marrow of one's bones, and the long tub was a good place to relax in blessed peace, and to think long, satisfying thoughts concerning the pleasures of some future, remotely possible seduction, revenge on some hated superior, of a good scheme to get to Paris, or some other laudable project, and there was a splendid resonance to make one's voice sound good, while giving out with "Aupres de ma Blonde," or "Le Chef de Gare, Il Est Cocu," or even better that stirring, marching song of the French infantry, which one rendered as:

> Le regiment de SAMBRE Y MEUSE uh!
> Ty-ara-RAH—Boomety boom de BOOM!
> Oh, le REGIMENT DE——

However, one rarely got beyond this line, when Madame la Proprietaire would burst in the door, ask if all was well with Monsieur le Lieutenant, and if he did not wish his back scrubbed by, what I judge may well have been the strongest pair of female arms in all France.

In addition to the above creature comfort, Issoudun had a locally famous restaurant, Le Coq D'Argent, which became our favorite night spot, especially of a Saturday night, when on pass to town. Le Coq, besides its famed cellar with its earthy smell of high stacked barrels of Bordeaux wine, boasted a fine *cuisine*, where they even made a good job of a Thanksgiving turkey, or *dindon* as they called it, which Jim Osgood had somehow procured from the Hotel du Commerce for that occasion, when several of us, including Osgood, myself, Soule, Conant and Estil dined together. The establishment had also a famed upstair parlor, all furnished with pink silk curtains, deep-cushioned divans, love seats, gilt mirrors, gilt, talon-footed, marble-topped tables, gilt clocks supported by cupids and the like, where the youth and chivalry of our camp would foregather for an evening of champagne and merry talk in the company of the daughter of the proprietress. This daughter was a most animated young lady, with a quick wit, a ready tongue, a mighty keen eye for business, and an upper development that would have made our most famed Hollywood specimens look like the side view of a shingle in comparison. Her name might have been Suzanne, Marie, Germaine, one of those, but she was universally known around the barracks as Mademoiselle Twin Cylinder. She also had a friend, blessed in other parts, and known to fame as Tail Skid.

Besides the town of Issoudun, there were some small local villages, where it was possible to get a simple, but well-cooked and satisfying meal, when the outlook of another mess hall supper of either monkey meat, goldfish, or corn willie, plus the insipidly prepared Brussels sprouts, had just become something beyond reason. To one of these hamlets, Pody by name, and but a few miles from camp, I walked one bleak and wintry Sunday afternoon, in the company of Harold Tittman and George Kenney. Our purpose was a decent meal, but arriving a bit early, we visited a farm, which was on the ancient site of some medieval count's stronghold, and whose present house and barns were enclosed by the remnants of a moat, and some ruined walls, including an old main gate. This latter was impressively flanked by two fairly well preserved stone towers, the protecting barbicans of a long ago.

This ancient remnant of a castle, which must have gone back to the days of private warfare, and the church's Truce of God, still boasted underground chambers, which had been used for the torture and imprisonment of captives, but they now served as root cellars, and winter pens for farm animals. In the company of the owner-farmer, who kept excitedly relating legends of the place, but in a local patois, all but unintelligible to us, we toured the site, and then ascended the spiral stairs of one of the gate towers. Here, we came upon an interesting but odd discovery.

The stairs ended on a floor, which might have a guard room, since it was built with slitlike openings for the discharge of weapons, and it contained a large fireplace. Besides this, it had a tiny stone cabinet that projected from the outside wall of the tower, and a good thirty feet above the ground. This roomlet had an impressive stone throne, with a practical hole through the stone seat, and there were numerous sketches on the walls, close and handy to any sitter, that looked as if they had been inscribed with some sharp instrument, such as the point of a dagger. All these were of medieval character, and there was one in particular of a knight and his war horse, both in full armor, that seemed authentic to the smallest detail, and it implied that the depicter of this good-sized figure, not only was an illustrator of considerable merit, but that he was also an expert on his subject, and one who knew it at firsthand. This clever scratch on stone, that could have well been done by some young page, or man at arms, as he sat and pondered in privacy, evoked a strange feeling of sympathy for these fighters of a long bygone age. This vivid and accurate drawing made them seem more like modern beings, who, reborn in some cycle of reincarnation, might now be drawing airplanes, or even space capsules, on convenient walls, and whatever ghosts there were that might still faintly linger in these ruins, they became more like normal, everyday human beings, than so many stiff and wooden actors in a history. Like the drawings of the aurochs, found deep in that Spanish cave, it made one wonder.

Outside the tower on our leaving, we glanced up at the tiny round room that projected from the tower wall, well above our heads. It was now that one of my companions made a critical observation.

"Functional, but badly placed for a siege," he said.

"No?" I said.

"Of course not. Why, just picture the old count, the once lord of this castle, up there taking his morning's morning, and perhaps reading the *Chanson de Rolande*, or figuring out a better thumbscrew or rack for his torture chamber, while his mortal enemy, the puissant and tough Marquis de Pommes de Terre, has suddenly and quietly surrounded his walls."

"I understand," I said. "The marquis and his vassals are all about, while the unsuspecting count sits and reflects, in that small but necessary bower of the tower."

"Exactly. Now, Jacques Tireur, one of the marquis's best crossbowmen, says, 'Monseigneur, I see a moon.'

" '*Mille tonerres*! I see it too. Well, rascal! Do I have to tell you what to do? Sight your base Genoese contraption, bullseye yon moon, and a purse of gold and a *permis* to Paris is thine. Miss, and by the twenty-four treasures of the twelve apostles, I'll make thine own moon a target butt for all our gallant company.'

" 'Monseigneur, I can but try, with hope to do as well as my good father, who pierced a Switzer cheese at twice yon distance, to gain a prize at our good duke's wedding festival.'

" 'Shoot, *scelerat*, shoot, before I swing this chain, and crack thy base peasant skull, with this spiked Star of Bethleham skullcracker of mine.' "

"Go on," I said to my imaginative friend. "Get the story's ending out of your system."

"It's obvious. The veteran crossbowman crosses himself and takes careful aim, zing goes the deadly quarl, 'Yeee-OWWW!' screams the count, the besiegers press the attack, and the now leaderless garrison surrenders the castle. Logical, isn't it?"

"Okay, Froissart Junior," I said. "But I would fain pierce a good cheese, with my own teeth. Let us hie to this goodly nearby inn, and try *pommes de terre frites*, and *omelettes*, and *vin ordinaire*, for we're all hungry."

Leaving the ancient farm, we had a good supper in the nearby village, when our attention was aroused by a screeching commotion, just outside the inn door. Going out into the narrow, muddy street, we saw two young girls clawing and pulling each others hair, while they screamed at each other.

"You are not respectable!" cried one.

"Miserable one! I, I am very respectable. It is not me but you, who has affairs with Americans."

"No, no, no, no! I have not had a single affair with the Americans. It is you who makes them. You are a true slut, a girl who is always making dirty obscenities with the Americans. Ein! Yaaaahh!" As we stood amazed, a bent old crone, who could have been one of the girl's great-grandmother, came hobbling out of a cottage door. "Ein! You, you are at fault, sow!" She shook a talonish finger at the other girl. "It is you all right, not her, who is the cheat from here. Prostitute, bad girl, you!"

Diverted, the second girl turned from her adversary, and seized the old beldam, with both fists by her hair. She shook her amidst screams and cheers from half the onlooking village, when a uniformed figure suddenly appeared from off a bicycle, and silence fell. It was one of the gendarmes, or national police, of the area, and law and order, if not true peace was rapidly restored. The gendarme now left, giving us a military salute, and also a faint smile with a knowing look, as if he suspected us of being some of *les Americans* screamed about. I have no doubt he related the incident with gusto to his comrades in the police station, and I recalled the old verse that goes:

Quand un gendarme rit dans la gendarmerie,
Tous les gendarmes rient dans la gendarmerie.

None of this has much to do with the strict business of flying in the first great war, but it was all part of the background of the French scene of those days, as it kept uncovering before our curious and wondering eyes. To us, the French were certainly a form of civilized people, but rather different, and there was some ribald verse of ours, that began, "Oh, the French they are a funny race" and so forth. As to that, they probably thought us just as odd. Concerning Harold Tittman, who was with me on this occasion, he survived terrible combat wounds, was decorated with the D.S.C. and followed a diplomatic career, years later becoming ambassador to Peru, among other important assignments. George Kenney, of course, became a four-star general, and General MacArthur's chief of aviation in World War II.

Chapter 12

DELIVERING PLANES FROM PARIS

After graduating from the acrobatic classes of Fields 5 and 6, our cadre was transferred to and also quartered at Field 7, generally known as Valentine Field from the nearby hamlet, for training in formation flying, as well as general experience on the Niewport 24 model. This airplane was a somewhat differently designed 15-meter job, with a more powerful 120-horsepower Le Rhone rotary engine, instead of the accustomed 80. This more powerful engine gave the plane a top speed of around 120 miles per hour, when flying at about 5000 feet, and with it, we were able to climb to an altitude of 19,000 feet, and sometimes considerably higher. One student pilot, Leighton Brewer, actually made over 24,000 feet on an altitude test, flying this model, although he may have profited from some special updraft, but around nineteen thousand feet was the normal limit, and that was well off the ground for a pilot who had no parachute nor oxygen mask.

As to formations, we practiced them in threes, fives, sevens and larger, in stepped-up V's somewhat like wild geese, and generally rather tightly knit, especially so after we had had considerable experience. Like all the Issoudun fields, the flight line at Valentine gave out the all-pervading odor of the castor oil then used in our engines, which oil stained our uniforms, soaked into the leather of our flying boots, perfumed sheets, blankets, towels and all, until we could taste the stuff in almost everything. While awaiting our turns between flights, we stood around on the hard frozen field, that was often covered with ice or hard-packed snow, and we warmed our numbed feet by small bonfires, so burning many a pair of soles that winter. Issoudun bore little resemblance to the fabled sunny France we had read about. It was a raw icebox of a countryside, alternately deep in mud or snow, and more like a region of a mythical Upper-Lower Slobovia, a land only fit for goons and halfwits to inhabit, rather than a domain for poets, troubadours, and fair ladies. It was not that it was not beautiful. The faintly pink and pearly grey sunrises, the flaming red sunsets, with the long rays of the sun stretching out over the vast white fields, and sharply defining the shadows and the vivid greens of the little forests, or revealing some tiny hamlet, sharp and distinct as if etched in color, all this could be and often was something to delight an artist's eye, but the winter climate was another matter, and it was a wonder that pneumonia struck so seldom.

We flew formations at all altitudes; from low, simulated strafing attacks, where the leader was frequently at less than twenty feet above the ground, and his whole attendant formation was forced to hedge-hop over the road bordering poplar trees, railroad embankments, telegraph lines and other obstacles, as if it were some steeplechase, to high patrols at fifteen thousand feet and higher. As mentioned, there were no oxygen masks for pilots at Issoudun, nor even later over the front lines on combat duty, but no one, to my knowledge, ever complained of any altitude discomfort, either at school or in the combat zone, although 18,000 foot patrols over the lines became routine for our fighter squadrons.

Concerning the above in connection with the modern policy of using oxygen breathing aids for all air crews at over ten thousand feet, I think the old-time pilots got used to breathing thin air, just like the inhabitants of the Pamirs, or the Indians of the high Andes. Years later, I did much hiking, above the eleven-thousand-foot level in the Sierras, often carrying a fair pack, but I could never notice any discomfort, nor any more fatigue than at much lower levels, and I have a feeling that today's aviation crews could readily become accustomed to dispensing with masks, until they reached a much higher level than present practice. If in 1897, a mountaineer could conquer 23,000-foot Mount Aconcagua without benefit of oxygen equipment, and if even higher altitudes were attained in the Himalayas by early expeditions lacking breathing aids, it might seem that a modern, sedentary aviator, one picked from the physical flower of the nation, should be able to fly as high as the old mountaineers walked, without donning a mask, and with no impairment to his faculties. This might be tested, and men might be conditioned, through physical training, to reach surprising altitudes, with much fewer gadgets.

Breathing thin air on our flights, as we did in World War I, seems to have been very beneficial to some of us. Previous to the first war, I had generally suffered one or two heavy colds during a winter. These nuisances ceased to trouble me, after constant high altitude flights, and since then I have all but never experienced them. In my case at least, altitudes of well over 15,000 feet, without oxygen masks, seem to have conferred permanent immunity from all respiratory troubles.

Formation flying was not just flying V's. In formations we were constantly practicing sharp right-angle turns, or crossovers, where on the abrupt change of direction, the right and left planes exchanged relative positions, the inside plane climbing slightly, and the outer plane nosing down a trifle, to avoid collision on the crisscross. At Field 7, this maneuver was usually practiced with small formations of three to five, but over the front lines, our squadrons executed these right angle turns, in tightly knit V's of seven to even as many as twelve planes, with great precision.

Another of our maneuvers was the so-called Taylor stunt, or 180-degree change of direction. For this, the leader gave a signal, such as wobbling his wings, then immediately executed a *renversement* or half-roll, to come out heading in the opposite direction, while the other members of this formation did sharp, right or left about-turns, according to their respective positions. In this manner, a formation, patrolling a section of front line, could instantly reverse its direction, with no loss of altitude and no departure from the patrolling flight line. With those tiny planes, that could seemingly turn on a dime, compared with modern, superspeed machines, this was easy.

In addition we practiced the defensive maneuver called the Lufberry circle, after our great ace of the Lafayette Escadrille. By this action, a formation that was about to be attacked from above by a superior enemy force, could quickly change itself from a V into a large, milling circle, where each plane protected the rear of the plane in front, and was in turn guarded by the plane behind. Maintaining this defensive circle, the threatened formation could often maneuver itself into a much more favorable position. On breaking formation at a flight's end, we often played at follow the leader, a spiralling, diving rat race one after the other, from a high altitude and often through clouds, until we had descended to a rather low level, and it was dangerous to continue this pleasurable romp.

Not all our duties consisted in formation flying at Valentine Field. The school was getting more and more students, and many planes were becoming worn out, or hopelessly wrecked in crashes. Consequently, new planes and replacements were frequently needed, and these had to be ferried from the factories and the assembly fields, that were mostly on the outskirts of Paris. For such ferry jobs, student pilots who had progressed as far as Field 7 were selected, and most naturally, since it involved a minimum bonus, in the form of an overnight stay in Paris, these assignments were highly regarded, and they were given out in rotation to the deserving. Almost every pilot was, like the poor in Victorian novels, considered deserving, but since not many pilots had yet reached Field 7, and planes were beginning to roll a bit faster off the production lines, most of us got in two or three pilgrimages to our Mecca of Meccas. Even though it was a necessity and quite justified, this ferrying job had all the joy of a congressman's junket. It was another aspect of the combination of business and pleasure, that grand old legitimate American racket.

On my first assignment of this pleasurable nature, three of us, including Walt Smyth and the dour Zacharias, made the train journey in a *wagon de première classe* as befitting American aviators, although previous to the war the French had a saying, that no one ever rode first class, except the fools and the English. Fortified by a good lunch and a couple of bottles of *pinot* in the dining car, and in high good humor, we disembarked at the Gare D'Orsay, and scanned the sky for a hint at the coming weather.

This was pleasantly dark grey and looked like rain, which put us in a still higher fettle, since it meant there might be no flying back to Issoudun on the morrow. In those days any sort of rain, except a fine mist, was apt to damage wooden propellers, and it was also hard to fly a true course over a low overcast that hid all landmarks, with no aid except an uncertain compass. As for low flying under the overcast, across wide stretches of country, this was poor policy with those unreliable engines, and far-apart landing fields. So rain, a bore and a malediction in Issoudun, was a boon from *le bon Dieu* Himself, to a ferrying pilot in Paris. It was one of those things we prayed for.

With a cock and a whoop, and arm in arm with the good demon Rum, we did the necessary reporting at headquarters, scorned some official hotel billet, which we suspected was a disguised YMCA and on the dull side, and took a suite at the Grande, which although not so smart as the Crillon, the Ritz, the Eduard Sept or such, was quite suitable for pilots, since it was lively and bustling, and its bars and lobbies were frequented by much gay life. That evening after dinner at La Rue, we tested the old Olympia dance hall, tossed some francs around various spots in Montmartre, and ended up at the Folies Bergeres, where we were invited behind the scenes to meet the whole cast, including Mistinguette and other principals. There was also a husky youth, somehow connected with the show, who was introduced as the current middle-weight champion of Belgium. This sounded impressive, until Zacharias observed in his dry bitter way, that Belgium was a pretty small country, and our new friend's status was comparable to being champion of Connecticut.

Back in bed around three, we were soon aroused by the wail of the sirens announcing a raid, and we stood on our room's balcony watching the searchlights sweep the dark, while antiaircraft batteries roared and rattled, as they lit up the northern skies. There were distant and nearer, heavy explosions, then a long silence, followed by the exultant notes of the Berloque, the all-clear played on bugles. This was our first experience with enemy action, and it did not seem much to worry about, even though a house had been gutted in the Rue de la Paix, not so far from us.

The raiders had been Gothas and about a dozen. None had been shot down, either by the archies, or by the venerable flying contraptions assigned to the rather futile defense of Paris squadrons, but the enemy had hit Paris in numerous spots with bombs weighing about ninety kilos apiece, and generally fairly close to the worthier targets. Although all Paris had been blacked out, the German planes had seemed well aware of the more important locations, and it was obvious that there were many spies and secret signallers in the city.

The next morning, no rain having developed, we left headquarters in a light Fiat truck, for the assembly field at Villacoublay. This grassy airdrome lay southwest on the outskirts of Paris, and its numerous canvas hangars housed an interesting collection of most of the French planes then in use on the front lines or in the flying schools, plus an assortment of experimental models, including a few freaks and oddities. One of these latter, in particular, seemed to have come from the drawing board of a genius, who had visions of grandeur, but little regard for air resistance.

This was a triplane, a huge, five-motor, wire, canvas, and wood cat's cradle of an erection, with a wingspan of well over a hundred feet, which was tremendous for those times. Designed for a night bomber with a crew of five or so, it had one tractor engine in the nose, and four pushers built into the wings. The rest of it looked like something inspired by a mad bridge engineer, being a maze of struts, wires and other bracings. I was told that it had not been flown, and a French pilot expressed doubts that it would ever leave the ground. If it ever did, the air resistance of the triple wings and the bracing would have been excessive, and it must have sounded like a huge harp in the sky. It probably never did take off, for we would have heard some rumor of the flight, but it must have cost the taxpayers plenty of francs.

Since the weather had definitely cleared, we were told that we would ferry three 23-meter Niewports to Issoudun, as soon as they were readied and warmed up. I was also told that I would have a passenger, a young first lieutenant of our medical corps, who was being stationed at the school and had never flown, but who was willing and anxious to entrust his valuable life and expensive education, to a tricky plane, an uncertain engine, a takeoff over suburbs and factories, and the skill and judgement of a mere student pilot, during a one-hundred-and-twenty-mile flight, mostly devoid of intermediate landing fields. As to all this, if those in charge had really known flying hazards, this doctor would have been shipped by safe train, but this was the age of flying innocence, when ground officers gave orders from a background of ignorance, and so my passenger eyed me, an actual certified pilot, with the trust of a small child in his daddy. As for this doctor, whatever eminence he may have attained in his subsequent professional career, that morning he was a sucker.

My plane was soon readied, and with my little Johns Hopkins graduate on the front seat, we took off from the somewhat boggy field, barely clearing the line of hangars. Then shortly, the plateau region dropped away in a sheer cliff, and clear of the Isle de France, we were well airborne over the level, far-reaching farmlands of central France, and enjoying good visibility to follow the tracks of the *Chemin de Fer d'Orleans*, due south to our destination. So far so good, and everything promised an uneventful flight, with a safe delivery of the doctor at Issoudun, where he could prescribe the usual CC pills, apply iodine, inspect kichens and latrines, and in numerous ways justify his alma mater. Then the engine began to sputter and miss.

At this time we were about five thousand feet up, and about halfway between Paris and Orleans, but I had vaguely noticed a small airdrome, not far behind on my left, around which a few slow and obsolete-looking airplanes had been steadily circling. Not wishing to take further chances with my motor, I made for this field and landed. It was French, the planes were ancient Farman pushers, and it seemed to be some sort of school for primary instruction in flying.

I was most hospitably received by the French commandant, who gave orders that whatever ailed my engine should have immediate attention. This was done, I was able to resume flight within an hour, and the incident is not worth mentioning, except that I was amazed at the general age of the student flyers. Many looked at least forty-five, and some had beards. To me, who then considered thirty an advanced age, they looked like a bunch of grandpas.

These older men were probably being trained to take over ferry jobs, and other noncombat flying duties, but back in Issoudun, my plain story grew with the retelling, until it reached the status of a minor legend. There was, the tale finally went, an old men's flying school, where the last possible flyers of a depleted France, were being trained to fight its air battles. It was now averred that, if one flew near this school, one could see ancient men, in old wobbling planes, flying round and round in a leisurely way, while their long white beards streamed backwards in the slip stream, long and wavy like the home-going pennant of a man of war. This was the Methuselah Escadrille, pledged to its last artery to the defense of *la patrie*. Of course, this was not taken seriously by anyone, but such yarns made for amusement in the barracks, and underlying the joke was the more sober realization that France was about at the bottom of her barrel for more soldiers.

Not all of us who ferried from Paris to Issoudun arrived without serious trouble. A pair of students—one may have been Ernie Giroux—on reaching the area of Orleans, flew very low to observe the famed historical city. Then their engine suddenly failed, and they landed their 23-meter Niewport, with no better choice possible, amidst the branches of several tall trees, in the city's principal park. They were unhurt, but the plane hung in festoons of torn fabric, and from it they were extricated by the fire department, then locked up in jail by the police, while their fate was debated. There they stayed for three long hours, while a fellow American officer, but of the infantry branch and stationed in Orleans on some billeting assignment, hinted strongly of the guillotine, and of the rightly inflamed indignation of the citizens.

Finally came the verdict from the mayor and the city fathers. This was that,

> The American pilots did wrong. Without reason, they endangered the population of Orleans. Their misconduct was very serious, a deed to be brought to the attention of General Pershing. But the American pilots are young and brave. They have come from America in the defense of our country. They are good fellows, and the city of Orleans wishes to invite them to dinner.

On this, the locks turned in their cells, the bars swung open, they were invited to spend the night at the nearby country estate of a local baron, and refreshed, were escorted, as guests of honor, to a banquet presided over by the mayor, and attended by all the dignitaries of the city. The infantry captain was also asked to attend, but pleaded sudden, acute illness. "These damn screwballs of the air corps should have been court-martialed!"

Chapter 13

GUNNERY PRACTICE AND FRANTIC FRENCHMEN

Having completed formation flying training at Valentine Field, our group was ordered to Arcachon, on the coast not far south of Bordeaux, in order to receive instruction and practice in aerial gunnery, at Cazeau, where there was a French school established, and which was a few miles south of the small resort city. Accordingly, after a tedious train journey, broken by an hour stopover at Bordeaux, where I remember seeing the tall, slender figure of the first Mrs. Vincent Astor presiding over the station's Red Cross canteen, we arrived at Arcachon, on the coast of the often stormy Bay of Biscay, and were assigned comfortable quarters at the Victoria, a small but very good hotel. For roommates I had Harold Tittman, ex of Yale, and Pat Herron, a most likable graduate of the University of Pittsburgh, and a member of the 1916, second All-American football team.

Arcachon was on a good-sized, landlocked bay, and it was well guarded from the sea by a rampart of dunes. Inland, the countryside was part of that extensive, flat and low-lying region of the coast, lying roughly between the mouth of the Gironde and Biarritz, and known as *Les Landes*. It was a thinly settled and rather drearily lovely country of marsh and moor, somber, pitch pine forests, shallow salt ponds and tidal estuaries, and lonely coasts of sand and dunes. It was a land of far-apart and tiny hamlets, a home for countless waterfowl, and a domain where solitary shepherds made their way through bogs and fens, mounted on gigantic stilts. It reminded me of Cape Cod, the cape, that is, of my boyhood, before its present, cancerous overdevelopment, and through a forest of this sad lovely country, a tiny, narrow gauge railroad ran the ten miles or so from the charming resort city to L'Etang De Cazeau, a fairly large lake, reed bordered and filled with brackish water. Here, the French had established their serial gunnery school, and here we were assigned for instruction.

Let it be said, that whatever were the merits of the French

aviation of those days, and it had a justly famed record, the aerial gunnery school at Cazeau did not do it much credit. It had competent enough French officers and instructors, a passably efficient, but utterly ragamuffin looking, and quite incomprehensible crew of Annamite mechanics, a camp of German prisoners to repair the levees and maintain the drainage ditches of the low-lying airfield, and the most beaten up old crocks in the form of 15-meter Niewports, ever collected together by some junkman, for us students to fly, in our gunnery training.

Their wing fabrics smeared and brownish yellow from old oil stains, and so patched that they rivaled the traditional seat of a Zuider Zee fisherman's breeches, their rotary engines reconditioned about as well as an old old man, after his second monkey-gland injection, these Niewports were a struggle to fly, since their wings were usually out of line, their fuselage seemingly about to buckle, and their engines always on the verge of going to pieces—literally, pieces! This last happened to a pilot named Sherry, who fortunately made a safe pancake landing in a cushion of thick bushes, after his engine had suddenly hurled most of its cylinders and rotating parts, through wing fabrics and struts, in an almost total disintegration. Sherry, well liked and humorously nicknamed Madame Sherry, after a then famed musical comedy, survived this and the dangers of the front lines, to become a combat intelligence officer in the second great war, and also a professor at Cornell University.

The gunnery instruction consisted of a certain amount of ground familiarization and target practice, with various makes of machine guns, followed by airborne practice. In the air, the guns were all Lewis models, and the single gun was mounted on the upper wing, immediately above and before the pilot. So mounted, they fired over the propeller, and they must have contributed no little added resistance to the plane's air speed. These model Niewports, and these Lewis guns had once been the mainstay of French fighter squadrons, but now they had been superseded by faster planes, and by guns mounted in a much more streamline fashion, on the hood of the fuselages, and synchronized to fire through the blades of the propellers.

To aim the Lewis gun at Cazeau, there was a ring sight on the plane's nose, and for firing there was a trigger on the control stick. The main trouble came from jamming, and the Lewis gun was apt to jam, even if the 30-caliber cartridges had been carefully calibrated, with elimination of those found imperfect in any respect. This job was certainly doubtful at Cazeau, where the Annamite ground crews jabbered like birds, played soccer with their bare toes, had their own women, disguised as boys, smuggled in over thousand of miles from their steaming homelands, and generally, from our American point of view, seemed as crazy as an army of monkeys. The French did not seem to understand them too well, either. For one thing, the French sergeants just gave up on their names. No Annamite, at roll call, ever had a personal name bawled out, in traditional army fashion. It was just, "*Annamite, numero un! Annamite, numero deux!* and so on. As mechanics, they seemed to have a certain cleverness and ingenuity, but we did not, rightly or wrongly, have much trust in them.

At Cazeau, it was easy to learn the clearing of a Lewis gun jam when on the ground; the problem was how to handle it when airborne. The airborne gun was mounted on a hinge that allowed it to be tipped back, either to replace an empty cartridge drum, or to clear a jam. This was feasible enough, if the pilot were tall and with long arms, but a shortish man had practically to unbuckle his safety belt, and half stand up, if he were to get at things. This meant not only letting go of the stick and control of the plane, but one risked a good chance of being pitched out, without benefit of parachute. Clearing a jam, or reloading a loft on those planes, was no job for a short-armed fellow. It was hunky-dory for your long-armed ape, but I never tried it.

Aerial gunnery practice consisted in our releasing small, weighted parachutes, on which we were supposed to dive and fire; on diving and firing on ground targets; and in firing at sleeve targets, towed by lumbering, twin-motored Caudrons. At this, we were always supposed to aim towards the sea, but due to our inexperienced excitement, our bullets might travel to all points of the compass. Luckily, it was a very thinly settled region, but the Frenchmen in the Caudrons risked their lives, on more than one occasion, for some students became so intent on riddling the sleeve, that they were blind to the firing angle. Then the Frenchmen landed screaming and cursing, and pointing to bullet holes in their wings or fuselages, and we almost fell down laughing. Unless it was a real tragedy, all such things seemed funny in wartime, and the sight of a screaming, bearded Frenchman dancing like a mad hornet, because he had almost been shot through his situpon, was good slapstick burleycue, and very risible—that is, if one were not the French pilot.

However, if one or two of us came near to perforating some target Frenchman, we ran many more risks from the old planes assigned to us. One day, up a good five thousand feet and practicing various acrobatics, I went into a wing slip. It was very steep to vertical, and the plane lost altitude rapidly, at the same time starting to vibrate in a manner I had never previously experienced while doing a similar maneuver. Alarmed, I throttled way down, and with great difficulty, for the plane seemed bent on diving backwards, regained normal flying position. Hastening to land, because I sensed the plane had been unduly strained, I informed the French officer in charge of maintenance, of what had happened, and that I thought the plane might be unsafe, unless carefully gone over. He muttered something, shrugged his shoulders, barked at an Annamite noncom, and strolled off. It was the lunch hour, and flying was suspended.

Some hour or so later, and flying resumed, a young Cornell graduate named Hagedorn, was flying in a normal position, a few hundred feet above the field, when one wing suddenly came off, and he plunged to death. I never cared to verify the number on his plane, for I had a dreadful feeling that it was the same one I had just been flying. It may not have been, since almost all the planes, used by the students at Cazeau, were similar, castor-oil-soaked derelicts, which flew around the field, like poor wornout racing thoroughbreds, competing in the leaky barn, county fair race meets, at the sad end of their careers.

Not all danger and death came from the condition of the planes. One hazard came from diving and firing on ground targets, where more than one pilot, too intent on a good score, flew into the ground, destroying mark, plane, and himself in a blazing pyre, so hot that the fire fighters could not approach it. Another risk came from the German prisoners. These Heinies did no particular harm of their own accord, but some were Prussians of the famous guards, who looked boldly and even arrogantly, when we passed by. They were still convinced that Germany would ultimately win the war, and "who were we, Americans, to try and hinder the aims of the glorious *vaterland?*"

We did not like their dirty looks, and when we caught them below in their drainage work, we buzzed them low, so as to make them lie flat, or even jump into drainage ditches. It was considered legitimate sport, and even if we had decapitated one, the French in charge would have probably done little, except shrug their shoulders, and mutter, *C'est la guerre*. No Boches were ever hurt, as they became as nimble and fast as rabbits in taking cover, but two pilots, both intent on the same quarry, locked wings and were lucky to come out with minor injuries.

Chapter 14

THE COLONEL'S CAT AND OTHER VIPS

After a few weeks of aerial gunnery practice, flying the wornout and horrible derelicts of the Cazeau school by day, but dining with wine, and generally living quite well at our pleasant hotel in Arcachon, we were ordered back to Issoudun, and assigned to Field 8 for both quarters and our final stage of flying training. Here, the field commandant was a captain, a decent enough kiwi, who did his best for all concerned, but who always seemed sad and lonely in his role of sole ground officer, as if aware that he was not quite accepted as a comrade and a complete human being, by us caste-conscious company of flyers. For the sad truth was that, in those days, to be a kiwi was to be not quite a *white man*, in the eyes of young and biased pilots, and it was hard on a kiwi, who might well be both able and a gentleman. The operations officer, in actual charge of the flying, was Jim Osgood, a pilot and one of the boys, although he could and would lay down the law to any one of us, if the occasion warranted.

At Field 8, besides more formation and cross-country flying, we practiced aerial combat tactics against one another, sometimes without, and sometimes with planes equipped with camera guns, which were similarly installed and vaguely resembled machine guns, but which took pictures instead of shooting bullets. In those days, the 30-caliber, airplane machine-gun fired about one hundred shots a minute and, in combat, a good burst might be around five to ten bullets per gun. At an average effective firing distance, such a burst fanned out into the base of a cone, with a diameter of some thirty feet, and it was thus possible to estimate the success or failure of a simulated attack, by one student on another, through the pictures registered by the camera gun. It probably did not tell quite the true story, since light's speed is far greater than any bullet's, but it was a fair approximation of the real thing, and good training for dog fights of the days to come.

In addition to these camera fights, we were given practice patrols, either singly or in formation, between designated points, during which we tried, through making good use of the sun, mists, clouds, superior altitudes and other tactical advantages, to make effective surprise attacks on other student patrols, and at the same time to avoid being attacked in a similar manner. This was good practice in patrol tactics, aerial observation of any given situation, both on the ground and in the air, and training in the all important necessity of a state of constant alertness, and quick thinking over the front lines. In subsequent months, the above type of training was greatly developed at Field 8, and it turned out well-prepared graduates for the real thing in store. However, we of the early cadres received far too little of it, mainly due to the lack of sufficient camera guns, and other equipment.

Since at first, few of the planes had camera guns for combat practice, the pilots not so engaged, were encouraged to practice acrobatics, and to fly across country as much as possible. For this, we now had the Niewport 27 model, a superior handling 15-meter, and a delight to maneuver in the air, as well as being of very graceful design. With it, one could cut the switch of its 120-horsepower rotary engine, while airborne at a good altitude, and then by steeply diving in slight turn, crank the propeller and start up the power again. As for cross-country flights, they were pure fun, for in those primitive days, once in the air and away from the field, there was no communication from the brass to cramp a free spirit, just as there were no prescribed compass courses nor altitude levels to bound a pilot, in most cases. Consequently, a Field 8 pilot felt as free as a bird, either to fly as high as the cirrus, or as low as the hedges, and to any point on the compass, just so long as he returned safely in an undamaged plane, and did not arouse too loud screams from mayors of little villages, railroad officials, and mad enough farmers whose plow horses had been aroused to gallop like Kentucky Derby entrees.

The French country folk seldom squawked, at least officially to the school's headquarters, about low flying, but on one occasion, the management of the *Chemin de Fer d'Orleans* all but died from apoplexy or ruptured ulcers, because one of their crack trains had been brought to a complete halt. On this regrettable afternoon, three *aviateurs*, in strafing formation, had been alternately skimming the brown, furrowed fields and leaping the bordering poplar trees, when the express, bound for Chateauroux and points south, came racing along at about seventy miles an hour.

Here was big game, that promised more of a challenge than a farm Percheron, a bull of the meadow, or even a work detachment of German prisoners. In no time, the train passengers were aware that planes were diving at their car windows, and coming alarmingly close before zooming overhead. Then the fireman became very excited, because three planes, one after the other, were skimming down the length of the speeding train, with a bare few feet clearance. With landing wheels about three feet above the cab, they passed the locomotive, flew some distance ahead, wheeled about and came straight for the engine, at all but track level. At the last instant, they rose like rockets and no damage, but the engineer had had his fill. The train stopped, and he ran out waving a red flag, and all but dancing the cancan. The game then ended with the score, American pilots 1, *le Chemin de Fer d'Orleans*, 0.

A dreadful protest at this outrage was made to our headquarters, but the engineer had neglected to note any identifying numbers on the Niewports, and since many planes had been, at the same time in the air, it was difficult to verify the miscreants. Of course these reprehensible young criminals were pretty well known to about everybody, but one became a decorated ace, and the other two developed as good combat flyers and, years later, kind fathers and very solid citizens. Of course all this sort of *esprit*—in these modern times, some crab would have called it a manifestation of juvenile delinquency—was very deplorable, and it was just the thing, if it had ever come to their attention, for the General Staff and the humorless, squads-right generals to hold against the Fancy Dan Air Corps. Their indignation would have been justified, one supposes, but more than one train, filled with German troops or carrying supplies to the German armies, was similarly approached by our boys, during the St. Mihiel, the Meuse-Argonne, and other engagements, except that locomotives where blown up, cars derailed, and the passengers, not lying on the ground, were last glimpsed, scurrying for cover like panic-stricken rabbits. The spirited lads of Issoudun became grim fighters.

Not all the amusement came from low-flying antics. Cross-country flights, planes powered by the uncertain engines of those times, gave rise to all sorts of adventures, from forced landings on the ample grounds of chateaux, to become the honored overnight guests of dignified and ancient provincial nobility, such as fell to the lot of pajama and flying suit clad Leighton Brewer on an early morning flight, to more bizarre finales resulting from a dead engine. One of these forced landings ended amidst an explosion of bricks, sheet-metal roofing and other debris, of a totally flattened, boulevard *kiosk de necessité*, from the center of which a French gentleman was seen to retreat was amazing rapidity, considering his pantaloons were down by his knees. Fortunately this mishap resulted in no serious personal injury, except to the French monsieur's dignity and aplomb, but the student pilot, one well and favorably known to the old air corps, was scarred for his days, which he always explained as due to the hazards of war, to admiring feminine inquirers.

One sunny afternoon, on a formation flight to beyond Tours and return, my 120-horsepower Le Rhone rotary engine began to miss and make other signs of quitting. Some three thousand feet below, was a lovely countryside of rolling hills, vineyards and orchards, but no open, level country, as around Issoudun. A cleared hilltop offered a possible landing, when a farm wagon suddenly appeared dead ahead, and only the good fortune that my engine came to life for a last instant, prevented a serious smash. My wheels had touched ground, but I was able to just bound over the cart, as the stupefied farm wench threw up her hands and went arsi-versi over the seat, and to flutter across the next valley onto the slope of a moderate-sized hillside clearing. There seemed no damage, but the engine was dead, and on three sides were enclosing orchards. Above was a farmhouse, from which the proprietor, his wife, his son, the son's wife, three large dogs and several children came running.

My trouble, an unaccountably empty gas tank, was soon determined, but the farm had no telephone, and there was no petrol in the neighborhood. The farmer was quite sure that there was *pas d'essence par ici*, but he had better ideas. "Regardez, mon lieutenant," he said. "*Helas!* It is true that we possess no single drop of *essence, pour faire marcher votre avion, mais nous avons chez nous*, that other but most excellent essence, which makes march *les soldate incomparable de France*. You, monsieur lieutenant, having escaped death by a miracle, have need of it."

White Mule, whether a product of the most remote hillbilly glens of the Blue Ridge Mountains, or doubly distilled from the vineyards of sunny France, has an equal potential to raise the human spirit, much like an astronaut lifted by a rocket. In my lame French and my new friend's rustic version of that language, we discussed the general situation, while the *petit vers* were filled and refilled, and the home brewed brandy scorched the inner man like liquid coals of fire.

"*Aha! J'ai une bonne idée*," said my orchardist friend, after the last drop of his *bon* but veritable hell-brew had been consumed. "*Tenez! Here is my bicycle*. Take it—ride it to the city hall in Losche. There you might very well be able to get some gas."

Taking his suggestion, I mounted the rusty object, and after six bone-shaking miles of pedalling, which cleared my head nevertheless, I arrived at the city hall of the picturesque river town of Losche. There, after signing all sorts of papers, I was assured of obtaining a small but sufficient supply of aviation gas, but since that would take an hour or so, I was advised to visit the ancient castle while waiting.

The old fortress castle, in an excellent state of preservation, was well worth seeing, but most impressive were the dungeons for prisoners of the royal power. They were all very grim, but the most terrible, the so-called *oubliettes* or dens, where a prisoner was left to be forgotten, were like something out of a Gothic novel, a horror of utter darkness, hollow groans, dragging chains, and the specters of madness and despair. Hewn out of the solid rock and deep under the castle, were several small, cavelike recesses, all reached by a corridor like a tunnel in a mine. By the light of our candles, I could make out that each cell, a few square feet in area, and much too low to stand erect, had a good-sized hole in its floor, opening on a shaft which led, so said my venerable and voluble guide, to the river flowing beneath. In these cells, the political enemies of medieval kings, most of them probably well born, and accustomed to the best in the life of their times, were thrust away to be forgotten, and their families and world did not know what became of them. It made me shudder. In 1918, the western world's rulers were all to some extent limited in their actions, and influence by the humane principles of Christian religion. The days of medieval torture were considered forever over, for Hitler was then but an insignificant corporal, Mussolini a nothing, and the Communist power was mostly unknown and of little account.

Driven back to the farm in a French army *camion*, with five 5-liter tins of the precious *essence*, for the payment of which I had seemingly pledged my life, my honor, the sacred word of the government of the United States, and the fortunes of the Vanderbilts thrown in for good measure, I spent the night in an all-engulfing, and very dampish feather bed, to be early awakened by the cock-a-doodle-doos of several raucous roosters, and the pungent aroma of a moist, conical dunghill, close by my open casement window.

Petit dejeuner—a big bowl of hot *chocolat* and a slab of bread—over, I filled the plane's gas tank, and then considered the problem of safely starting the engine, and taking off. The clearing was not much over six acres, but the slope was fairly steep, and a downhill takeoff was possible with a very short run, provided the engine was sufficiently warmed and turned up, before departure. It was plain that no one, except myself, could start the engine by cranking the two-bladed propeller, but others might be entrusted to holding back on the leading edges of the lower wings, and some one of the family could sit in the cockpit, with instructions to depress the tail, by holding back the control stick.

For the wings, the farmer, his son, the farmer's sturdy wife, and a neighbor were assigned as the anchor team, and since there was no one else, the son's wife, a plump young girl, with a rosy and pretty peasant face, was boosted up with many a guffaw and near hysterical giggle, and crammed into the cockpit. Once in, I carefully showed her how to hold the stick, and warned her not to touch anything else, above all the little throttles by her side. I then primed the engine, adjusted the spark and the manettes, readied my rustic crew, and gave the propeller a sweeping yank.

The engine started, but turned over faster than expected, the plane began to move despite the efforts of the four on the wings, the son's wife screamed and excitedly opened the throttle, the engine roared, the frightened ground crew scurried out of the way, and I was just able to reach the cockpit and cut the switch, before plane and shrieking passenger took off into the blue for an unknown destination and ending. Disaster averted, the son volunteered for the cockpit's hazard, some big stones were found for blocks, and I was finally able to make a rough but successful takeoff from the farm. Inside a half-hour, I arrived safely at Field 8, where Jim Osgood took a rather dim view of the whole adventure. Although he did not say so, he seemed to put little faith in my account of running out of gas, but mumbled something about "monkey business," and having a good mind to report me as awol. He grounded me for two days.

I was unjustly in disgrace, but our field was soon enlivened by an episode which put my joked and talked about adventure into the shade, and all but caused a small international incident. It did cause some sort of protest, but much more laughter. This was the case of the colonel's cat.

Although in those days, the term VIP was unheard of, its ranks were legion. France was full of such inspectors and official visitors, and Issoudun, as the chief aviation training center for the AEF, had a steady influx of important guests, all on more or less important errands. Among these were generals and congressmen, cabinet members, heads of war production and other top ranking nabobs, and also a host of lesser personages, such as second assistant secretaries, low ranking brigadier generals, and even mere colonels, who suddenly arrived from somewhere, opened briefcases, showed impressive credentials, inspected, asked questions, disrupted schedules, looked wise and departed, no doubt back to their very important bureaus and headquarters.

Among these lesser but very respectable visitors, was a certain British colonel, a pilot and a very good one, who arrived in his own special plane, with his own private insignia painted on the plane's fuselage. Colonel X was quite dashing and very correct, his fighter plane was of the latest model and the object of admiring comment, and his private insignia was very striking and conspicuous. It was a cat.

This cat loomed large on the plane's fuselage. Its back was arched, its bristling tail was straight up, its ferocious head was turned to glance behind, and its elevation was like a view of a horse from the driver's seat in a sulky, an aspect from south to north. Also, except for its baleful yellow eyes, it was coal black. No other spot of color marred its glossy but utter blackness. It was a witch's cat, very large, very black, malignant and very eye catching.

Arriving at this time on some errand, Colonel X was anxious to see the camera-gun training at Field 8, and deciding to spend the night, he left his plane on the flight line, before our row of hangars. One of these was being used for vehicles, and their upkeep and repairs. In this one, a Ford tin lizzie ambulance was being repainted, including the big, Red Cross emblem on its side. This ambulance and the colonel's fighter had little in common to the unimaginative mind, but most of the early air-force pilots had considerable imagination—perhaps too much for the strictly military regulation way of thinking about many things. Admiring the colonel's plane, a small group engaged in comments.

"A good job, except for that cat," said one.

"What's wrong with the cat? He looks all right. A fighting cat! Ready to spit in your eye, he looks to me."

"That's his trouble. He lacks something vital. You'd be mad too, if you didn't have what he ain't got."

"I get the point," said another. "As a supporting member of the S.P.C.A., I make a motion that this unfortunate cat be taken care of. What we need is in that hangar, and tonight after dark!"

The next morning, the enlisted men were in convulsions, and delighted to see that the cat, on the colonel's plane was no longer in such an ugly mood. He seemed to be smiling with a happy expression. However, he was no longer completely black. The unknown artist, years later an architect of some merit, had with steady hand, and with unerring precision for the exact location, centered an orb, the size of a silver dollar, and as red as the setting sun. What the colonel said was unprintable, apologies were in order, but the miscreants were never discovered.

Not long after this, my training at Issoudun was over, and with barely enough hours of flying time to my entire record, I was considered officially ready to engage in any flying activity, over the lines or behind. Our cadre was given various orders, and in company with some dozen others, I was assigned to Orly Field, near Paris. Somewhere around this time, all hell broke out in the north. The Germans had launched another great offensive.

Chapter 15

ASSIGNMENT—ORLY FIELD

Orly Air Field, on the southern outskirts and not more than an hour's truck drive from the heart of Paris, where a good number of our just graduating, Issoudun cadre were now assigned as ferry pilots, had not been long established, and by today's standards for an important airport, it was a very primitive layout. Bounded on the west by a tree-lined highway, it consisted of no more than one hundred acres of level cow pasture, a not numerous collection of one-storied shacks for headquarters, barracks, messhalls and such, and the usual line of small, wooden framed, canvas covered hangars. These were all dusty, musty, smelling of dope and castor oil, and as hot as hell under the noonday sun, but on one was a short pole and a wind sock, which was considered quite adequate to police all incoming and outgoing aerial traffic.

This deduction was not quite justified, since the wind sock was subject to all sorts of diverse gusts and eddies that might swirl around the hangar, so it often indicated any but the true wind's direction, for a takeoff or a landing. However, we pilots of that remote era were well aware of that, and we were more apt to consider the smoke rising from the chimneys, the flutter of the leaves in the trees, the waving of the wash on the housewives' lines, and even the directional landings of the bigger birds, in order to determine the wind's real bearing. There was no control tower, naturally. There were no control towers on any airdromes in all France, even Le Bourget. Up to a few years previous, all aviation had been strictly for the birds. It was then still not much further advanced over nature.

At this time in the early spring of 1918, Orly Field had been taken over by us, as an assembling depot for the various models of planes that had been procured from various factories, mostly in the Paris area, although some from elsewhere. In consequence, its flight line and its hangars contained not only a good representation of the latest French fighters, bombers, observation, and reconnaissance airplanes, but also several British models, and in addition, several specimens of most of the lingering, flying fossils, that for some obscure reason or other—political, ultraconservative, or just no brains in high places—were still deemed necessary for the preservation of democracy.

Concerning these all but obsolete airplanes, like the tourist attraction argument, given to retain the quaint cable cars of San Francisco, there seemed to be no other reason for their being of interest to us, except that the French had gradually come to regard us as a great horde of touring Americans, rather than a serious army. At this time, although we had declared war on Germany a good year earlier, and had transported many men to France, we had done little fighting of consequence. France was being bled white with enormous losses, and the ordinary Frenchman, seeing Americans only as incredibly well-paid troops, well armed and uniformed but all safely back in areas that were far from the blazing front lines, was beginning to mutter that we had only come over for the joy ride. In the opinion of many Frenchmen, we were merely armed tourists—*des soldats Americains qui ont beaucoup de francs, mais des vauriens pour la guerre*" (American soldiers with a lot of money but worthless in war).

Fortunately, within a few weeks, the action of the 2nd Division at Chateau-Thierry completely changed this unfavorable opinion, but on our arrival at Orly, that event was still in the future, and it was obvious that the French, still polite to our faces, were saying to each other, *when are these goddam bastard tourists going to fight*? Such words in the French equivalent were the universal question, and even the *petites femmes*, the cute girls of Paris, were privately thinking that we were little better than so many *sales embusqués*, although that did not quite stop them from sipping our wine, and from helping to spend our francs. In all, the general atmosphere was becoming a bit embarrassing for a decent American soldier, and we pilots began to feel less and less like *heroes of the azure heights*, a phrase in an American paper, but more like an army of jolly quartermasters, something like a herd of Ferdinands of the Bulls. It was as if the AEF were in France not to fight, but to sniff the flowers.

From Orly Field, where we had been assigned as ferry pilots, it was our job and pleasure—the latter sometimes a bit dubious—to take off, fly and deliver almost any model airplane, to wherever it might be called for, whether in any part of France, perhaps even to Italy, and certainly across the channel to England. This last, just an insignificant hop for today's light planes, was in those days of frequently failing engines, no plane-to-ground communication, and no survival equipment save for nature's, something rather for aspiring channel swimmers, than for the average intrepid birdman, who might prove to be an eagle over the front lines, but would be no penguin in the icy tides off Dover. This was my opinion; luckily I never drew a British mission.

I had not much more than checked in at Orly, when M.E. Carter, a sterling character as well as a competent pilot, but also one of the smooth Memphis crowd of ace crap shooters and virtuoso blackjack players of the long voyage over on the good ship *Manchuria*, strolled out of the operations office, and hailed me.

"Ever fly a Salmson?" said M.E.

"Ever fly a what?" I had never even heard the name before.

"A Salmson. No matter. None of you birds ever have. It's new, and we have one ready. They want it up at Colombey Les Belles, as soon as possible. You fly it there, right away, now."

"To Colombey Les Belles?" I said. "That name sounds very nice, but what is it, and where the hell does it lie?"

"No matter. I've got your map all ready, and the route is easy to follow. Your ship's now warming up."

"But what about this ship?" I said. "I don't know the first thing about it."

"You know as much as the others. So what! It's a bit bigger than a Niewport, and you sit way up in the nose. Outside of that, it's just another airplane."

"Okay," I said. "I'll get ready."

"Well, step on it. It's a good way, and you want to be sure to get there before dark."

Down on the flight line before one of the hangars, a big, strange-looking plane was being revved up. It was a two-seater job, brown and green in a camouflaging pattern of those colors, with a more or less barrel-shaped cross-section through its fuselage, and the pilot's cockpit right up in the nose, and before the wings. It had three machine guns, a fixed one—I think it was a British Vickers—for the pilot to shoot dead ahead, and a brace of Lewises, that could be trained and fired over a wide angle of coverage, by the gunner-observer in the rear. As was universal in those days, these guns were blocked from shooting an enemy who might attack from a blind angle, beneath and to the rear. This warplane, like the porcupine, had a vulnerable belly, but all the two-place bombers and observation planes had a similar handicap.

A sergeant shut off the engine, clambered out and saluted. He was tall, and bony, and solemn like an undertaker. "You, the lootenant as is going to fly this ship to Colombey?" he said, in deep, funereal tones.

"Yes, sergeant," I said. "I'm it, but you've got to instruct me in all the engine controls, and the other dinguses. I've never seen this make of a ship before now."

This latest model of a Salmson was being ordered and received by us, for service in some of our photo-reconnaissance squadrons, that were in the course of being activated and trained. It had a radial engine of around 270 horsepower, which proved unusually reliable for those days, it had one of the first of the to any extent successful, self-sealing gas tanks, and for its type of work, it turned out to be a very decent airplane. However, I knew nothing about it, even by hearsay. Now I was to fly it, for a good distance over unfamiliar country, and on a half hour's notice.

This experience was to be expected. In those days, planes might be two place or one place, single engined or double, tractors or pushers, land planes, sea planes, or flying boats, but all were relatively very simple compared with today's complicated machines, and the difference between one model or type and another was not too great. Consequently, any pilot who had graduated from an advanced flying school was supposed to be able to fly anything, whether he had had any experience on a given model or not.

Like all fond theories of the higher ups, this was not always true. Theoretically, a commissioned officer was ready to handle any job appropriate to his rank and category. In the old, prewar, regular army, where promotion took years, and war had been much less technical, this was true, but it was so no longer.

Officers, commissioned after only ninety days of training, were not always able to handle an unfamiliar duty and Blois, filled with unhappy officers up for reclassification, unjustly stigmatized many a good but inexperienced man, and scarred his soul for a lifetime. However, no pilot ever went to Blois, that I know of. Some failed through inexperience, but they went to the hospital or the graveyard, and more often the latter.

Clad in a fur-lined flying suit, for I expected it to be cold above, I got into the pilot's seat, and was instructed in the instruments and engine controls by the sergeant, standing on the stepup to the cockpit. There were the usual throttles or manettes, oil pressure and temperature gauges, an RPM indicator, an altimeter, a gas gauge, and a route-inscribed map mounted on a framed set of rollers. There was no compass nor air-speed indicator, although some planes had them, and of course no kind of climb or bank indicator, since they were then unheard-of.

To me, there was one more thing, strange and obscure in purpose. This was a hole, about the size of a saucer as I remember, in the cockpit's floor, and about between the pilot's legs. It may have been for the use of some sort of camera or sighting device, but Ihave never known. Or this afternoon, it was just a round hole through the floor, which seemed to have no apparent function, except possibly to spit through. Since the front gun was not loaded, I played with the trigger, and tested the ailerons and elevator controls, while the sergeant made a few somewhat disconcerting observations.

"The last flyin' lootenant, I showed the controls to, was killed, sir."

"Too bad," I said. "What happened?"

"Don't know, sir. One of them accidents that happen. He was a real nice-looking feller, too. Real young, and about your build, sir. Course, come to remember, he had never flown this type of plane, before. It was just like you, sir."

"I've had a lot of friends killed," I said. "Maybe I knew him. What was his name, if you remember?"

"Can't recollect at this moment. Only saw him once, sir. I did hear though, that his plane was smashed up something awful, and him too for that matter. They said his head was all blown up like a balloon, and one of his eyes was lying in the grass, a long ways from the rest of him. Didn't find it 'til the next day, neither. They said it looked like a china marble, a blue and white one, a-starin' up there from the grass at them. It was kind of unpleasant to see it, just a-starin'. That's what they told me, sir."

"Enough please, Sergeant! I think we had better start the engine. It's getting late, and I want to be sure of getting there before dark."

"Right, sir. 'Specially as this plane is new to you. Just like that young lootenant, that was killed, sir."

The Salmson's engine fully warmed up, I taxied to the far east end of the field, and swung around for the takeoff. Giving a glance at both wings, I realized that they had, apparently, considerably less, relative camber than the familiar Niewports, and that the leading edges seemed set at a much smaller angle of attack, but I attached little significance to my observation. There was little wind according to the listless sock, but the field stretched out well over fifteen hundred feet, which was a lot of run for those days, so with a quick look around for any possible, landing plane, I gave the engine full gun, and with wings and fuselage parallel to the ground, started rolling.

Over halfway down the field, I was rolling a good seventy or more miles an hour, and the plane—any plane in my experience—should have become airborne, for with the Niewport, one had merely to keep the nose slightly down or level, and the plane would take off automatically, after flying speed had been reached, a speed even less than I was now doing. Soon, I was travelling at close to one hundred miles an hour, but the Salmson still hugged the ground like a desert road runner, the end of the field was nearing fast, the highway trees loomed tall and thick dead ahead, and the confounded plane seemed incapable of reaching flying speed before crashing. Then at the last split second, I yanked back on the stick, and the Salmson shot up like a rocket.

I cleared the trees, brushing the top branches with my landing wheels (as was reported by fascinated observers), but I cleared them. I now knew how to take off a Salmson. I knew it the hard way, with the aid of a guardian angel, and one jump ahead of the devil. No one had warned me that, unlike our familiar Niewport, a Salmson had to be lifted off the ground by the pilot. Perhaps, no one at Orly had known this. Today, it is inconceivable that a pilot would take off an unfamiliar type of plane, without at least some minimum oral instruction. In those days, many a pilot just learned, with the help of God, through the hard way, or else he was just another poor dumb bastard, bumped off.

Climbing to about three thousand feet, I headed for Colombey Les Belles, our principal air depot in the Zone of Advance, and in the department of Meurth and Moselle, about 170 miles due east of Orly. In clear weather, such as it was, the route was easy to follow, and I figured on arriving in a little over one hour and a half, since the Salmson was said to cruise at around one hundred and fifteen miles per hour. If all went well, I should land well before dark, even though I had taken off very late in the day for such a ferry job. The trouble came from my flying suit. It was fur-lined, and it would have been all right in a Niewport, where the air-cooled rotary engine was several feet in front of the cockpit.

In this Salmson cockpit, a snug little well, close behind the big 270-horsepower, water-cooled radial engine, the suit was too hot. Too hot soon became a gross understatement. I felt as if I were being smothered in a sweatbox, but strapped and cramped in the little cockpit, it seemed impossible to get out of the terrible suit. I began to feel faint from the heat, and the sight of the earth below, through the hole between my feet, began to give me a nightmarish, dizzying effect, which I had never before felt, even in the most strenuous aerial acrobatics. At the same time, the hole started to have a semihypnotic influence, and it was hard to keep from staring down into it. It was a little hole, that led down, down, down to hell, I kept thinking. The combined heat of the engine and the suit was beginning to put me under, and as it would take too long to climb to at least ten thousand feet and cooler altitudes, I had to make an immediate landing.

Fortunately, I had arrived at about the halfway mark of my flight, and below was Haussimont, one of our airfields, close by to Sommesous on the road to Vitry Le Francois. Here with aid of some saint, who must have taken over pilots for his special care, I made a safe landing, and was welcomed by the commanding office and the local squadron. This squadron was, if memory is not at fault, the 96th, although it may have been the 90th. At any rate it was one which a few months later, made a famous record as one of our day bombardment squadrons, during our battles of the St. Mihiel, and the Meuse-Argonne.

At this time however, it was only being trained and broken in, with flying mostly confined to practice, well behind the front lines, since the squadron's planes were of a model of two-seater Sopwiths, which featured only moderate speed under wide open power, but had an almost sailplane range of glide, in case of engine failure and dead stick. Once they had been of some account, but at this stage of air progress in warfare, armed or not, these Sopwiths would have been sitting ducks for any German fighter, since they were slow to fly, slow to turn, and quite likely to snap off a wing in a dive. Regardless of these deficiencies, members of this squadron were wont to sneak across the front lines, for a quick, practice reconnaissance flight, after first making quite sure that none from the redoubtable Richtofen Circus were lying in ambush from behind some cloud bank.

Concerning the gliding range of these obsolescent two-place Sopwiths, it could not have been less than forty to one, and it was probably much greater. Even with a completely dead engine, they seemed to float like thistledown, and a first landing with one could prove an embarrassing experience. A pilot, named Downes as I remember, and I, flew a pair of them to Haussimont, on our initial flight in these models. I landed first and safely, but came to a final, rolling stop—planes had no landing-wheel brakes in that era—only about fifty feet short of a line of hangars, and utterly amazed at a plane that seemed never ready to settle its wheels on the ground, but kept on floating beyond anything conceivable. Then Downes came in, or tried to.

At the far end of the field, he was but a few feet above the ground, and his stick had gone dead, but his Sopwith would not settle. It floated, and floated, and floated, with its wheels not over five feet from the ground, and this for a thousand feet and more, while Downes tried vainly to stall and ground it. Then still gently and steadily sailplaning, it struck a hangar, its nose went in, the wings folded back into a vee, while the canvas hangar went way in, like a fat man's well-punched stomach, then collapsed in ponderous, elephantine folds, over Downes and his evergliding albatross. From this, he finally emerged, unhurt, but very dusty, very red-faced, and completely speechless. However, everyone laughed, and all agreed, that Downes had made the Sopwith resemble a Burgess-Wright flying boat.

As to this, Downes was a careful and competent pilot, but this was his first landing on this model of a Sopwith, and no one had warned him of its peculiar tendency to keep gliding. For all of us pilots, in that rather happy-go-lucky age of aviation, there was always some surprise in store, before landing at our destination, when flying some unfamiliar contraption. Models varied greatly, and whatever they were, they seldom gave us a dull journey.

At Haussimont, an after-supper ball game was in progress, between the pilots and the squadron's ground officers and headquarters' enlisted men, but all quit to inspect and admire the Salmson, which looked so modern, powerful and formidable alongside their own outdated airplanes. The pilots were mostly old friends from Issoudun, and a gay and lively lot, although one was a Quaker, and could have, quite legitimately, been a conscientious objector. His name was Sid Marine, he was from Brooklyn, a little known region of the United States to most of us, and his church had ousted him for wanting to fight, as he told me. He fought in plenty of engagements, returned to Brooklyn in the best of health, his church treated him like a hero, and reinstated him.

My stop at Haussimont was necessarily short, and I was soon airborne once more, but not quite soon enough, for a head wind had arisen, and I still had more than eighty miles to cover before dark. At flying altitude, the head wind must have been very strong, as I seemed to crawl over the unfolding map below, and it seemed almost forever before I left the town of St. Dizier, a bare forty miles beyond Haussimont. At this point, the sun was rapidly sinking out of sight, and the night was advancing, like a dark storm in the eastern sky. Then by the time I passed Gondrecourt, the stars were out, the earth was in deep shadow, and few lights burned, especially in the tiny villages, such as nearby Domremy, where Joan of Arc was born.

Although night had come, the white and dusty roads were easy to follow, the Meuse River reflected the shining stars, and I had little trouble in reaching Colombey Les Belles, and in making out the shadowy outline of the big, unlit airfield, its lighter, bordering highways, and the darker line of hangars. A landing, even if it was night, did not seem an unduly risky venture, so after circling and surveying the field a couple of times at low altitude, I throttled and glided in for the landing. Shortly, my wheels touched smoothly, and with tail down I was rolling over the slightly undulating ground, and congratulating myself on a safe arrival. Then suddenly dead ahead on the dark ground, a previously unnoticed, ink black ribbon stretched clear across my run, the ground gave way, my wheels were gripped, and I felt the rear of the plane rising over me. Then with a rending crash, the Salmonson was over on its back, and I was hanging from my safety belt, my head not over two feet from the ground, and the smell of gasoline in my nostrils.

Most of the field heard the crash, scores came running, and I was soon extricated, unhurt, but very thankful that the plane had not caught fire in the crash. The trouble was a big ditch, very recently dug for a drainage culvert, and not yet refilled. No warning lights had been set, for after-dark landings were not looked for, and the showing of a light was also unwise, since the front lines were only thirty miles or so to the north, and a visit from enemy night bombers was always possible.

Apart from the engine and the guns, which did not suffer much damage, the fine, new, expensive ship was a total wreck, and my return journey (by rail) to Orly was filled with gloomy forebodings of being courtmartialed, in the name of our suffering taxpayers, of my wings being ripped off by some aviator-hating colonel of the general staff, and of being transferred to the derided S.O.S., the Service of Supply, of which the soldiers' song ran:

> Oh mother take down your service star,
> Your son's in the S.O.S.!

However at Orly, it was decided that I had been despatched a little too late in the day for a flight to Colombey, and little more was said about my mishap, except that it was too bad that it had to be a fine Salmson in the ditch, instead of some perambulating chickencoop of a Voisin, or other obsolete flying erection, and that I was a lucky bastard not to be pushing up daisies. That ended that, although I had two other experiences in a Salmson.

Chapter 16

GETTING TO KNOW THE FRENCH

My second experience in a Salmson was when I made a short hop from Le Bourget to Orly, and is only worth mentioning to contrast the Le Bourget of 1918, with what it has since become, the modern French counterpart of La Guardia Field, and other world renowned international airports. At that time, outside of a smooth and level grassy field, quite a bit larger than the general run, and a greater number of, as well as larger and more substantially built hangars, Le Bourget had next to nothing deemed essential to a modern air terminal.

Most obvious to modern pilots and air travelers, it had no vast network of concrete landing strips and runways, and no control tower. Neither had it any organized system for regulating plane arrivals and departures. There was the usual pole and airsock, and a big arrow on a turntable in the center of the field, that might indicate the wind's true direction, provided the French gentleman of leisure in charge of it, had not forgotten to adjust it. Sometimes he had, but there was always the smoke from the factory chimneys, the ladies' underwear on the lines, and if William Wordsworth had been a flyer, there would have been the daffodils dancing in the breeze, and what more did a pilot want to guide him to a good landing.

Landings and takeoffs were as casual as the birds, but since traffic was very light by modern standards, few individuals were ever killed in collisions, and such would only be pilots, poor bloody observers, or some lowly mechanics, but no passengers who had paid good money for a ticket, and who was lost as a good customer. To the French, an occasional mishap through collisions was all part of the game, and when one occurred, they merely spat and shrugged their shoulders. *C'est la guerre*, they said, as they nodded philosophically, and that was that.

After presenting my orders at Le Bourget for a brand new Salmson, the French mechanics wheeled the machine to the flight line, and cranked the propeller. The engine warmed up, they lit a couple more of their horrible Algerian cigarettes, turned to me, spat, shrugged, eyed each other like leering brigands, and indicated that the ship was mine to take off, when and how I saw fit, and to fly straight to hell, or smacko into the Eiffel Tower for all that it mattered. It was early morning as I took off, and in no time I was a good thousand feet over Paris, the mist-covered windings of the much bridged River Seine, the butte of Montmartre, the Place de la Concorde, Notre Dame Cathedral, the Arc de Triomphe, and the streets and radiating boulevards of the incomparable City of Light.

In the pearly grey morning light, the ancient city looked like a melancholy painting in brown, ochre, and slate grey, its myriad chimney pots and dormered attic windows suggested the shivery abodes of starving artists and writers, as described in French novels, and one could almost smell the most remembered smell of Paris, which was not the perfume of bediamonded dames in the Ritz, nor the stench from untold automobile exhausts, like in most of today's great cities, but the wonderful odor of fresh baked bread. Much of Paris then smelt like a bakery, instead of like a garage, filled with the fetor of the gasoline engine, although that is true no longer. A few minutes' flight, and I had delivered the Salmson at Orly.

A third flight in a Salmson proved more adventurous. Although the weather looked a bit dubious, I had been ordered to take this ship to Colombey, and I had proceeded some distance, when a considerable storm enveloped me. There were strong and gusty winds, thunder and lightning, and such terrific rainfall, that it was impossible to see ahead, and one could only follow the map by looking straight down at the highway. This I could readily do, and all might have gone well, except that my engine began to miss, for the rain, driven in sheets of water, had short-circuited some connection. Then suddenly it stopped for good, and there was no way to go but down, and in the safest way possible. I searched, and some thousand feet below were the tossing branches of dark and rain-glistening woods, but there was a clearing which my glide might reach, if stretched to the utmost.

It was a very roly-poly pasture that offered asylum, but I made it at the cost of a couple of bounding jumps, a blown tire and a cracked landing gear. Then hundreds of grey uniformed men swarmed out of the surrounding woods, and crowded around me. They jabbered like madmen, and neither their speech nor their uniforms were American, British, or French. They could not be Belgians, since their caps lacked the silly little tassel, dangling over one eye, that the Belgians affected for some historic reason. My heart sank. I feared that like an idiot I had somehow strayed from my true course, crossing the not so distant front lines, and into the domain of the *Boches*, and that I was a stupid prisoner.

However, the excited and sibilant sounds did not quite suggest German. At college, I had acquired a rudimentary acquaintanceship with German grammar and prose, but no great facility in conversation. To be sure, one summer before the war, a large family of German tourists had been my fellows in a small Paris hotel. There, each morning at breakfast, I had heard the formidable papa lecturing, or rather haranguing his docile wife and subdued children, like a marine drill sergeant admonishing recruits. From then to my ears, all male German conversation had sounded like rumbling thunder and growling dogs, and nothing like the liquid sibilants and other mellifluous syllables that came from the excited throng surrounding me. In addition, there were many un-Teutonic gesticulations, and in spite of the grey, suspicious uniforms, the heads were not close cropped, nor were the occiputs flush with the backs of beefy necks. Therefore whoever these soldiers were, they no longer seemed in keeping with the Kaiser's own squarehead Krauts.

A young man, in speech and from his red *kepi* to the *galons* on his sleeves a French lieutenant, broke through the crowd, addressed me, and my fears were ended. These grey-uniformed men were Italians. A half-year or so previous, they had been part of an artillery brigade, a unit of a brave but inefficient army, that was opposing an equally second-rate army of Austrians. Between these inauspicious adversaries, there had been some fighting—minor skirmishes, though, and with little real victory for either. As between the modern, classical British heavyweights, and similar featherduster punchers, blows had been exchanged, but nothing packing a knockout. In a way, the war on their front had been comparatively polite and restrained. There had been shots and barrages, raids and sorties, a little ground gained here, a little lost there, some brave deeds and some losses, but there had also been plenty of leaves taken, plenty of singing, plenty of Chianti. Then one day, a horde of Germans came, the *sole mios* turned to yells of alarm, and the next twenty-four hours saw the terrible slaughter and rout called the Battle of Caporetto.

Completely defeated with over three hundred thousand losses, leaving three thousand cannon, and most of their supplies and equipment on the field, the survivors fled south, and all of North Italy to the River Piave, came under the Germans. What was left of Italy's greatest army was demoralized, and practically disarmed of all heavy weapons. Allied troops had to fill the gap, and in the meantime, some use had to be found for the broken Italian units. Here, where I had just crash landed, were artillery survivors of that terrible debacle. Not knowing what else to use them for, but anxious to keep the remnant organization together, they had been transferred to France, for duty as a labor battalion.

Among the thousand or so here, I did not see one single rifle nor pistol, but I did see several bottles of wine and cognac. These men gave me the impression of a very depressed lot, who felt keenly both the humiliation of their defeat, and their present ignominious situation, for to front-line fighters, nothing was considered lower than a labor battalion. Wine might dull the frustration, but there was no singing of arias among these men. In the headquarters hut, an unshaven Italian officer greeted me, and smiled after a fashion, but another sat at a rude table, his head pillowed in his arm, an empty bottle at his elbow, and snoring heavily. Outside, the rain fell steadily, and sodden tree branches scraped the hut's low roof. Inside, it was dim, bare, and cold, and men merely stared at the blank walls. Brooding melancholia pervaded the atmosphere, and these unfortunate Italians seemed prisoners, not of the Germans, but of that huge and grim keeper of the dungeon, as related in *Pilgrim's Progress*, Giant Despair.

The minor formalities taken care of, the French lieutenant took charge. Quickly he arranged for my plane to be safely lashed down to stakes, and for a guard to be posted over it. Then he suggested that I accompany him to his local headquarters, and his commanding officer. A short ride in a French truck brought us to the village of Champeaubert, the site of some minor Napoleonic battle. Here we drew up to a roomy farmhouse of the better sort, that had been taken over for the temporary headquarters of a French howitzer battery. This unit was now *en repos* after many months of combat, including the second Battle of the Marne. Inside, I was formally presented to the commander, le Capitaine X, a gray-haired but very keen-looking and handsome officer, who was treated with the greatest respect, even pronounced deference, by his men and his staff.

After listening to his lieutenant, and assuring himself of my proper identification, the captain gave me his hand, bade me welcome, and assured me that there would be no delay in notifying Orly Field as to my safety and whereabouts. In the meantime, quarters would be assigned me as an officer and an ally, and that he and his command would be happy to consider me their honored guest.

Until a truck from Orly arrived, with mechanics and spare parts to put my plane in flying shape, I spent several pleasant days with this French battery. Measured in millimeters, their howitzers were about the equivalent of a British 9.2 in caliber, and they had seen action near Chateau-Thierry, not much more than twenty miles distant, only ten days previous. I have no doubt that my welcome was all the warmer because the recent gallant and effective action of our troops in stopping the German advance, had brought back the respect of the French, who had been wondering whether we would ever do any real fighting. We certainly had taken our own good time in getting ready to fight, but finally "The marines had arrived," just like in the old movies, and Americans were once more regarded as brave soldiers, and not as so many tourists, barrack fighters, and cabaret heroes. Our stock was up with the French.

The officers of this battery were of the best type of French soldier, being young, well educated, vigorous and gay, but they stood in great awe of their commander, who although only a captain, seemed to have more presence and dignity than many a major general. It was obvious that discipline was very strict, with no slackness tolerated from anyone, but orders were quietly given as if they were merely polite suggestions, instead of commands to be precisely and swiftly obeyed. At mess and in his more leisure moments, Capitaine X displayed a friendly and gracious manner, but was always rather reserved and serious. He may have been a viscount and from an ancient family in civilian life, for he certainly seemed to be *le grand seigneur* to his organization, but he was very well liked in spite of his aloofness, and I got the impression that everyone trusted him in all things, and regarded him with an admiration not often bestowed on commanding officers.

Quartered in a farmhouse room that had a stone floor, a huge feather bed, a commode, a long wooden chest, a primitive washstand, a wooden chair, a pot under the bed, a candle and a wall crucifix, I was early awakened by the inevitable crowing cock, one who might have stepped out of Rostand's *Chantecler*, and the usual pungent smell of the farm's wealth, a high and steaming manure pile in the courtyard, close by my half-opened casement window. That, I did not mind at all. After all, this was all part of the true rural France, and not the Paris Ritz France, of elegant ladies and rich acquaintances. It occurred to me that both Paris and rustic France could be enjoyed by us military tourists, just like caviar and turnip soup.

Breakfast with the French army was at six, and was nothing more than a hunk of bread, and a big bowl of hot chocolate. From then on, the French soldier was expected to put in a hard morning of work or exercises, until eleven, when a small *dejeuner* of eggs and coffee was in order. The only real meal was *le diner*, mercifully served in the late afternoon or very early evening, just before a famishing hunger had become all but impossible to bear any longer, and I felt as desperate as a starving tiger. To our small officers' mess, everyone arrived with a very *bon appetit*, and no wonder.

This evening meal was always very good. The French army did not have the numerous canned varieties of foods that we had, but they had cooks, and what they had was always prepared in a very tasty fashion. The mess sergeant and his cooks did not completely depend on the quartermaster's allotments; they also rustled for the edibles of the locality. They poked around gardens for snails, haggled with farmwives for eggs and chickens, and not infrequently took old, muzzle-loading, black powder shotguns and muskets, to hunt the game of the area. From these forays they might return with hares, pheasants, ducks and other small game for the command's stew pots, and with the right kind of sauce, of which they were masters, even a crow or an owl might have been eaten with relish. Once in a great while, if stationed in one of the more heavily forested areas, they might take part in some traditional, community boar hunt, and bring back a haunch of wild boar.

There were still some wild boar in parts of France, and these could prove ferocious animals to encounter. Three pilots, motoring through woods, saw a very young animal by the roadside, and stopped to capture it. It squealed loudly, and something with bristling hair and small blazing eyes came charging out of the bushes, looking so formidable and determined that our flyers made a scrambling rush for their car, stepped on the gas and departed as fast as possible. Eddie Rickenbacker figured in the tale of this trio. However, to my direct knowledge, it was only a story told at a bar by a flying gossip, and it may have happened to three other fellows. At any rate, the piglet went back to its mother, and our aces did not, for once, bring home the bacon. As for the community hunts, a pilot friend was invited to one, and from what he said, it was something fantastic. As related, everyone had his assigned post to shoot, his being next to the local mayor. This official was dressed in keeping for the great occasion, which was an annual affair and taken rather seriously. For a weapon, the portly mayor, leather gaitered, hat with a feather, hunting jacket fastened with huge brass buttons, inscribed with deer heads, had a most formidable firing apparatus that looked like a cross between an old-fashioned, muzzle-loading, four-gauge duck gun, and a musket from the times of Napoleon. This, His Honor kept patting, while assuring my friend that it could kill anything—"*un tigre, mais oui. Un elephant, je crois bien, mon lieutenant!*"

To this, X agreed, for the mayor's gun looked as powerful as antitank rifle, and then suddenly, there was an outcry of yells and barking dogs, and a huge boar dashed out of the nearby woods, and raced about, while guns went off in every direction, and general pandemonium broke loose. When it was over, and the boar, apparently untouched, had again vanished into the heavy cover of the forest, the mayor was sitting in a ditch, where he had been propelled by the back-kick of his weapon, which had also burst near the end of the muzzle. That ended the boar hunt, but like the duels in France, where shots are exchanged but no one may be hit, the honor of the village and the honor of the boar were both, seemingly, satisfied, and with *bon appetit* everyone repaired for a very fine repast, also traditional of the great occasion. As for the huge boar, he had been unsuccessfully hunted on several previous village turnouts. He had become something of a local celebrity, and X had a suspicion that everyone was rather glad the boar was still a living inhabitant, for he added an element of glamor to the area.

Unlike our usual officers' mess, which had about the elegance of a "come and get it" feeding in a cow camp, *le diner* was somewhat formal. Besides Capitaine X, there were some good half-dozen French offices, but no one sat down at the long table until the commander had taken his seat at the head. We then sat down in order of rank, except that I, as a guest, was on the captain's right. The table was laid with china and a clean white cloth, and there was a bottle of the better *vin du pays* for every two men at table. The first course, *le potage*, a huge steaming tureen of vegetable and chicken soup, was brought in by a mess boy, and ceremoniously placed before the head of the table.

This mess attendant was a private, but in civil life he had been a trained waiter. His manner of serving was like that of a butler in a well-managed and cultured household, for no one can hope to become a waiter in the highest classes of French hotels and restaurants, without years of apprenticeship in lower positions. During this, the future waiter must not only acquire the suavity, the dexterity, and precise knowledge of setting and serving a table, but he has to learn the ingredients and preparation of each complicated dish, and to be a connoisseur of wines, so that he can advise a guest if called on. Above all, he must have the correct manner and bearing for his calling.

In this tiny mess at Champeaubert, we had such a paragon of a waiter. This was an officers' mess, more as I had pictured one, before joining our army. As a boy, I had been an avid reader of Kipling's tales of the British army in India, and my idea of an officers' mess had been, vaguely, a service of gleaming silver, fine china, and cut-glass wine goblets on a snowy, damask cloth, and gentlemanly officers of good family, in impeccably tailored mess jackets, with a handsome, imperious and eagle-faced, white-moustached colonel presiding.

In the background of the handsome dining room, would be tall, silent mess attendants, their dark faces topped with snow white turbans. The dinner would be formal, conversation would be both serious and witty, and at the proper moment, the colonel would rise and say, with upraised glass, "Gentlemen. The President of the United States!"

On this, we would all rise and say, "To the President. God bless him!"—Democrat though he might be—and we would drink bottoms up, and snap the stems of our champagne glasses, lest the same ever be used again for a less noble purpose. This was the very vague, but rather high-minded dream, and rude was the awakening when I joined our army.

This dream was a bit different from filing up to a greasy counter, and having a hunk of meat and a gob of potato slapped on one's plate, as in our banquet hall at Orly. In our army, we pilots—America's own commissioned intrepid birdmen, the envy of all men and the darlings of the ladies, according to the magazine writers, and to the fury of the rest of the army—did not eat very nicely. We just slipped on the nosebag, as the old cavalry used to say, picked the first seat at a hard bench, and gobbled up the drably cooked fodder. There was no breaking of glasses after toasting the president, for that would have been impossible. Our thick mugs were of the kind forbidden in prisons, lest the convicts use them to hurl at and brain the wardens. As for the storied, tall, turbaned mess attendants, our kaypees did not come even close to them. Now, here in this French mess, we did dine more like civilized people, and if circumstances had ever made it crow for the entree, it would have been *corbeille a la sauce howitzer*, I feel certain. That was the difference. The French army dined; we just ate.

The captain ladled each of us a big bowl of this soup, which was served by our waiter, and we fell to with alacrity. It was very good. The next course was new to me, a huge dish of garden snails, served steaming hot in their shells and cooked in butter. Collected from nearby by the cooks, they were very tasty, and no more strange to eat than so many oysters. A taste for snails can be acquired, without too much trepidation, by the average American, but some French dishes, although reported as delicious, would be hard for us to swallow.

In some parts of the south of France, they serve a soup made of white mice. A pretty lady whom I knew, learned of this tidbit, and she learned it the hard way, and *ex post facto*. She had sipped the last spoonful, when the truth was sprung. *Potage aux souris blancs*, said the smiling waiter; white mouse soup, in plain English. The rest of the meal was never eaten, and this has nothing to do with aviation. However, it was all part of France and the lands of democracy that we were fighting for, and if our boys ever fought for mom's apple pie, as alleged by some sickening sentimentalist, some French *poilus* might have fought for their grandmothers' mouse soup, for *chacun à son goût*, as they say in Gallic.

The good mess over and famine averted, the red wine flowed, and there was considerable conversation, much of it stemming from a general curiosity about America, and American ways. To all this, I answered the best I could, but very poorly on the subject of our latest popular music. These young French officers were all very keen over our ragtime and earlier forms of jazz music, and they knew the words and airs of many of our latest popular tunes. I knew far less than they did, and it surprised them. They thought that all Americans could play ragtime on the piano, or the banjo, just like many Englishmen have the conviction that no American ever takes a good long walk. It was all part of most men's stereotyped thinking about other races and nationalities, like my schoolboy idea of a Frenchman, an *après vous, Alphonse*, always bowing, and fond of dancing and light wines.

During much of the general conversation, the captain was silent, but when he spoke he had something to say, and everyone listened attentively. He also asked questions, especially about certain aspects of our aviation. He told me that he had known, very well, several of the early flyers, such as Louis Bleriot, the first man to fly across the English Channel. He had also known the Brazilian Santos-Dumont, the aeronaut who had made and flown the first dirigible balloon. "But," he said, "that was back in

1898, the time of your Spanish War. You would hardly remember that far-off time, mon lieutenant."

Although I did not mention it, I did remember the Spanish War, or rather some small incidents connected with it. I remembered our brownstone, green shuttered house, with the wrought-iron grillwork fence before it, on Lafayette Square in Washington, the excitement in the capital city, the grave talk of my elders, and most especially of a very popular reminder of the sinking of the battleship *Maine*, in Havana harbor. This was a drawing of the battleship in a harbor, with the picture of a very villainous-looking Spaniard crouching on the nearby shore, with the end of a fuse in one hand, and a match in the other.

My uncle brought one of these home, showed it to the family and some guests at tea time, and then put the flame of a match to the fuse of the unspeakable villain, the Spaniard, who dressed something like a bullfighter. The fuse burned slowly, and a smoldering paper trail approached the doomed vessel, whose bow concealed some sort of a firecracker. The end was a considerable bang, the total disintegration of the *Maine*, and everybody was then supposed to get howling mad all over again at this reminder of Spanish perfidy. It was a good, rousing gimmick, and something similar might have been devised right after Pearl Harbor, and sold for a tidy profit, except that our laws now allow the detonation of atom bombs, as in Nevada, but forbid touching off Chinese firecrackers.

I remembered one other thing about the Spanish War, besides the Rough Rider suits, complete with tin sword and pistol, that all the small boys wore, and that was Theodore Roosevelt, the nation's one and only *Teddy*, in the company of Colonel—in World War I, General—Leonard Wood. They arrived in New York at TR's sister's home, and they had sabers and pistols, turned-up campaign hats like Australian soldiers, yellow leggins, spurs, and to my eyes, a look of glory that today even Colonel John Glenn could not evoke, for I doubt if our country ever had anything more romantic in all its wars, than the Rough Riders, who epitomized the great Americn dream of hard-riding, straight-shooting good guys, and our own Far West version of the same recurring legend as found in the Arthurian Round Table, or the paladins of Charlemagne. Of course, there had been malaria, yellow fever, typhoid, utter confusion, and very rotten meat, for our army to contend with, but in some ways the Spanish War had been more fun than our later ones. San Juan Hill did have to be taken on foot, for the Rough Riders, somewhere on the line, ran out of horses, but to most Americans it stands as the last of our glorious, whoopee-yelling, cavalry charges. Probably, that is the way TR would have liked it.

After a few days, a truck, with a sergeant and mechanic, arrived from Orly, bringing a spare undercarriage to put my Salmson in flying order. Orly was not much over seventy-five miles, as the crow flies, from Champeaubert, and a few hours should have sufficed for them to travel the distance, even under the road conditions of that time. They claimed that they had been detained by a breakdown of some part of the truck, and not having personally suffered from the delay, I did not question their statement. However, I strongly suspected that they had, in truth, lost their bearings, and had found themselves unavoidably delayed in Paris.

At that time, French roads seemed oddly confusing to many American soldiers. No matter the compass headings and destination, Paris could pop up anywhere to obstruct the way of an honest American soldier on a legitimate journey. Our boys did not want to go to the wicked city, but it seemed to move around so. It was most distressing.

"Damn it, we're in Paris, and it's so late we'll have to spend the night here," would say a broken-hearted but clean-cut American youth to his buddy.

"The pity of it," would reply the other. "But be of good cheer, comrade. We will seek out the good YMCA, and theywill take good care of us."

Well, war was long, life was uncertain, I had passed some pleasant days with the French army, and had certainly got to know them much better than just seeing them around on streets and in restaurants. Whatever may have delayed them on their way, our mechanics wasted no time in putting my Salmson in commission, and soon I was able to resume my flight to Colombey Les Belles, and to land safely. From the latter, I had

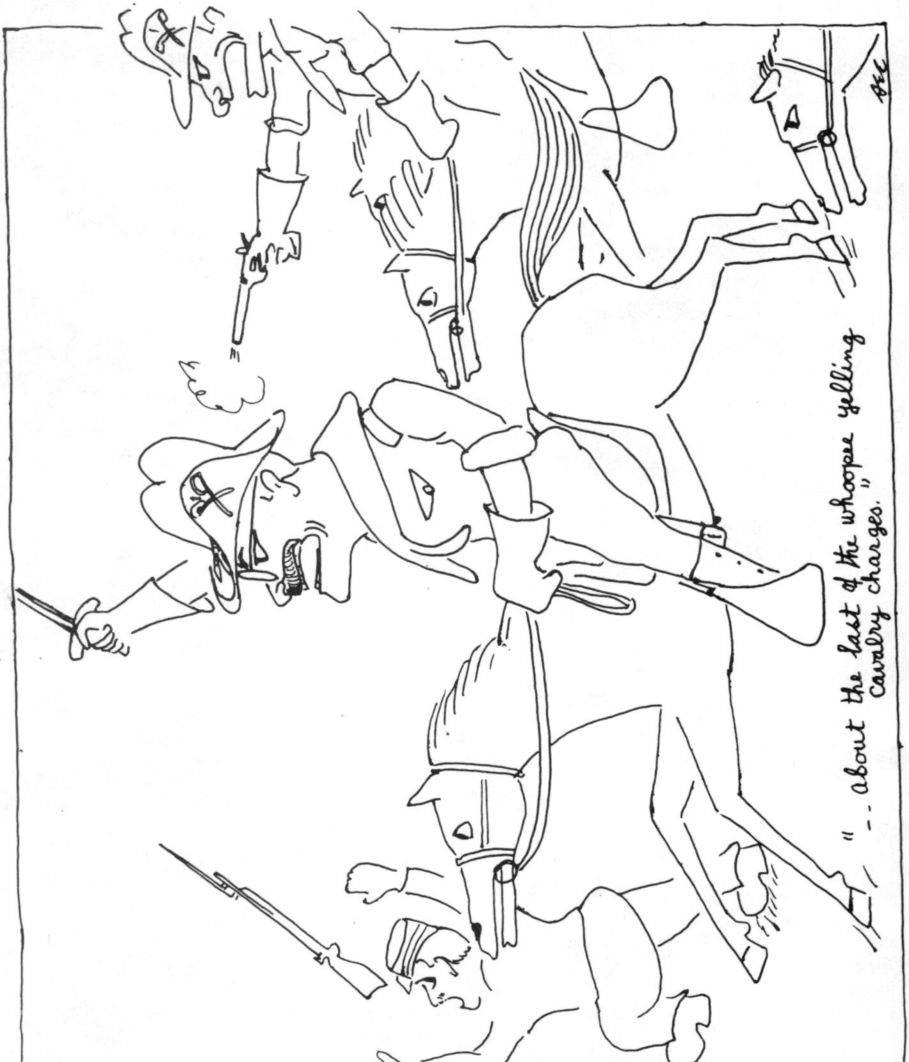

"... about the last of the whoopee yelling cavalry charges."

the usual slow train journey back to Paris, and the truck ride to Orly. Once in Paris, the truck ride could wait a few hours. Strange as it may seem, the City of Light was about the best part of being a ferry pilot. It was mighty educational.

Chapter 17

THE NOTORIOUS BATTLE OF PARIS

Orly Air Base, being the assembly airdrome for the product of surrounding airplane factories, saw a great variety of models, and we, as testers and ferry pilots, had the opportunity of flying about everything the field had, which ran from the latest designs such as the Salmson, and the Niewport 28 model, to the most curious and primitive flying erections, still used for some obscure purpose or other. Among these freaks were wing-warping Caudron primary trainers, and certain earlier model Farman, and Voisin, antique contraptions.

The Farman relic, a flying rat trap of wooden struts, canvas wings, and a maze of crisscrossing wires, was a pusher. Being slow, it had a huge rudder, and it had no proper fuselage, but a kind of a bathtub-resembling receptacle, called a *nascelle*. In this nascell, the pilot and his observer sat like two missionaries in a cannibal's stew pot, and the pilot gripped the main control, which looked something like the handlebars of a bicycle. The nascelle's crew seats were well in front of the wings, but the engine was just in back of the wings and quite a bit above the heads of the crew, from which perch it could readily tear loose, to land on the pilot's neck, in case of a severe forced landing. That this seldom happened was due to the plane's considerable wing area, and its relative light weight, which generally made for a very gentle landing. In the air, this type Farman had a top speed of around sixty miles an hour, and it could land at about twenty-five miles an hour, if the head wind were little more than a zephyr. With a deadstick and a strong head breeze, it might be in danger of landing, running backwards, but since it had a large tail skid, this did not necessarily involve any damage. This aerial chickencoop merely coasted backwards to a stop, like some rubber-tired baby carriage with wings attached to it.

I have no idea why this obsolete model of a Farman was still in demand at this time (spring of 1918), except for use by the mythical old men's flying corps previously mentioned, but in earlier years it had been much used for artillery observation. Its function then had been to fly at a moderate height, over a given front-line area, and there to direct and report on the effect of French fire, from their 75s and larger guns. For this, the Farman's slow speed had been an asset, but only up to the time that pursuit aviation had been developed, when the slow and defenseless Farmans became sitting ducks for attacks from above, and perfect setups for aspiring German aces to increase their combat scores.

Previous to this development, and especially in the early months of the war, Allied and German aviators had been little more than observers and reporters of enemy action, and although the eyes of the armies, they had hardly been an arm of battle. At first, flyers had carried no more than a pistol, for use in case of forced landings in hostile areas, and they had been accustomed to exchanging no more than a hand wave, or if in a vulgar mood, placing a thumb and extended fingers in juxtaposition to the nasal beak, on meeting an enemy plane while on a mission. As one captured German pilot said to a French aviator, "Why fight each other? Isn't flying alone a dangerous enough business?"

This nice understanding did not last long, and soon pistol shots were substituted for the old hand signs. Then some spoilsport brought along a shotgun, loaded with ball ammunition, although this was not very effective. Finally, one of these muskets did a job. A Lieutenant Franz of the French service shot down a German plane with one, and the French assert that he is the very first man to have scored a victory in aerial combat. If true, this Frenchman should be enshrined with the boy who first picked up the football to run with it, as one who initiated a new game. Soon after this exploit, planes were equipped with one machine gun, then two or more, and finally some were armed with 37-millimeter cannons. However, from the very first, a few planes had carried small bombs to harass the enemy. Others had also carried and released great numbers of steel darts on marching troop columns. These were not successful, for the chances of spiting a man, even with troops in close order, were not better than ringing a cane at Coney Island.

The Voisin model was an improvement on the Farman model,

but it too was a pusher, a wallowing goose of a plane, a skygoing cat's cradle of the same order. I flew one once on a short tour of the countryside, and it was like flying an old-fashioned hay wagon. Accustomed to the Niewport, which could turn on a dime, I was amazed at the response to the controls of this Voisin. I used the controls and nothing seemed to happen. More on the controls, and then it came around, ponderously and slowly like an ocean liner in a tideway. On all responses to the rudder and the stick, it seemed as deliberate as a country banker endorsing the note of a local farmer. Landing, it felt more like a balloon slowly settling earthwards.

Yet in its heyday, this Voisin model had been an effective bomber, and one of the mainstays of Allied aviation. It had been armed with machine guns, and eight bombs, each one of about fifteen kilos. Bombing by both day and night, such Voisins had even bombed as far across the front lines as Karlsruhe in the German state of Baden. There they had created a great panic, which was especially featured by the queen of Sweden, who was visiting the city of that time. Surprised in her bath, she had fled down the main street, like an unhorsed Lady Godiva, or so swore the French aviation.

There were also other, more or less obsolete Voisin models that were still being used at night in the so-called defense of Paris squadrons. At this time, Paris was subject to air raids on almost any clear night, from Gothas and other German bombers, for the front lines were only about seventy miles from the city, and that was easy striking distance. These German bombers were powerful two- to four-motored planes, bristling with machine guns, carrying crews of three or more, and generally capable of releasing at least one thousand pounds of bomb load. These Gothas and Friedrickshavens, the British Handley-Pages, and the Italian Capronis were the B-29 equivalents of that war, and that the German bombers did not do more damage to Paris seemed mainly due to the many searchlights and antiaircraft batteries, collected for the city's defense. These guns threw up such a continuous curtain of fire around the outskirts of the city, that few planes got through to the heart of the capital.

However, a certain percentage always got through; bombs crashed, railroad stations and other targets were hit, and the people complained to the government. No first-class pursuit planes of the latest model, could be spared from the vital front lines, but something had to be done, or the heads of politicians would roll in the gutters, for that machine with the keen blade and never missing chop was always oiled and ready for action. Accordingly, Niewport squadrons were organized for the daytime defense of Paris, and among their assigned pilots, the sacrificial goats for panicky bureaucrats, were some of our best graduates from Issoudun. For night-bombers, Voisins were used and that few of these were shot down in night missions, as they sought out the powerful German bombers, seems a miracle, for not only were these Voisins no match for Gothas, but the French ack-ack showed little discrimination. At night, all cats are grey, and the itchy-fingered French just banged away, hoping to hit a Gotha, but no matter otherwise. *Helas! C'etait bien dommage* if a shell brought down a Voisin, *mais quoi donc? C'est la guerre, mon vieux*, and pass the pinot, *s'il vous plait*. Well, with the French, it was *pas de pinot, pas de guerre*, as swore the *poilus*.

One of the bigger German air raids came in early May, well after dark, but in the height of the evening. In company with Harold Tittman and other Orly pilots, I was in the lobby of the Hotel Crillon, which elegant resort was currently housing many celebrities. Among these were General Pershing, General Tasker Bliss, Mr. Newton Baker, our very able as well as erudite secretary of war, and a famed and much loved actress, justly called the Sweetheart of the AEF, Miss Elsie Janis. It was a gala evening for wartime, and there had been nothing more explosive than the popping of champagne corks, when the alert sounded, the drum fire of antiaircraft started rolling, and bombs could be heard exploding on the outskirts of the city. Soon, the rhythmic beat of multiple propellers proclaimed that the Boches were right overhead. From the shelter of the hotel's arcade, we were watching the sweeping beams of the searchlights, and the fireworks of the bursting shells, when I overheard a firm voice not far from us.

"Mr. Secretary," said the voice. "I must insist that you take shelter below. It is much safer."

The voice was General Pershing's. For a moment, Secretary Baker hesitated. The sweeping, crisscrossing searchlight beams, the red fire of the exploding shells, the meteoric tracks of the trace bullets, the general roar and rattle of the defense; all this punctured by the heavier detonations of the bombs, made for an exciting and truly beautiful spectacle, and the heavy masonry of the arcade seemed shelter enough, save in case of a direct hit. However, General Pershing's request was all but a command, for he was responsible for his distinguished visitor's safety. Like a small boy reluctantly obeying his father, *Newtie Cootie*, as he had been dubbed by a famous publisher, a bitter political enemy, meekly followed the grim-faced *Black Jack* inside and below, down into the deepest wine cellar of the hotel.

However, down there was not without likely compensations. During raids, such vaults were apt to be filled with ladies, many of them young and beautiful, and such were seldom averse to jumping on a gentleman's lap, and hugging him close when bombs fell near, and shook even the deepest foundations. One knows of certain of our intrepid birdmen who delighted in raids, since they could gallantly extend great comfort to the trembling fair, but one could not imagine this in the case of the dignified Mr. Baker and his granite-faced companion. They were not the type for young ladies to dare to jump on, or even to speak to, without a proper introduction.

Although a later generation may minimize the effect, it was still no pleasure to be bombed in World War I, and what our big raids were to German and Japanese cities, in World War II, cannot readily be comprehended, by a bomb-free America. Some of the bigger raids, such as on Dresden and Tokyo, must have seemed like the destruction of the Twin Cities of the Plain did, to the panic-stricken sinners of Sodom and Gomorrah. The smell that comes from great fear, must have permeated all through the flames and crashing ruins of such cities, but there will be no similar reek from the eventual, inevitable falling of the first H-bomb. These instantly dead cannot fear, and if their souls survive in Heaven or in Hell, according to the decision of some utterly wise, and incorruptible justice, they can no more than exclaim, like those blown up in comic strips, "Wha' happen?"

Mr. Secretary Baker had not long gone to his deep abri, when a bomb struck the Ministry of War with some damage, which proved that spies were, in some fashion, guiding the aim of the

Germans. A pattern of dim lights, flashed from the confines of chimney tops, could have been one method, but it was evident that the Huns seldom wasted their bombs on chance targets. Within the limitations of their primitive bomb sights, they dropped their loads with discrimination, and with far better effect than the government reports and the press admitted. For those days, they were good, they caused a great deal of consternation, and a considerable exodus from the city to safer regions, by the families of those able to afford it.

This bomb had no sooner flowered like a great red gernaium, when the searchlights concentrated on some object above, and the antiaircraft burst all around it. A hit, and something in flames was seen to hurtle downwards. A crash, and the object landed in the Place de la Concorde, not very far from where we were watching.

"*On a un! On a un! On a un Boche! Un cochon, un salaud!*" arose the cries of frenzied Frenchmen around us, and despite the danger from falling fragments, many started running towards the blazing wreckage. Alas! It was no Gotha nor Friedrickshaven that had been whacked out of the sky that evening. It was a Voisin, and two poor French flyers. "*C'est la guerre,*" the politicians probably remarked. It was just too bad, that the Germans had not blown up the entire Chamber of Deputies, swore many a French pilot.

Besides the frequent bomb raids, Paris was then the target of another regular visitor. This was the shell from the mysterious and famous, long range cannon. I was still stationed for my last few days of Issoudun, when we first heard of the new arrival. At first, no one dreamed that it was a shell from a super long-range gun, this thing that had suddenly come from nowhere, to explode in various parts of the city. Most of these startling visitants had come in broad daylight, and from a cloudless sky, and yet no enemy bombers had been sighted. What a whoop and holler arose! Tongues wagged, the press screamed, politicians made promises of taking necessary steps—except out of office, as normal—military intelligence went into high gear seeking the answer, scientists and eggheads went into a huddle, and all the wiseacres and long-winded bores gave out with their explanations and theories, in all the salons and cafes of Paris.

It was, said many, a German bomber, flying at the unheard-of height of twenty-five thousand feet, and painted with a special paint that made it so transparent, that it was invisible. This sounded rational to some, until it was pointed out that the crew would also have to be painted invisible. If not, someone would have reported the most amazing sight of men riding through the skies, sitting on nothing. Another idea was that German spies had cannons with silencers, hidden in secret parts of the suburbs, even in innocent-looking houses. These cannon could be disguised as stovepipes, and the German cannoneers as so many maids and housewives. And so it went: an *aperitif*, a theory; a *cognac fin*, some other cockeyed opinion. For a few days, never had Paris listened to more pure baloney, for a regiment of horses could not have spread it so thick, even in a month of Sundays.

However, it was soon found to be a gun, unbelievably but truly firing from a distance of over seventy miles from the heart of the city. The German technical brains had pulled another rabbit out of the Kaiser's spiked helmet, and all Bochie gloated. The mystery solved, more of the richer citizens left Paris, but the government accepted it. "*C'est la guerre*," they shrugged and said again. Pass the pinot! "*Sacre nom, ces maudits deputés!*" swore many citizens.

The long-range gun or guns, for eventually there were more than one, were more of a remarkable tour de force, than an effective threat to the city. Lacking the directional precision of the bombers, these missiles could only be fired to hit somewhere in the city, and the shell, approximately nine inches in diameter, might drop on any sort of a target, but with no warning as in the case of a bomber. Almost invariably, as if in keeping with the methodical Teuton mind, these shells would arrive at intervals of exactly fifteen minutes to the tick, for perhaps a dozen or so a day, and usually in the afternoon when people would be on the streets, and there could be the maximum casualties. Very few came at night, when the good bourgeois would be under cover.

In the huge city, the total effect of such shells, from the first shot in spring, until the guns' abandonments after the German retreat, was physically unimportant, but psychologically of some significance. For a few days, the gun had Paris almost in a panic. Then gradually it became another accepted phenomenon of war, and regarded as not much more dangerous than a bolt of lightning. It was never more than a very remote chance of death to any one individual, even if one shell did hit a church, collapsing much of its roof, and killing some seventy-five people.

The long-range shell might strike in any ward of the city, but from personal experience, it seemed to hunt out the more fashionable localities. Two landed, much too close for personal comfort, one in the Tuileries Gardens, near which I was strolling, the second hitting the Church of the Madeleine, but sparing a nearby bar, where I was pleasantly relaxing. This shot snipped off the head from some saint's statue, but spared the scarcely saintly noggins of several well-known flying characters of our air force. Although somewhat jolted out of our previous alcoholic equanimity, we returned to our stools to resume our diversion. Again appeared the potent, if gagging and hair-oil tasting, French versions of dry Martinis. "Comrades! Fellow flyers, glorious!" said someone, his name but not his face forgotten. "Behold! Across the street is a direct sign from heaven. The saints above will sacrifice even their own heads, rather than have harmed a single hair of American aviation."

As a military participant in both world wars, although only an inglorious, grounded retread of kiwi status in the second, it has sometimes vaguely seemed to me, that the average overseas pilot of our relatively tiny World War I air corps, was somewhat gayer, more humor-loving, better educated in the humanities and in the classic, liberal sense, and more worldly wise and sophisticated, than the average flyer of our modern, enormous air force, vastly more technical and scientific though it be. With few exceptions, the student flyers of that first winter at Issoudun, most of whom composed the original pilot personnel of our combat squadrons, averaged considerably younger than today's air force pilots, and they were mostly unmarried college graduates, or even undergraduates on leave of absence, who had come from more or less cultured and conservative homes. Previous to the war, their lives had been well ordered, rather easy and happy, and their personalities had been subject to, and stimulated by much that was most cultural, interesting, exciting, and desirable in American life. They had had opportunities denied to the great majority of even today's young men, even though attending college is so much more general, and the average standard of living so much higher.

All this relatively cultured background did not, probably, make for any better flying ability and combat determination, for as to that, the near stone age Sioux warriors who destroyed Custer, had the hearts of lions, the eyes of eagles, the cunning of serpents, and they, without much doubt, would have made splendid fighter pilot material, if aviation had then existed, just as they had, in that age, made the finest of light cavalry. However, the general background of the old Issoudun gang did not make for any worse flying and fighting, and it did make for generally urbane and very sociable companions. At Issoudun, there had been farmers' sons, mechanics' sons, doctors' sons, and those representing families in many walks of life, but to an extent not found today, Wall Street and rather prominent families were markedly represented, and there were numbers of what some red-bloodied, one hundred percent Democrat might label as "young sassiety squirts, and Park Avenue kind, city slickers." To a certain extent this was so, and during our first war our air corps had the glamor and somewhat the same social prestige as the officers' corps of a crack British guards regiment. However, underlying all this, and what really made it something apart, was the intense and youthful spirit of high idealism. It was this burning idealism that distinguished our first air corps, and gave it a feeling of knighthood, like some order of medieval chivalry.

All the boys flew, fought, were killed or survived in the best traditions of American fighters, but the *squirts* had more worldly education, and they knew how to get around, and how to handle the best places. These lads would rather have been found dead than in the equivalent of a USO—although that war had mighty little of that, to my recollection—and sucking an ice cream soda. An ice cream soda was a *ghawstly concoction* as said the British; but brandy was for pilots. In those days, our air force could not only shoot down the enemy, they could also command attention and respect from the most insolent headwaiter. The famous so-called Battle of Paris was spearheaded by the old air corps. Our pilots carried the citadels of gastronomy, entertainment, *l'amour*, even of fashion and snobbery. The infantry, the artillery, the navy, even the marines only mopped up the leavings, so help me Hannah!

We Orly ferry pilots were naturally in a superior position to engage in that famous battle that is never mentioned in the history books for schoolchildren. Whenever we had to fly and deliver a plane, we had to return by train, and whether it was Gare du Nord, Gare de l'Est, St. Lazare, or Orleans, it was always *Gare Paree!* that awaited us, for thanks be to the saint who watches over pilots, there was no other way of returning to Orly.

From Paris, the ferry pilot rode by truck to Orly, but that headquarters vehicle made its daily trip in the mornings, and no ferry pilot's train ever arrived before the afternoon, unless he had a hole in his head, or was too good for this world and bound to die early. Debarked at the city, the cheerful pilot sought out his headquarters. This might be the Hotel Grande—strictly for those of the rougher sort, according to the more fastidious souls in the service—or the Hotel Castglione on the Rue de Rivoli, or the Crillon on the Place de la Concorde, the Ritz on the Place Vendome, or the Meurice, the Eduard Sept, or most any truly elegant hotel, deemed worthy of an American flyer. There, properly installed as befitting his station, a wholesome pilot's probable first move was to order up a bucket of ice, containing a champagne bottle. Then bathed, shaved and fortified, he was ready for enjoyment.

To be sure, there was a necessary first visit to official headquarters, where clerks filed papers, MPs stood around, looking stupid, or solemn, or both, as the case might be, and there was a book to sign, and a hard look to receive from a ground force major in charge, who regarded pilots very dimly. I knew this sour-puss a bit better, and once he frankly told me that he considered the air corps the ruination of the army, and that most pilots gave him ulcers. There was also some recommended official billet, where a night's lodging cost next to nothing, but they had the usual drab atmosphere of an army BOQ, and few flyers, unless in temporary financial ruin, ever made use of them.

Unlike our second world war, with our forces composed of young husbands and fathers, as never before in history, our first war's flyers had all but no wives and babies to provide for, and their pay went a long way, even in Paris. In those days, a luxurious double room at an elegant hotel, with a ten-foot ceiling, tall Venetian doors leading to a balcony, and a private bath, large enough to swing a cat with room to spare, and complete with a mysterious object called a bidet, all this could be had for the equivalent of three dollars a day, and a hundred francs—then, about twenty dollars—went for a long evening of fun, doing the hotspots and seeing the most fashionable places. That is, it took care of dinner with wine at La Rue, the old Tour d'Argent, Pruniers, or similar restaurants, seeing some show at the Folies Bergères, the Grand Guignole, or the Comedie Française, and ending up doing the rounds such as Maxime's, the Bal Tabarin, and the more hectic dumps on Montmartre.

Naturally, a soldier could spend much more money. Nighttime Paris, even in wartime, was like a race track, but with *petites femmes* running the courses, instead of horses. Like the equines, these fair chics also ran in classes, from cheap claimers to handicap stake entries. The run of the mill, selling platers were prancing all over the city, but the more expensive fillies hung around the best places. Each one of these last, inevitably, had a husband on the front, who was at least a baron, and every other one had a grandmother, who was no less than a marquise, or a vicomtesse. True or not, this was the regular line they handed us simple Americains, although none of us ever swallowed it. For one thing, it seemed quite improbable, the French trenches being so filled with counts and barons. It was as if we had regiments, made up solely of tycoons and millionaires, and all in the Social Register. Of course today, nearly sixty years later, that would not be so impossible, for millionaires have become a dime a dozen in America, and any line of drafted recruits has a number of them. As for the titled fair ones, they could also eat and drink like healthy race horses, but when the bill came, it did not seem like hay, to use the homely vernacular.

Financially unburdened with family allotments, the average flying lieut—as most enlisted men referred to us, sympathetically regarding us more as a special class of aerial jockeys, rather than regular officers and bosses—was a comparative gilded youth in Paris. With ten percent overseas, and twenty-five percent flying pay added, he drew down the equivalent of twelve hundred francs a month, and his common necessities did not come to over two hundred. Besides this, we ferry pilots collected mileage for every return train trip, and this generally added several hundreds of francs a month to our free spending money. Except to the taxpayers, this was all very nice, like all legitimate government rackets.

However at the same time, a French captain of infantry only drew about three hundred francs a month, on which he had to support a family in many cases. This did not seem right to us, when we reflected. We did not want to throw our weight around, and spoil Paris for a poor French officer *en permission*, but that tended to be the outcome. Our army was just too well paid for a European soldier's comfort, and although a French captain might have the wound stripes and decorations, he was outgunned in the Paris battle by an American second lieutenant. On looking back, all this difference in the pay of Allies seems a bit disgusting. It should have been equalized by some withholding plan if possible, or at least made not so glaring.

Wartime Paris was then the most hectic and colorful of cities. It was a modern Babylon, where there were as many tongues spoken as at the Tower of Babel. Ciro and the more expensive and glittering places might hum and clatter to the best Parisian French, this intermingled with the American language and its British version, but haunts of the ruder sort rang out, as will the chattering, jabbering gatherings of all souls on the Great Day of Judgement. Belgian, Italian, Portuguese, Arab, Nigerian, Afrikander, Annamite, Egyptian, Greek, Maori, representatives of every nation, color and creed, in any capacity aiding the Allied war effort, tried to get to Paris for their leaves, and many, by hook or crook, succeeded. Paris was *Panam* in the words of the French soldier, the fabled Eldorado of fun, splendor, beautiful women, and luxury, of which they had dreamed in the dugouts of the foul and muddy trenches. Paris was the apple of the nation's eye, and its heart and soul, as is no other capital city, not even London.

There was nothing drab about the throngs jostling around the crowded bars, shouting at waiters, singing famed songs such as "Madelon," or "Le Chef du Gare, Il Est Cocu," laughing uproariously and embracing old comrades, weeping into beers, crashing over tables, and then suddenly parading around with girls on their shoulders, all with the pent-up enthusiasm, and the lust for life, gaiety and expression, that had been bottled up by months, even years of filth and hardship, all under the ever present shadow of death.

In Paris, there was little of the dull garb of the trenches. Everyone who could, put on the old colorful uniforms, reserved for dress occasions. There were reds, robin's-egg blues, chocolates, golden yellows, maroons, blacks, silvers and others, so that scenes looked like patterns in a rotating kaleidescope, the spectrum of the rainbow in ever changing crystals. Every bar, bistro, and estaminet was a wonderful subject for some great genre painter, and there was need of a modern Franz Hals to do full justice to the types. Amidst all this splendid splash of color, only we Americans, and our equally dull looking British cousins, kept going around in our eternal brown suits, like a joyless delegation of Cromwellian Roundheads, visiting the court of Versailles.

Many of us would have loved to have donned red pants, and sky-blue tunics, fourageres, and gold-banded red kepis for these occasions, and if we had earned them, we might not have been averse to wear medals that jangled with extra citations from breast pocket to belt, and even to have risen and bowed to applauding audiences, from boxes in theaters, as did some of the best-known French aces. Of course, the British, with their national affectation for something called good form, despised the French for all this display, as too flamboyant for a gentleman, and they only wore ribbons, but never medals. We did not feel so strongly on the subject, for after all, we were from the same native soil as the legendary Diamond Jim Brady, whose answer on the wearing of his gems was, "I notice that them that has 'em, wears them." The French had that philosophy, and there was no hypocrisy about it.

Always in some shade of brown, like a brown study or a brown taste in the mouth of a morning, our strictly utilitarian uniforms were rightly representative of modern war, technical, mechanical, regimented to a degree undreamed of by Napoleon, a war of semirobots, who mostly slew without bodily contact, and often without even seeing their enemy, a war that was so huge, that even major generals were as nothing. Homer's war, although bloody and brutal, had been one of poetry and athletics, filled with the feats of stars and heroes, like a great football contest, and with valiant kings leading in the forefront of battle. Modern war was mass man, little better than dumb cattle driven sacrifice, under the directions of rulers back in cities, and a huge bureaucracy. There was nothing glorious, dignified, nor aristocratic about it. It was a socialistic, totalitarian kind of war, that not only killed the body, but also stultified the soul. War had finally developed into the stupidest kind of dangerous contest.

The bar at the Hotel Crillon, then on the ground floor and not, as later, tucked away down in the basement, was one of the great rendezvous for such pilots who could visit Paris. It was very fashionable, gay in a decorous manner, and there one could see, hear, and sometimes join over a friendly glass some of the most distinguished Allied officers, and also admire and perhaps be introduced to some of the best dressed and smartest ladies. Wartime or not, many Frenchwomen dressed to perfection, and down the avenues of the Bois de Boulogne or the Champs Elysees, one still encountered shining carriages and glossy horses, driven by smartly liveried coachmen, with a footman on the box.

Some of the elegant and serenely reclining occupants of these landaus and victorias, were of the real nobility, even of the *ancien regime*, and a promenading, gallant and worthy flyer might get a gracious nod from a beautiful and bona-fide vi'tesse, if he had the good fortune to have been received in some home of high society. On such an occasion, a graduate of Issoudun should have been sporting a benny with an ostrich plume, to doff and sweep with a low bow past his bended knee, but even Cyrano de Bergerac could not have done that gracefully with one of our overseas, monkey caps, so we just had to salute, as if it were to no more than some mere brigadier general.

The Crillon bar was *pour le cocktail*, but an honest-to-goodness, American breakfast, or a lunch of southern fried chicken could be had at a little American restaurant, called the Chinese Umbrella, to stave off starvation, since the croissants and coffee served in our hotel rooms, were hardly sufficient to keep a man going. Of course, those of the coarser sort loved to remark that nothing, absolutely nothing could beat a French breakfast of a roll in bed with honey in the morning, not knowing that this same crack had been bandied about in the army of the Black Prince, that it had been the cackle in Rome on the return of Caesar's Gallic legions, and that the primitive hunters of the wholly mammoth, driven south by the advance of the ice, had so jested in their caverns.

Chapter 18

SOPWITH CAMELS AND WOMEN DRIVERS

In Paris, for our dinners there were many fine restaurants, and there was also the Allied Officers' Club, which was housed in a ducal mansion, set back in a beautiful garden, off the Champs Elysees. This beautifully run club served very good but inexpensive meals, and it was the setting for many dances and social gatherings. For partners at these dances, there was quite a variety of young ladies.

As to the ladies of the Allied Forces, the British were said to have WACs, but we never saw them. They did exist, but they must have been kept locked up in barracks when off duty, or they were watched by the grimmest of British matrons to preserve their virtue, or perhaps their horribly sensible boots, of regulation British issue, might be fine to stamp the pavement on sentry go, but were so heavy that dancing in them was all but impossible. In *Punch*, these WACs were always depicted and described as of a wholesome and sensible type of British womanhood, which stigma was about enough to finish any girl's sex and social life, for keeps. In fact, the WACs must have had intense patriotism to have put up with that damning designation of wholesome and sensible, for the old verse, by some forgotten humorist, spoke truth in saying:

> Be a sensible girl, and wear heels that are flat,
> And comb back your hair without curl,
> And if you don't put on make up, or look at a man,
> You'll remain a nice, sensible girl.

Besides French girls for our dances, Paris was now filled with female Red Cross and YMCA workers from America, and since the former ban on girls under thirty-five had been lifted, there were many attractive girls from the United States stationed in

Paris. In addition, there were many English and Canadian equivalents, who—almost—spoke our language.

As for the English girls, they were nice and very often attractive, but many of them could not conceal their fixed idea that Americans were some species of outlandish colonial, and probably half red Indian. To these young Britannias, our speech and idiom seemed utterly hilarious. If you said elevator instead of lift, they giggled. If you spoke of baggage instead of luggage, they snickered. If you said truck instead of lorry, they gazed pityingly, and one does not know what might have happened if one had said suspenders instead of braces, but fortunately we used belts to keep our pants up.

"Oh, I say! But you really are most frightfully American, aren't you?" said one of these little Englanders to me, when I had said something in a different way from the dialect spoken on the banks of the Thames. Right then I should have answered that my Bostonian-American language was modern, highly expressive and subtle, pungent as pepper, lucid and logical as Emerson, and powerful as Daniel Webster's, while her precious *righto lingo* was affected, senescent, and sometimes as hard to understand as would be the early Saxon yammerings of Hengist and Horsa. Unfortunately, I did not think up that answer until the next morning while shaving, for it would have pulverized her. Looking back, these young British damsels had plenty of good points but a girl who actually said *manglewurzle*, when she meant plain, red beets, needed an interpreter. Otherwise, an American might have thought she was ordering up a plate of ground up weazle meat, or one of those Scottish blood-pudding things, that go with the other horrors of bagpipes and Highland Flings.

Most of the dances at the Allied Officers' Club were conducted under British influence, and very correct in the spirit of a dying Victorianism, even though there were plenty of high spirits, and lots and lots of the old do-good, in all sorts of bottles. However, once in a while, someone, like the Norse god Thor trying to drink the whole Atlantic Ocean, got a bit under the influence and things happened. On one occasion, three of us pilots strolled into the club bar, where two marines were telling the bartender how good they were, and how they had saved the world at Chateau-

Thierry. Both were captains, built like fullbacks, great powerful fellows, and beside them the average pilot of those days, a man who had to fit comfortably in the tight cockpit of a pursuit plane, looked forty pounds lighter, and more like a terrier compared to a mastiff. Now in a forcible and convincing manner, elbow on the bar, one size-twelve cordovan boot on the brass rail, one of these marines was telling the barman, how he and the 2nd Division were winning the war.

"*Mais oui, monsieur. Le Deuxieme Division est tres bon,*" said the polite Frenchman.

"You're goddam right it's *bon*. And where the hell would you Frogs be, if it hadn't been for the 2nd Division?" And the 2nd Division did this, and the 2nd Division did that, until enough was enough for the Air Corps.

"Oh, to hell with the 2nd Division!" This was not whispered, but roared.

"What! By God, I'll show you!" The marine's fist was a big as a small boulder, and his eyes glittered with the fury of too much cognac. Buck, our pilot, was a lightweight, and quick on his feet, but the room was cramped and small. His chances did not look good, when just as in Homer's *Iliad*, where Aphrodite or Athena always intervenes in the nick of time when some favorite hero is about to get the business, the as yet unindentified saint who watches over flyers, took remedial action on the imminent, painful scene. Suddenly the alert sounded, the lights went out, and a successful retreat was made during the confusion. Such things were bound to happen occasionally, for as the saying went, the British were fighting the war on scotch, the French on pinot, and the Yanks on any kind of hootch they could lay their hands on.

However, our relaxation was not just eating, drinking, and dancing, while stationed near Paris. The museums were closed and sandbagged against bombing raids, and their more precious contents had been removed to safer places, but one could visit Versailles, Fontainebleau, and other famous places of historical interest. Many men did, and profited by it, for a great many American soldiers were much soberer, and more interested in better things, than as depicted in so many war novels, where a Paris leave is always a sordid and mighty dull routine of coarse drunkenness, vulgar doxies of various descriptions, and a brutal military police. There was that of course, but only as part of the scene, just as the ill-famed, sadistic *Hard Boiled Smith* was not the typical provost marshal. Among other Paris relaxations, one could take the local train to St. Cloud, and there play golf.

The club at St. Cloud having extended guest cards to many Paris-stationed Allied officers, two of us played a round of golf with a British major who had lost an arm during the famous retreat from Mons. This veteran of the gallant *Contemptibles* must have once been a pretty good golfer, for even with one arm he beat the pants off the intrepid birdmen, and took our money as well. The major's drives were, understandably, not very long, but they were right down the middle, and around and on the greens, he was a demon. Our slices and swipes went all over the lot, but too often into the rough, including the bushes. There, our balls were in great danger of disappearing for good, and not unlikely into some small boy's pocket. The St. Cloud Club commanded magnificent views and vistas, and its rolling course was beautiful, but there were too many bushes where urchins lurked, and our girl caddies could not cope with them, although one suspects they knew them well, as living in the neighborhood.

One remembers beautiful St. Cloud, the stately trees bordering many of its fairways, and the misty view overlooking distant Paris. It was lovely in the style of a Corot landscape, except that Corot never inserted larcenous small boys lying in wait and running out of bushes. I think we lost several balls to these little wretches, and on the train back to Paris, my companion showed me a sketch he had made on the back of an envelope. It was a design, he said, for something much needed in France—a junior-size guillotine.

Flying, of course, was our main occupation at Orly, but that could be something besides a ferry job on many occasions. Each newly assembled plane had to be given a test flight before being flown to Tours, Issoudun, Colombey Les Belles, or other destinations. No special pilot was assigned for these tests. It was just another job for any pilot handy, and there was not much to it, being just a little tour of the area, with some acrobatics, and few dives and pull-ups. It did not mean much more than trying out a new horse at a dude ranch, except that in an emergency, a man can bail out from a horse, and not need a parachute; an ordinary horse, that is, and not some creature of a Western tall story. In these tests, a wing might snap off, and once in a great while did, but there were no extraordinary demands on a pilot's body as today, and any competent pilot was considered good enough for this kind of testing.

Concerning all this, it was still a very simple age of aviation, and the old horse-and-buggy days, army way of thinking was quite prevalent. For example, any officer was considered fit to handle any assignment in his province. The old Indian fighters could do that in their heyday, for they could all ride, shoot, boss their commands, and read the reports prepared by their sergeants. Outside of that, many of them knew next to nothing, for the isolated little army posts tended to be mental Siberias, utterly outside the vital life of the nation. Before World War I, the average army officer might be married, and with a quota of army brats to his name, but he was to all intents a military monk living in great seclusion, from the rest of the nation. As a class, he was almost never heard of outside his own profession, and in turn, he knew mighty little of the rest of the country. Quite naturally, his thinking tended to become rigid, and too many years of army life could produce a barnacle of the first water.

For a while, too many old barnacles were in certain places of authority in our air force. To these old bourbon-drinkers, a pilot was a pilot was a pilot, period. He was a cockeyed aerial cowboy in their regular army minds, and as such was supposed to be ready to ride any sort of sky-going mechanical cayuse, and right off—"Just like Grant took Richmond, sir!" So, by guess and by God, we flew anything right off, and somehow got away with it, in the great majority of cases. If as the song says, "Heaven shall protect the working girl," it also took some time out to protect the early flyers.

By chance and as a diversion from routine, some of the gang discovered a new way to liven up test flights. This was steeplechasing. The race track in the Bois de Boulogne was but a short hop across Paris from Orly, and it was closed to racing in wartime. However, brush hurdles were still in place around one of the courses, and the sport was to take a couple of Niewports or Spads, and race around, landing wheels about one foot from the green turf, and jump the hurdles. There was about enough room to fly, wing tip to wing tip, and come skimming down the stretch, like the finish of the Grand National. No spills ever came from this, and there were no official squawks from the French grounds keepers, until a future ace—Avery, I think was his name—landed at Orly with his landing wheels trailing a festoon of light wires. Somewhere about the race track, he had collected some part of an electric system, the wires had snapped, and he had known nothing about it. No great harm had been done, but the glooms at headquarters took the expected dim view, and our pastime was over.

Another interesting project was debated, but never—by us at least—put to the acid test. This was to fly through the Arc de Triomphe. It was agreed, after pacing it off, that the famous arch was wide enough for a Niewport to skim through, if aimed dead center, but there were trees all around it, and a plane would have to come in on a dive, swoop through, and go out on a zoom to avoid them. It would have to be like a cat jumping into a garbage can, skinning through a croquet wicket, and leaping out, except that the cat would have to be flying at one hundred and thirty miles an hour. At that, a cat had nine lives and we each only one, and that single one on too much mortaged time for comfort.

This proposition was never ventured, there being none of us quite that reckless, but months later I did hear a rumor that it was tried by some mad Frenchman during the celebrations of the Armistice. If true, he undoubtably went, right off, to wherever pilots go at their endings. As to that exact location, the air force has its opinion, and the army has quite another, but it could be they are now handling flying saucers. This is what is known as metempsychosis, and it is as good an explanation of the saucer sightings as the official gobbledegook that has really settled nothing. I will lay a guinea, as say the British, that holy science in the Pentagon can not disprove it.

The test flights, even without race tracks, could be exciting. We used to fly most of the models, both French and British, then being used in some capacity or other, in the war effort. Among these were the previously mentioned Farman and Voisin pushers, the various type Niewports and Caudrons used in training, and such models as the French R-4s, the two-place Breguet day bombers, the Salmsons, the British two-seater Sopwiths, the Sopwith Dolphins, the Camels, the SE-5s, the FEs, and the earlier model Spads. There were no big night bombers, such as Handley-Paiges, at Orly, but I did have a brief experience with a twin-motored Caudron, although not at Orly, and much later, several flights in the American manufactured, British designed DH-4, powered with our famed Liberty engine.

Among the mentioned models at Orly, the R-4, better known as the French R-Quatre, was another long gliding kite, rather slow and obsolescent for the front lines, but remarkable for the extreme back staggering of its biplane wings, so that in profile it reminded one of the undershot jaws of an English bulldog. Much more exiting to fly, and the doom of more than one good but unlucky pilot, were the Niewport 28 Model, and the redoubtable Sopwith Camel.

The Niewport 28, the latest model of that make, was a beautiful single-seater; fast, delicately responsive to the controls, and well armed for combat, but it had two unfortunate defects. In a sharp pull up from a steep dive, often a combat necessity, it had a tendency to imitate a stripteaser, and to shed an alarming amount of the canvas fabric of its wings. This occurred with several pilots, including Eddie Rickenbacker, who managed to get one home and make a safe landing, although he appeared to be flying something of rags and tatters, on not much more than the bare skeletons of wings. The Niewport's other fault involved its engine.

The Niewport 28 had a rotating engine of some 160, or a bit more horsepower, which was designed with no inlet valve, and which was regulated by no throttle. The engine was a monosoupape, with an exhaust valve, but no carburetor. Gas was admitted by being sucked up through the base of the cylinders, and the engine was speeded up or retarded, by cutting in and out the numerous cylinders, by means of the spark. There were nine cylinders, and by manipulating the spark control, one could run the engine on a choice of one, three, six, or the whole battery, with sounds varying from the put-put-put, like the one-lung auxiliary in a Cape Code cat boat, to a final high pitched *Waaaaaaahhhhh*!, that sounded like a myriad fire sirens. It was an engine with a repertoire like an opera singer, but like many a headlined diva, it could prove hot to handle on occasions.

Flying was mostly done on nine cylinders, although one could loaf along on six, and not lose much altitude. To come in for a landing, it was either dead stick, and undesirable for that reason, or on one or three cylinders, which could be a considerable hazard. This came from fire, because gas was unconsumed, and this might accumulate in an undercasing of the engine, where a chance spark could set it off. At a safe altitude, this flame might be snuffed out in a near vertical wing slip, as was done by a few survivors, but on a gliding approach for a landing, there was nothing to do but to get down and out, as fast as possible. A very close friend of mine could not quite make it, and perished in this manner. I made several flights in the Niewport 28, but on one short hop at Orly, the gas in the casing caught fire just as my wheels touched for the landing, and I did not think it quite so humorous as did a small group of onlookers, including one young lady.

"Oh, you looked so funny, hopping out just like Charlie Chaplin!" exclaimed this pretty laughing hyena.

The field's fire crew had quickly smothered the flame, and there had been no great damage, but I had felt the blast of heat, and it had not been pleasant. However, I said nothing, for she was obviously one of that type of ever trilling, oh-so-gay young females, who are the life of every party, but a suffering husband's bane.

Besides the above young woman, Paris had some other American filled-with-joy-of-life females who should have never been born. One of these was a member of some motor corps auxiliary or other, and back in the States she had most appropriately come from that region of our country that had once been known as the *Dark and Bloody Ground*. Unfortunately, her family knew my family, and hearing that I was at Orly, she arrived in her tin lizzie with an invitation to drive me to Paris for dinner, at the expense of some relation, sent over on some mission.

It was some ride! "Oh, I would love to fly," she said, as she missed a Frenchman only by inches, and this only because he had jumped like lightning. "I would just love to be an aviator," she said as more Frenchmen flew over the gutters like bullfrogs. I felt like saying that at the speed we were going, we would soon leave the ground and be airborne, but the hurtling bumps made conversation impossible. Finally the terrible ride was over, and there was no more need for me to press on imaginary brakes every other second. "I suppose motoring is awfully tame for you flyers," she said brightly. She was a pretty girl then, and she may well be now a sweet and white-haired grandmother. I can vision her, happy and serene amidst her numerous and loving grandchildren —all horrible little hot-rodders!

Returning to flying, the other tricky plane was the Sopwith Camel. This particular model had a rotary engine of around 120 horsepower, and it was not especially fast, not much over 115 miles an hour. However, it had been a most effective combat plane over the lines, because if some planes were said to turn on a dime, the Camel could turn on a pinhead. It was well armed with two machine guns, both synchronized to fire through the propeller, and the pilot sat rather close up towards the nose, like a jockey on a horse's neck, this horse having rather a short back and hindquarters.

With the engine, the gas tank, the guns, and the pilot all well up forward, and with the rear fuselage, seemingly, not much more of an appendage than the tail on a Manx cat, the Camel could have probably been spiraled within the wing span of a big, modern bomber. However, its great maneuverability demanded expert handling at low altitudes, for if a sharp turn were not made correctly, the ship could spin without warning, there being little longitudinal resistance to the sudden dropping of the nose with which the spin started. On taking off, it was wise to reach a good altitude before attempting a turn, unless one were a veteran Camel man, for a short but fatal spin into the ground was much too common, and such was the end of many inexperienced flyers.

For once, I had been given some warning hints before my first flight, and I did not venture to turn my Camel until I had reached a good fifteen hundred feet of altitude. Gradually I got the feel of the plane, and enjoyed putting it through some acrobatics, including spirals that felt like corkscrews. Landing it was also a bit tricky. With a short fuselage and the weight all forward, there was little longitudinal stability on the ground, and a consequent great tendency to bird hop. Some planes, like the Spad on landing, would hug the ground and roll like a Pullman car on a rock-ballasted track, but the Camel, in green hands, was apt to act like a worm hunting robin, making a series of hippity-hops which might end with the nose down in the turf. Coming back to the Niewport 28, our first fighter squadrons in combat, the famous *Hat In The Ring* 94th, and the equally fine *Kicking Mule* 95th, used them on the then quiet Toul defensive sector, during May and June. Some victories were scored in them, but they gave trouble until they were replaced with new Spad 13 models, to everyone's relief and satisfaction.

It was at Cazeau that I had a brief experience flying a twin-engine Caudron, the model being the G-11, if I remember correctly. At any rate, I had met this French pilot, and had offhandedly said that I would like, someday, to try a twin-engine job. To my surprise and some consternation, he said, "You weesh to try. Why not? There is *mon avion*. Come, I show you. There is nozzing to it."

There seemed to be no honorable way out, so I was led to the unfamiliar monster, now being warmed up by an Annamite mechanic. My orientation course was very brief, being little more than a demonstration of the twin-engine controls, and a warning that it would be best to avoid any sharp turns, as with a single-engine plane, until I was fully accustomed to the different behavior. "Be careful, *mon vieux*," said this Frenchman.

This Caudron was a three-place job, there being a cockpit for a gunner-observer aft of the pilot, and another gunner's cockpit way up in the nose, which projected considerably beyond the wings. I got in, took off, made a very wide sweeping, conservative, and gingerly tour of the area, and managed a safe landing. This Caudron was a good airplane for those days, and safe for an accustomed pilot, but my introduction had been pretty casual. Today, no pilot goes from single engine to twins, without some further training. However in that age of aviation innocence, some Frenchman might have as casually handed over to me a four-engine bomber, like a Handley-Paige monster. It was a good thing that there were none handy. It would be like having a fair horse-and-buggy driver take sudden charge of a twenty-mule team, borax wagon.

There was another very exciting plane which I never had a chance to fly, but wish to mention. This was the latest model,

Moranne-Saulnier monoplane, perhaps the fastest plane in the world at that time. It had a monocoque fuselage, the same engine as the Niewport 28, and I have a feeling that this small, streamlined, single seater monoplane could outspeed, by at least twenty miles or more an hour, the swiftest combat biplane, at the war's end.

I saw the first one of this model at Issoudun, where it was being flown and tested by a short, stumpy pilot, generally known to us as Guy Wire Gates, and also by Ned Post, who skimmed it through the skies, at an amazing speed, and as smoothly as if the plane and engine had read his mother's *Book of Etiquette*. This plane could, probably, do at least 170 miles an hour, since it had far less drag and air resistance to overcome than the best designed biplane. However, although it might have been used for reconnaissance, being next to uncatchable by any enemy fighter, it was useless for combat and pursuit work. This was before the days of metal construction, and cantilever wings. This monoplane, lacking the strong truss bracing of a good biplane fighter, would have snapped off its wings in normal but violent, combat maneuvering.

Chapter 19

THE EVER FASHIONABLE GENERAL PERSHING

Our 1st Pursuit Group, made up of the 94th, 95th, 27th, and 147th Fighter Squadrons, had seen some action on the relatively quiet defensive Toul sector for a good many weeks, and they had already begun to cover themselves with glory, and quite a lot of publicity writeups in the Stateside papers. They now had had their breaking in against the German 2nd team aviation, and they were considered ready for much more active fronts, and the really first-class, enemy squadrons, even the dreaded Richtofen Flying Circus. They were now to be transferred to the critical Champagne region, just as soon as new American squadrons could be readied to take their place.

This operation was now underway, and about the first of June, I was transferred from Orly to the 1st Air Depot at Colombey Les Belles, where I was assigned to the pilots pool, to await future orders to some new combat squadron, whenever it should be ready for front-line duties. As flying at the front was the ambition of ninety-nine percent of Issoudun graduates, those of us now transferred from Orly, held a jolly celebration over the news. Ferrying had been all right, and Paris had been great fun, but the front was the only place to be for any pilot who aspired to be in the best fashion. At the front line was *la gloire*, the Arena of Honor, the storied, heroic region so filled with gallant gentlemen, and the very best of all fellows, and if death was quite likely, he was also around in all our locations.

To us, the worst thing was to get killed in some routine crash, before having any combat experience, for life then would have been in vain. "If I have to die young, then let me die in combat, Lord!" If not quite in those words, I heard many pilots express this feeling. To be killed in action was a glorious finish, but to crash and die on a ferry job was not. In that case, as all said and remarked on each such occasion, you were just another, poor, dumb bastard bumped off. Like on an old western so-called Boot

Hill, with its gravestones ironically inscribed "Slow On The Draw," "Too Many Aces," and the like, this was the unwritten but common epitaph of many a nice family's darling son. War had made us cynical on the surface, in self-protection.

Colombey Les Belles—it must have been some medieval prototype of a real estate developer who gave it that name—was some ten miles south of the city of Toul, in the Muerth and Moselle prefecture, and it was just another one of the dreary villages of that region of France, noted for its poor agricultural soil, and a general look of wide open and barren spaces. Further east were the French hillbillies of the Vosges and German-ruled Alsace, but Colombey Les Belles lay in a kind of small-scale French Wyoming. It was all right for forced landings, for there was plenty of flat land, with very little on it.

Here, the 1st Air Depot was a big field to the north of a highway and a branch line railroad track, and with the usual setup of barracks, headquarters, guardhouse, and the rest, lying south of it. It was drab, and for a pilot waiting his turn in a pool, there was little to do, except reread old letters, take his turn as officer of the day, and hit the sack when not eating. Colombey Les Belles soon became Colombey Les Bums. Like all pools, for those waiting in them, it was a kind of limbo of homeless spirits, but occasionally there was some excitement, and even some humor.

German bombing raids were one source of excitement. The front lines were only some twenty miles to the north, and if the weather was good and the stars were out, German bombers were apt to follow the dusty white French roads, and come over. In the two raids I witnessed, they never hit anything with their ninety-kilo bombs, except a latrine and some poor peasant's pig pen, but they made some very large holes in the field, and they did afford us some much needed practice, and the thrill of combat to our antiaircraft machine-gun crews, who yelled and shrieked and fired with enthusiasm and vim, but likewise hit *nawthin'*. For the suffering taxpayers of both sides, these two battles were a complete waste of expensive ammunition.

Almost as much excitement, and more real damage came from the English. Not far distant was the field of a British night-bombing squadron. They had giant Handley-Paiges, and they were a good and enterprising outfit, but one night on returning from a raid, one of their planes got a trifle off its course, flew too low, and hooked its huge tail onto the village church steeple. This came toppling down, and minus part of its tail, the plane still managed to make a safe landing. During the entire war, this was one of the high spots for the villagers of Colombey, but some of the peasants grumbled to their cure, that *le bon Dieu* was not taking any too good care of his own property. Colombey was one of those places that exist, without ever really living, a locality of poor farmers living off submarginal land.

The air base at Colombey saw some of our first Liberty planes, the British designed, but American made DH-4s, that had been shipped to the depot to be assembled. This model plane was powered with our famous 400-horsepower Liberty engine, and they arrived at Colombey sometime after my departure for the front, but I had occasion to see something of them, and fly them as well, much later.

In profile, the DH-4 vaguely resembled a sperm whale, for its nose and forward fuselage were big, squarish and blunt, and its head looked as if it extended for two-thirds of its entire body length. It had a big, thick, two-bladed propeller, that looked like two huge clubs compared to the slender blades of the Niewports, and for those days, it was a decidedly hefty airplane—almost too hefty, and in some danger of bogging down on takeoff runs, in the often muddy fields of the airdromes. Its Liberty engine was a good one, which proved to compare most favorably with the famous Rolls-Royce airplane engine, as readily admitted by the British. These Liberty planes were much used in day bombing, and they received a great deal of highly unfavorable publicity as so-called *Flaming Coffins*, but this was not the fault of the Liberty engine.

After the Armistice and while awaiting orders to return to the United States, I made several short flights in a DH-4, and found it easy to handle for a plane of its size and weight, although for delicacy to the touch, it could not, of course, come close to the Niewport or the Spad. DH-4s had been used for day bombing and reconnaissance, by certain of our squadrons, whose total casualties had been excessively, and perhaps unduly heavy. An unusually high percentage had been shot down in flames, by enemy aircraft, and this gave rise to a very bitter criticism of their design, and the scornful appellation of Flaming Coffin. It was said that they were too vulnerable to the usual fighter attack from below and to the rear, there being too many blind angles for the defensive rear gunner to contend with, and that the non-self-sealing gas tank had been placed in an unusually vulnerable location.

All the above might well be a major reason for our Liberty squadrons' heavy losses, but although I never flew a Liberty in combat, it has strongly occurred to me, that there were other and great reasons for these disasters. The Liberty-engined DH-4 was supposed to be capable of a cruising speed of 128 miles an hour, at an altitude of ten to fifteen thousand feet or higher, and it had been the theory, of some authoritative mental giant or other, that this speed could outdistance enemy pursuit ships, and that they could operate far within the enemy lines, without Allied fighter protection. This idea may have arisen through out-of-date intelligence reports, for by the time the Libertys appeared in action, the latest German fighters could easily do 135 or more miles per hour, and nosing down from some high ambush in clouds, attain speeds very much greater. Lying in wait well behind their own lines, at altitudes of 18,000 feet or more, a flight of fast Fokkers could pounce on an unescorted flight of our day bombers, and raise havoc with them, especially if the bombers had already used up much of their ammunition in beating off a previous attack.

Charles Drew, a close friend who had been shot down, severely wounded over the lines, and who was being treated in a German hospital in the city of Metz, saw one of these attacks from a window next to his cot. He later told me that he saw seven of our unescorted DH-4s attacked by successive waves of perhaps forty Fokkers, and that in no time, all seven of our Liberty bombers went down in flames. At this time, the heavily fortified German base at Metz was almost twenty miles within enemy lines. In broad daylight, and without any fighter protection, our day bombers were like sitting ducks to the numerous enemy.

Few things can more hurt morale, more than a person in authority with a conviction based on an untried theory, which he thinks ought to work, can work, and will be worked, not by him, but by the unfortunate beings who happen to serve him. Such a one was a certain field grade commanding officer, who had mathematically figured it out, that the DH-4 could carry four 90-kilo bombs, instead of the regular load of two. His pilots, while granting that the ships might stagger along under the extra four hundred pounds of bomb load, were dubious about takeoffs, and also about reaching reasonable altitudes. However, the professor was all for efficiency, a greater load per gallon of gas consumed, a greater punch delivered to the enemy, per airplane mission, all of which would look good on his official report.

Orders were orders, and two extra bombs were duly affixed, but the first plane took off, wobbled around, and crashed shortly after. This ended the experiment, and also the pilot and the bombardier, as I heard the story from one of the squadron. Soon after, this commanding officer was relieved, perhaps to do more figuring but not to command flyers, but such stupidities hurt, and left a legacy of bitter feelings. The DH-4 squadrons did have very heavy losses in combat, but from what I heard and saw while on the lines, their excessive casualties were certainly as much due to unescorted daylight missions far within the enemy lines, as to defects in their design. The DH-4s did have blind angles for the rear gunner's guns, and it did take more than the usual muscular effort to swing the brace of Lewis guns against the wind streaming past the bombardier's cockpit, and the tank was so placed that it was easily hit by enemy bullets, and so set on fire. However, these disadvantages were found, to a lesser extent, in all combat two-seaters, and in those days of no armor, few self-sealing gas tanks, and blind defensive angles, any plane was easily set on fire by enemy incendiary bullets, and most especially if far within the German lines, where the tank was half empty. Allied or German, any unescorted two-seater was about the easiest mark for an experienced pilot in a fast fighter, and many an ace built up his score on such lone targets.

Time hanging heavily on our hands while we awaited assignments in the pilots pool, some of our more sartorially conscious flyers reflected that our present uniform, although strictly regulation, was too drab, too uncomfortable, and too utterly regular army, for the free spirits of this new arm of the service. The blouse, with its high, Prussian style collar was a hindrance to a flyer. So, out! The cap, the regulation, overseas cap! More fit for a monkey, than for a pilot. So, out! The pants! Brown or olive drab, and decidedly on the dull side. To hell with these uninspired nether garments, good enough for the gingerbread troops of the ground forces, but not fit for the air corps. Come comrades, fellow flyers glorious, blazers of new trails, beloveds of the fair sex, and shining apples of the American public's eye, let us intrepid birdmen don fancier plumage!

The sartorial revolt was on, and the first roll-collar coats appeared. Since these really made good sense, they were, from the first, generally allowed on the front lines, and much later, almost officially adopted, but the new style shook the holy inner temple of the General Staff, and caused a terrible struggle before it became really regulation. Then, the cap! For that, we just bought and wore the Royal Air Corps version. This, much more smartly designed than our own, God-awful, organ grinder's monkey headpiece, sloped fore and aft, following the natural curve of the head, and it did not offer two floppy points with a saddle between, like a profile of San Francisco's Twin Peaks during an earthquake. Then, the pants! Rose beige, cafe au lait, milk delicately tinted by the juices of peach or strawberry, the Ice Cream Pants now blossomed in all their glory. One thing more. Ah, the overcoat! A leather buttoned, beige or light chocolate British Warm, with a fur collar of racoon, of fox, even of mink, was very, very swell, and this too was adopted, and with one more accessory. A stick must be carried, a stick to swagger with, and to swish with a nonchalant manner. Thus arrayed, the air corps had really become birds of a fine feather, although of course, we did not exactly look as if we belonged to the American army.

Certain things, seen in the past, are never forgotten: a black and towering waterspout off Nantucket; the white cloud, bounding boulders, and high tossed pine trees of an avalanche in the Sierras; a flash flood, with a mud-colored, twenty-foot wall of water in the Silver Peak Mountains of Nevada; the tree-rendering, high-shrieking fury of the 1938 hurricane in New England; that awful explosion in Tokyo, when dandyish Colonel X stepped proudly but hurriedly out of his new command car, to put his highly polished foot, and one leg of his new uniform trousers, almost knee deep into a misplaced, but brim full, ironically called *honeybucket*. All these were dire manifestations of fury, but no more than on that morning that first Lieutenant C, one of the pilots in the pool, appeared before Lieutenant Colonel J, in all his exquisite new regalia.

"Sir, I am reporting as new officer of the day," said our lieutenant.

For a seeming full minute, there was nothing but an awful silence. In the headquarters office, typewriters ceased clacking, clerks gazed with pallid countenances at one another, and the long service, regular army top sergeant braced himself for what he knew was coming. Good Lieutenant Colonel J had been a Spanish War veteran, and of the cavalry. He knew how to ride like a Cossack, how to shoot like an expert, how to mow them down with a saber, and he knew all the army regulations. He barely knew one end of an airplane from the other, but he had become increasingly aware that this new breed of junior officer, these monkey-business pipsqueaks that flew, had yet to learn what it was to really be in the army. For a long moment he glared, just as a lion might have glared at a Christian in the Roman Colosseum, for a good hard look, before leaping on him.

"Young MAAANNN!" The sound was like a choking explosion, as if it came from deep in a cellar. "JUST WHAAAT DAMNED ARMY DO YOU BELONG TO!"

Soon after, it was known all over the base, that the subsequent, full fifteen-minute chewing-out was in the highest tradition of the service, and almost on a par with the alleged, awe-inspiring reproof administered by General George Washington to General Charles Lee, at the Battle of Monmouth. Thereafter, the ice cream pants and the rest of our fancy duds were put away in lockers for our remaining days at Colombey.

There was, however, a sequel to this. In our American squadrons, engaged in combat over the lines, the roll-collar coat, although still unofficial and not to be worn on formal occasions, became the accepted working uniform of all pilots. A man could not fly over the front, and keep turning his head on an all-around lookout, without seriously irritating the back of his neck, while wearing the regulation high-collared tunics, which had originally been designed to keep a foot soldier, chin up and face forward on the drill field. These were simply not functional for flyers. As to breeches, most squadron commanders cared little what their pilots wore, provided they were neat, of military cut, and of hues within reason, which did not preclude rose beige, silver white, and similar fashionable shades.

After I had been at the front, about one month after leaving Colombey, a small dance, with nurses, Red Cross and YMCA girls was given in the city of Toul, a few miles from our airdrome. Most of our pursuit group attended, and also several officers stationed at Colombey Les Belles. Among the latter, was Colonel J, who greeted us pilots very warmly, and who seemed surprisingly mellowed since the days of our pilot pool. He pumped my hand, suggested a good big drink, and was very buddyish to us horrible noncomformists. This was not all. Not only was he gay and jolly in manner, he was dressed in a gala fashion. His breeches gleamed like silver, and I had seen him check in a British Warm, one with leather buttons and a collar of fur. Colonel J had had a brief leave in Paris, and there he had seen a great light. He had seen General Pershing. General Pershing had had on ICE CREAM PANTS.

Chapter 20

A WARTIME TRAIN JOURNEY

On 1 July 1918, I received Special Order 246, Headquarters Advance Section Air Service, AEF Zone of Advance, directing that I *proceed at once from 1st Air Depot to 2nd Pursuit Group, Toul, reporting on arrival to the Commanding Officer thereof, for assignment to duty with the 13th Squadron.*

Excited and very happy at this news, I lost no time in obtaining transportation to Gengault Airdome, which lay a few miles to the east of the small, ancient and fortified city of Toul, and not very far from the banks of the Moselle River. There, I reported to the Commander, Major (in World War II, Major General) Davenport Johnson, and then hastened to my new squadron's headquarters, where I was welcomed by the adjutant-executive, First Lieutenant Hugh Ellis.

Lieutenant Ellis, a most excellent ground officer, had been the squadron's commander during the months that its mechanics and other ground personnel were being thoroughly organized and trained in their various duties, and he now informed me that he was immediately cutting orders to send me, and a small group of just assigned pilots, to Paris, there to meet our newly appointed squadron commander, and then to fly back several of the very latest Spad models from Orly. This was the best of good news, and a day later, four of us left for the big city, entraining at the Toul station. The subsequent journey, like all long and tedious train rides of that time, developed some aspects of distinction, but not in the mode of the Royal Scot, Le Train Bleu, or our Twentieth Century Limited.

Toul was less than two hundred miles from Paris by the most direct rail lines, and in peacetime, the trip would not have taken much over four to five hours, but it was then a much longer and slower journey, for much of the main line was under shell fire, so that trains had to be routed through a much more southerly route. A great deal of this had to be over single-tracked, meandering, connecting lines and branches, where most passenger trains had to run very slowly, and often stand for many hours on end—in one personal experience, an entire night and day—on sidings, to allow free passage of interminable military trains, hastening supplies and troop reinforcements to the battles on the lines. If one were lucky, one might reach Paris from Toul in twelve hours, but it could take two days, as well as give a taste of near starvation to unprepared passengers. As for the trains, once they had been good, but now they were dingy and overcrowded, being mostly filled with hairy and hardy Frenchmen, who feared and hated something called a *courant d'air* more than the devil.

Why French soldiers fresh from the trenches, where for months they have braved not only the weapons of the enemy, but also mud, rain, snow, sleet, and raw cutting winds in the open, should show such concern over an open window, and a slight draft of fresh air, is a mystery, but it seems to be some part of a national phobia, perhaps inherited from their Cro-Magnon ancestors of the caves. At any rate in all our train, there was not a single open window.

Our train left in the late afternoon, and for hours we stood in a narrow car corridor, since every compartment was filled with French soldiers, going on leave or to other assignments. Night came, black curtains were drawn over the windows, and the air we breathed, if it really was air, seemed redolent of powerful cheeses, sour red wine, black and pungent Algerian tobacco, coal dust, and the smell of unbathed bodies, and moldy, long worn uniforms. Lit by a few feeble bulbs, it was a Rembrandtish scene, a chiaroscuro of dark shadows and dim yellow lights, where tired, silent soldiers stood, propped up and motionless like mummies in a closed museum, or sprawled in our passageway, in attitudes of utter resignment. Our train crawled, speeded up for a time, stopped for long intervals, then resumed crawling. Finally it stopped, seemingly forever, and at nowhere in particular.

"Maybe the engine's just quit for good," said one of us. "I saw it in the station. One of those real old ones."

"Everything's old on this train," said another voice. "We started this trip one hundred years ago, when I was twenty-one. Now, I am one hundred and twenty one, and very tired. A bed I need, and a bed I see. I will have it."

In a nearby compartment, into which we could glimpse through a glass partition, a more comfortable scene presented itself. Within its privacy, a group of French officers were seated, some dozing, some smoking in a silent and philosophical manner, some quietly conversing while sharing a bottle of red wine. Above their heads, the personal effects jampacked the hammock-netted, hand baggage racks, in a confusion of paraphernalia. In the compartment, there was no more apparent space for man or bag, for even the floor was encumbered, and it was fully occupied with no rank lower than a *capitaine*, and there were several *commandants* (majors) in attendance. There was a printed sign, *complet*, on the door. Thus, the dignified, bearded conclave within seemed serenely at ease, and utterly safe from any intrusion.

"Camerades, pardon!" A person had slid back the door, and now stood in the opening, saluting in a vague but amiable manner, as the smartly uniformed but weather-beaten inmates took sudden notice of this intruder.

"With your permission, I will lie down here. *Comprenez?*" said the apparition. "This looks like a good place to rest, *n'est-ce pas?*"

"Monsieur, mon lieutenant, regardez. Ici, nous sommes complets. There is no more room here, as you can see," said a French officer of artillery, whose sleeve insignia proclaimed him to be a major.

"Complet, complet, absolument complet!" agreed several deep voices.

"Avec votre permission?" The intruder now entered. Reaching up with long arms, he carefully removed all the hand baggage and parcels from one long rack, and as carefully deposited them on the floor, where they made a small mountain. "*Avec votre permission*!" Carefully, finding a place to put a foot, and grasping whatever afforded support, the intruder eased his six-foot body along the full length of the emptied baggage rack. "*Merci bien, camerades.*" The intruder closed his eyes and sighed contentedly. The Frenchmen gazed in dumbfounded amazement, and so did we through the doorway. The intruder once more opened his eyes for a brief moment, and a broad grin lit up his amiable, dog-like face as he saw us. "*Bon soir*, you guys," he said." See you in the morning." It was another scored victory for

the air corps. Lieutenant C had found himself an upper berth for the long night's journey.

Later that night, the remaining three of us found seats in a partially evacuated compartment. We slept at times, but the night was almost one long battle, a desperate struggle between Americans, who needed some minimum of fresh air to live, and Frenchmen, who resembled anarobes in being able to do, almost completely without it. Not only were they able to dispense with it, they regarded the night's fresh air with a seeming horror.

It was a stealthy war. "The frogs are all asleep," a voice would whisper.

"Gently does it," another whisper would answer. Slowly and silently, the car window would be opened. A bare crack only, but it helped. Life might be saved until morning, if only the Frenchmen kept on sleeping. They ought not to feel that minimum of fresh air, from that tiny opening. And so it went, for fifteen or twenty minutes, and for almost an hour, in one life-renewing interval. For a little while, we could enjoy our triumph, and breathe what was intended by nature, but this could not last.

"BRRRrrrrrr!" A Frenchman would suddenly awaken, and sit bolt upright, hugging himself and shaking. "*Sacre Nom, la fenetre! Sâcre Nom d'un Nom, d'un Nom, quel courant d'air!*" Bang! He would slam down the window, awakening all the other Frenchmen, who would look fiercely at us, and also grumble about the *courant d'air*, implying that hardly anything was more dangerous to life, than night air circulating through a window.

This went on for much of the night, although there was one other incident of a very different, and more serious nature. We had stopped at some station—Sezanne, it may have been—when there came a terrific bang close by, and loud screams from the next compartment. Although there followed some shouting and considerable commotion, we were too tired to even glance out of our compartment at what was taking place. From the sounds, it seemed obvious that some people were badly hurt, and that they were being taken from the car to the station. The next morning, we heard the story from the conductor.

In the next compartment to ours, a hand grenade had

exploded. It had detonated in the breeches' pocket of a French soldier, a young farmer who was going home on leave, and who had taken a grenade with him to kill fish in a river. At the time of the explosion, he was not only wearing these trousers, but a young woman was also sitting on his lap. "*C'etait bien dommage*," said the conductor, for the soldier would probably die, and France needed strong, young soldiers.

"But what of the girl?" we inquired sympathetically.

"She'll probably die also," said the conductor. "*Mais, quoi donc?*" He added with the usual Gallic shrug. With so many men being killed in France, what matters a woman?"

This was war, trains were slow, and even to things concerning death and great suffering, there was attached a certain grim humor. We had never laid eyes on this unfortunate couple, we had never even heard their names, and sudden and violent death was always peering over our shoulder. On the surface, death had become a figure of jest, something to be avoided with honor, if possible, but not to be taken too seriously. In this case, we were not struck by the horrible suffering and tragedy of two human beings, for it all seemed so impersonal, and not of our world. A grenade going off in a soldier's pants was pure comic strip, like a slapstick applied to a bending, fat man's fundament. It struck us as funny, as funny as all hell—then!

"The bomb, that killed poor momma, went off in poppa's pants," said a friend to whom I related this incident several days later. "Could write a song about that, one of those Frankie and Johnnie sort of things."

"Sure thing," said someone else. "Make a million out of it."

Odd things like that, although seldom so grim, were apt to happen on those slow, wartime trains. Trains were sometimes routed to the wrong tracks, got lost, wandered around strange countrysides, and never did arrive at their proper destinations, until days had elapsed after their due arrival. Concerning this, there were many legends, and also myths and tall stories. A train full of skeletons, the passengers having starved to death, was one of them, and there was another to the effect that a group of starving officers had cooked and eaten a sergeant. This last one was never quite accepted by our soldiers. It was not that they thought any better of the ethics of officers, but eat a sergeant? As an erudite private said, "Too far fetched. Only a school of piranhas could stomach a sergeant." As for our trip, we finally arrived in Paris, not too much worse for wear, only about fourteen hours later than the normal schedule.

Chapter 21

AT THE FRONT

After signing in at Paris headquarters, we met our new commanding officer, Captain (later, Major) Charles J. Biddle, Jr., who made the welcome suggestion that we have lunch with him at the Crillon Hotel. This at once confirmed the very good impression he had immediately made on us, for we had not eaten since leaving Toul, almost a whole day previous, unless one counts a piece of black, sour bread and some bitter coffee, gulped at a way station, and hardly adequate for a jockey, or a skeletonized, fashion model.

Captain Biddle, Princeton and Harvard Law, and a Philadelphian who would have warmed the heart of both William Penn and Benjamin Franklin, had been a distinguished member of the Escadrille, Cigognes (the Storks) and had already accounted for four German planes, before he was shot down and severely wounded. A quiet spoken man, he still carried a cane and walked with a slight limp, but that did not interfere with his continuing to be a first-class combat pilot, as was proved by his subsequent record of four more victories to a total of eight enemy shot down. We saw at once that we were to be commanded by both a gentleman and a real combat pilot, and not by one of those loud-mouthed blusterers, under whom both flyers and ground troops have sometimes suffered.

Our morale went up from that meeting, and it was further boosted when our captain told us about a new model Spad that would be ours to fly over the lines, against the enemy. This model plane was, according to all reports, the very latest and best fighter model, and we, the 13th, would be the very first American squadron to be equipped with it. The next morning, we hastened to Orly to inspect and obtain our planes.

Guynemer, the great French ace, had been killed in action. He had flown a Spad, but it had been an earlier model of about 180 horsepower, armed with but one machine gun, and with a top speed of not much over 130 miles an hour. Ours, the Spad 13 Model, had a 220-horsepower, V-8 Hispano-Swiza engine, and it was armed with two 30-caliber Vickers machine guns, both mounted flush on the cowl, and synchronized to fire between the fast-revolving blades of the wooden propeller. As to its speed, it was officially rated at 136 miles per hour, cruising at 6000 feet. However, official ratings have to be conservative and based on an average performance, and I am fairly certain that this model Spad, equipped with the excellent Belleau manufactured engine of the Hispano-Swiza design, with a superior Eclair propeller, and sharpened up in little but effective ways by clever American mechanics, could easily do 140 miles an hour at twelve thousand feet, and with the engine wide open to 2150 revolutions per minute, it might go considerably faster.

As to all this, opinions vary, and the Pitot-tube air speed indicators with which our Spads were equipped, were probably not precise, although they were of some value as a rough approximation. A plane's performance over a measured ground distance in still air, gives a better indication of its speed capabilities, and on my first cross-country flight in this Spad, I checked the distance on the map, and carefully noted the exact time of takeoff and arrival.

On the map and as the crow flies, the distance between Orly Field and Toul is 159 miles, and as our group's field, Gengault Airdrome, was some 5 miles east of the city, the total flying distance, from Orly to our destination, was a good 164 miles. That afternoon, the wind was very light and quartering from the north, and its effect on a plane flying due east was minimal. If anything, it may have impeded ground speed a trifle. On this occasion, my flight took exactly one hour and eleven minutes, making my average speed, over the entire distance, just a fraction under 139 miles an hour. When one considers that this included a climb to three thousand feet, and a good half minute's circling of the field before landing, and that the entire flight was at normal cruising speed, as revealed by the engine tachometer, it would seem that the Spad may have been capable of close to 145 miles per hour at level flight, when wide open.

Later, other timed and map-measured flights gave similar results and I feel reasonably certain that it was the fastest plane that saw combat up until the time of the Armistice. Flying this Spad for the first time, I got a feel of speed appreciably greater than with the Niewport 28, and that was capable of at least 130 miles an hour. At the Armstice, the three best fighter planes were the Spad, the British SE-5, and the German Fokker D-7, each model with its peculiar advantages and disadvantages. The Spad had the disadvantage of a limited angle of vision from the pilot's seat, but it had speed, it could climb fast and attain a high altitude, it could dive like a thunderbolt, and it was extremely rugged and strong.

Gengault Airdrome, the base for our newly organized 2nd Pursuit Group, lay just outside a ring of modern forts, which defended the old, walled city of Toul. Our airfield, a level meadow of perhaps fifty acres, lay at the foot of a fortified hill of a few hundred feet elevation, from the summit of which, brave and worthy Frenchmen, but not very good shots, banged away at visiting night bombers with little observable effect, but with lots of noise and fireworks, lots of searchlights sweeping the skies, and the scattering of considerable shell fragments over our location.

On our raid nights, a man had an equal chance of getting his ticket to Heaven, Hell or the hospital, from either a German bomb or a French fragment, which was something like an eighteenth century patient's choice between his disease and his doctor. The field had some good points. It had the Sebastopol Barracks, made of stone, with individual rooms for each pilot, it had a good bathhouse with hot water, it had a primitive, but rather superior French style gents' room, it had a reasonably firm and well-drained field, and it was close enough to the front lines to fly there within a few minutes, but not so close that it could be shelled by an enemy gun in the sector.

Aside from that, the nearby city of Toul had some attractions, including a small group of Red Cross and YMCA young ladies, who were of better than average looks, and of very nice American background. With a fine Spad to fly and, on this rather quiet defensive sector, a not too aggressive and dangerous enemy to contend with, our first month's taste of combat was rather pleasant, having all the thrill and not much more danger than an African big game expedition—that is, a true-blue and honorable sportsman's hunt, and not one of your modern, foolproof, one-sided, butchering safaris, now so popular with any slob with money, where the animals have but their old-fashioned teeth and claws, tusks or horns, while the well-guarded fat men and their dull wives have helicopters, and magnum rifles that hit like cannon. Our sector was like big game hunting in the days of Frederick Selous, but it changed a great deal a few weeks later.

The 2nd Pursuit Group was at this time composed of the 13th, 139th, and the 103rd pursuit squadrons. The 103rd had been the famed Lafayette Escadrille, before it was transferred to the American service. At this time, it was commanded by Major William Thaw, who had accounted for five enemy planes while with the Lafayette Escadrille, and it had several Lafayette Flying Corps veterans on its roster, including Lieutenant G.D.F. Larnett, and Lieutenant George Turnure. Some time later, the 103rd was transferred to a more newly formed, 3rd Pursuit Group, and its place was taken in our group, by the 22nd and 49th Pursuit Squadrons. All these squadrons were soon equipped with the Spad 13 Model. The organization of each squadron in our group, was far simpler than today's, and our 13th was typical of that era.

The 13th Squadron was commanded by a captain who was a pilot, and he had under him twenty pilots, most of whom were first lieutenants at the beginning. A little later, the General Staff, having considered in its divine wisdom that a first lieutenancy was too good for an air corps pilot, sent replacement pilots with only the rank of second lieutenant. These gold-barred, flying *shave-tails* were as well educated, as old, as well trained, and had graduated, on the average, just as well from the flying schools, as us higher ranking subalterns, but they had received their commissions just a little too late. The General Staff had had its will, and a second lieutenancy was considered more than enough for a flyer. That is the way it went and, in a later war, a still lower rank, *flying officer*, was invented for many a pilot. Gentlemen of the U.S. Air Force, consider yourselves fortunate. If you had not become a separate service, a generous PFC might have been your reward for completing flying training.

The above may be a bit of hyperbole, but in World War I, the General Staff, with some notable exceptions, looked with a stepmother's eye on this youngest child of the army. It did not really understand what it was, nor how to handle it to the best advantage of all concerned, and its collective imagination could not remotely conceive what it would become in the future. The air corps was a fancy frill to most old-time general officers who, although good men in their line, were mighty set in their opinions about flyers and flying.

As to first and second lieutenants in our 13th Squadron, we were all pilots together, members of a special brotherhood, a class different and light-years apart from the ground-huggers, and a little difference in rank meant less than nothing to us. However, the difference in pay was something else, and that was an injustice.

As noted, the tactical force of the squadron was twenty-one planes, twenty commissioned pilots, and a flying, commanding officer. In most cases the latter was no more than a captain, Eddie Rickenbacker being a notable example. Later, some squadron commanders were promoted to major, while due to the usual red tape, some able pilots were given commands while still only lieutenants, even second lieutenants in one instance. Job and rank often had no correlation. An able man might rise to command like a rocket, but no rocket ever pushed promotion papers through the usual channels.

Our tactical force was divided into three flights, each led by a flight leader, with a deputy to replace him, in case he were shot down. Each plane and its pilot had a ground crew of three mechanics, one generally being a sergeant. There was no executive as such, but the adjutant did that difficult and very responsible job, in addition to his paper work. Other ground officers included a supply officer, an engineer officer, an armament officer, a medical officer, and a kind of commissioned general handyman, procurer of whatever was needed, but not covered by regulations, and a Mr. Fixit for this and that, labeled for lack of a better name, an operations-confirmation officer. All these ground officers were first or second lieutenants, for even First Lieutenant Hugh Ellis, who had commanded and trained the squadron before it was ordered to the front, and who as executive had administrative supervision over 250 men, did not rate a captaincy according to our table of organization, although his job was a big one.

Our T.O. had one big and serious lack. This was an Intelligence Officer, one especially trained and solely assigned for the job of combat intelligence, a need that was well taken care of in World War II, where combat squadrons had two officers and an organized and well-equipped intelligence section, to keep pilots posted on the latest vital information. In all of World War I, I never heard of such a job as intelligence officer. If there were any for the ground forces, they were not for us, probably on the assumption by the General Staff, that combat flying did not require much intelligence, anyhow. Looking back, and also from the experience of going through the Air Combat Intelligence School at Harrisburg, during World War II, our old 13th's and other squadrons' greatest lack was a well-trained, well-supplied intelligence section, to keep us posted on the latest information as to the enemy. We could have used that to the greatest advantage, to increase our effectiveness.

As to what intelligence we received, we found our own, scratched like hens for it the hard way, pieced it together as well as we could, and made the best of it, under a general policy towards combat flyers, which seemed to resemble the motto of some ancient cynic regarding women, "Catch them young, treat them rough, tell them nothing!" Due to this lack, our briefings were rather skimpy, and too often we had only a rather vague picture of the forces opposing us, the lay of enemy installations, and what we should expect to encounter on a given mission. Our substitute for a well-equipped intelligence office was a small tent with a map, kept up by a sergeant, and very little else. There was none of the elaborate briefing, and detailed information concerning the enemy, as in the second war. It was often not much more than a there are the lines, and we're heading for such a spot, and let's go, boys!

As regards the other side, I am convinced that the Germans had good aviation intelligence, and knew far more about us than we knew about them. As to this, on his release from captivity after the Armistice, a friend told me that the German interrogating officer had not only known the name and experience of every pilot in his prisoner's squadron, but he had also related some jokes and minor incidents that had taken place among them, a few days previous to his capture. "How's Lieutenant B," he said of a pilot who had taken on the additional duty of mess officer. "Have you given him the grand bounce yet, for serving up too much crabmeat?" In addition to such tales, but never actually verified, there were rumors, even assertions, that German officers, in French uniforms and flying captured French planes, had landed on British airdromes, and vice-versa with British planes on French front-line fields, with some story that they had been lost from their flight on a mission, and had run out of gas. They had been good enough to fool our side, had been entertained, refueled, and had departed, back to their German field, with a lot of valuable information. True or not, it would have been easier for the Germans to pull such a fast one, than for the Allies, for on one side was a single language, German, while on our side, there was French, American, the Walloon or Flemish, both spoken by the Belgians, and of course the various dialects of Anglo-Saxon spoken on the west side of the Channel. Such being the case, only an officer who was an expert linguist would have detected some faulty idiom.

After a week or so, although we lacked our full complement of pilots, we made our first venture over the lines. Six of us, all greenhorns, were in the first flight, but we were fortunate in having for our flight commander, on this maiden venture, First Lieutenant Hobart A.H. Baker, a veteran of the Lafayette Flying Corps and, previously, a famous hockey and football captain at Princeton University. It was fine to see Hobey again, for I had known him well at St. Paul's School in New Hampshire, where he had brilliantly starred in every sport, even gymnastics, in which his great *giant swing* on the horizontal bar, that ended with a breathtaking *fly away*, was always the sensation of the annual winter gym exhibition. Hobey could do about everything much more than well, that involved muscular and mental coordination; he thought fast and did the right thing instinctively, and it was no wonder that he was a beautiful flyer. There is no question that he was one of the greatest all-around, natural athletes our country ever had, although he was no more than five-feet-ten, and around one-hundred-and-seventy-five pounds.

Under the leadership of Baker, it did not take our flight very long to get the feel of flying formation together. Our practice was to take off, in quick succession one by one, with a rendezvous over Mont Saint Michel, the fortified hill overlooking our field.

There at about three thousand feet altitude, we would circle clockwise, dropping into our assigned positions behind our leader, who was circling in the opposite direction. Our V quickly formed, we would steadily climb towards the lines, which were about a dozen miles to the north. There, our patrolling sector, extended from the town of St. Mihiel on the Meuse River, to Pond à Mousson on the Moselle, and eastward of that ruined little bridge and town, to a region marked by the villages of Nomeny and Bey, which lay north of the city of Nancy.

The total length of our sector was around forty miles of front line, and for practical purposes with due regard to gas tank capacities, it extended in depth from Colombey Les Belles, ten miles or so to the south of our field, to the rail center at Conflans, or even to the town of Briey, some twenty-odd miles across the lines, and well into German-held territory. That was our jungle and hunting ground, save for special missions, and as our Spads had a fuel supply of about two hours and fifteen minutes, not counting the emergency tank situated on the upper wing, which had an extra supply of some twenty minutes, an average patrolling mission could cover the total length of our sector, for some 3 1/2 round trips, before it was necessary to return to our field.

At this time, before mid-July, and up until mid-August or later, we ran into little danger from the enemy on our quiet sector, except for a few night-bombing raids, and the usual antiaircraft salutations which greeted us at the lines. These latter sometimes gave us a good shaking up, and might put a few tears and holes in our wing fabric, but with most batteries the percentage of effective hits to shells fired was very small, and we usually regarded the Boches' archies as one regards lightning, something to keep a person awake, but a remote danger.

As to enemy aircraft, they were at first mostly Rumplers, and other two-place reconnaissance planes, which now and then sneaked over our lines to take pictures. These were comparatively slow, were vulnerable, like most two-seaters, to an attack from the blind angle of their rear, and they could not attack us, while we could attack them from the best position, and choosing the right moment. We had the weather gauge, as was said in the days of Lord Nelson and sailing-ship battles, and accordingly, it was seldom that a lone two-seater shot down a well-handled attacking fighter. Aside from the Rumplers, an occasional small formation of Albatross, Pfalz, or other somewhat obsolescent German fighters might be discerned at a good distance within their own lines, and difficult to contact. These Germans were probably like us, inexperienced combat flyers, being broken in on a quiet front. On this, at this time, unimportant sector, the Huns were not wasting their crack squadrons, and their veteran flyers.

The latter, including Jagdstaffel Boelke, Jasta Eleven, the Richtofen Flying Circus, and other famous German aviation units, were all down on the blazing Champagne-Marne sectors, where they were desperately battling, suffering heavy losses, but also inflicting heavy casualties, while engaged with our finest squadrons, such as the Escadrille Cigognes of the French, the superb British groups, and our own 1st Pursuit Group. It was down there that Quentin Roosevelt was shot down, and one of our fighter squadrons, in the brief time of a few weeks, needed over one hundred percent pilot replacements to make up combat losses, nor was this especially unusual.

It was about this time or a little later, when a front-line flyer's life expectation, in that sector, averaged about three weeks, that some brain in Washington came out with figures to prove to the public that it was not an especially dangerous duty to serve in the air corps, for the percentage of those killed to those enrolled was very small. This was true, except that the report did not mention that there were some thirty men who remained on the ground to each one that flew, and a good hundred ground-huggers to one pilot on a hot sector. Applied to front-line flyers, especially during a major battle, such percentages meant as much as figuring out a commando's chances on a desperate raid, by using the life expectations of the armed services as a whole, including WAC, base quartermasters, and the paper pushers at general headquarters. As to this, cold figures do not lie, but the Democrats can figure it one way, the Republicans another, and in any form of government, there are always plenty of good jobs for liars.

Although the Richtofen Circus was still manned by the cream of German fighter pilots, Manfred Von Richtofen—the Bloody

"...a ghastly guest..."The Baron Richt ~!" they cried."

Baron, the King Cobra, the Circus Master—had been shot down dead at the Battle of the Somme, some months previous. He fell behind the British lines, and concerning his end there is a tale, which may be more legendary than strictly factual, but which nevertheless represents the truth, from the consequent implications.

Frenchmen, Russians, Canadians, Englishmen—the Baron Von Richtofen had shot down eighty airplanes. He was the idol of Germany, and the most feared of enemy flyers. Finally, surrounded by a superior number of British planes, and under fire from the ground as well, he crashed in his all-red Fokker triplane, within Allied lines. Then respectfully, and in an atmosphere of awe, his body was placed on a broken wing, and carried to the mess hall of the British squadron that had shot him down. There, it was propped up in the seat of honor, at the head of the table, a ghastly guest now white and peaceful looking, who had been the fiery-souled terror of the skies, so short a time before. For a long moment, all the British pilots gazed at their dead enemy, and did not speak a word. Then, one and all rose from their chairs, with glasses in their hands. "A toast," they cried. "To the Baron Richtofen!" So they honored him, who had been their foe.

Legend or fact, this story could not have circulated, except that in our first great war, all flyers felt a certain kinship for each other, and being a front-line flyer was like belonging to an order of warrior aristocracy, that crossed all political boundaries, and set one apart from other men. Members of this vague brotherhood would readily kill one another, if on opposing national sides, but there was little feeling of hate, such as found among other sorts of deadly opponents. It was more like the respect, even liking, that Richard the Lion-Hearted felt towards Saladin, or General Grant's feelings with regards to General Lee at Appomattox Courthouse. Although deadly serious, the gentlemen recognized the gentlemen, and there was a spirit of knightly contest between opposing flyers.

In our second great war, one senses very little, if any, of that sentiment. Military aviation was so much more technical and science-dominated, the numbers engaged were so vastly greater, that the individual enemy was hardly known, except as an anonymous member of a huge organization. In addition, the air war was so much more ruthlessly waged on the civil population that it inspired great mutual hate, and there could be no more knightly game to it. Flying had become the efficient business of mass extermination. There were many heroes and great aces, but the gentleman concept of air warfare had gone to the fabled isle of Avalon, like the knights of the Round Table.

Chapter 22

FIRST PATROL MISSIONS

During that July, more and more pilots trickled into our 13th Squadron, until we had our total complement and, by the end of the month, we were able to put three full flights on general patrolling, and convoy protection missions. In our flight, besides Hobey Baker, our veteran leader, there were Harry "Buck" Freeman, a square-jawed product of Yale, years later a suave bank president, but then a soldier full of strange oaths and pungent, rapid-fire remarks; and Leighton "Laddie" Brewer, another blue-belly from New Haven, a good pilot and companion, although of a bookish, egghead turn, and much too abstemious. There was also Rob Roy Converse, as vague in speech as he was persistent in his pursuits, and Charley Drew, who gained the DSC, but lost an arm to pay for it, and one more was Dave Howe, a good flyer filled with homely Vermont wisdom, who fought well and lived to become an editor and publisher in a hilly region of Vermont, where the cows are said to browse all day, and the very rare and timid Democrats come down to drink at night, together with the deer and the cougar.

Our second flight had also a veteran leader. This was First Lieutenant Maury Jones, a rather huge fellow to fit in a Spad's tight cockpit, and formerly of the Lafayette Flying Corps, where he had accounted for at least one enemy. The leader for our third flight was Lieutenant George Fisher, an old friend from the crossing on the *Manchuria*, who had had combat experience with our 1st Pursuit Group. Later, he was given command of the 49th Squadron, when it became a part of our pursuit group.

Among others of our pilots, were several destined to become decorated aces, such as William "Hank" Stovall of Issoudun days, Murray Guthrie, Frank Hays, and John Seerley. They are listed with their records in air-force histories, but there were also Dick Este, another winner of the DSC, and Guyon Armstrong, Robert "Red" Stiles, and the two Brodies, not brothers, but Big Steve and

Little Steve, as they were called. Besides these, there were George Kull, the friend of countesses, Dick Richards of artistic bent, Henry Riley, a quiet Irishman with a quiet sense of humor, and others, of whom later. This was our company, and it proved a good one before the end, but at this time, with the exception of Captain Biddle and our flight leaders, we were all novices on the lines, and in many cases, with far too few hours of preparation for what lay ahead of us.

In our total advanced flying experience at that date, few of us had had much more than two hundred hours in the air, and some had far less. During all my stay at Mineola, Issoudun, Cazeau, and Orly, I may have totalled 225 hours of flying time, but far too little of this had been formation flying, and above all practice in aerial combat with camera guns, and simulated patrols under hostile conditions, where one might learn the lessons of how to observe, to guard against surprise, to maneuver to the best advantage, which was the most realistic and best flying training for what lay ahead, on the lines.

Of the best and most advanced preparation, I and others had
ours, which was mainly due to so much very bad
that winter at Issoudun, and an insufficiency of
especially those equipped for the most advanced
s, as the school got more supplies and better
uch improved, and later cadres were better
bat duty, but at the time of our arrival at Toul,
s that it was much worse with the British, and
hard pressed for replacements for those lost in
at eighteen-year-old boys, with no more than fifteen
lo flying, were being sent to the front. Of such, some
a very few even became aces, but a great many were
in their first week by crack German fighters, as if they
no more than so many clay pigeons, or sitting ducks. It was often not much more than murder, but what saved the situation, although we did not know it then, was that the Germans were beginning to scrape the bottom of their own barrel of adequately trained pilot replacements.

In our quiet sector of that July and much of August, our two-hour-and-twenty-minute patrolling missions were mainly to watch for, attack and destroy any enemy planes that might venture on or within our lines, or that could be contacted at a reasonable distance within the zone of German occupation. This reasonable distance might take us as far in as the German airdrome at Mars La Tour, or even the railroad center and supply depots at Conflans. This last was a good twenty miles across the lines, and a bit far into the German domain for safety, unless with a good-sized formation of at least six planes. As a general practice, unless on some special assignment, such as protecting a photo-reconnaissance Salmson of the 91st Squadron, whose field was not far from ours, or convoying a flight of day bombers on one of their missions, we rarely ventured beyond the regions of Thiacourt and Vigneulles, some ten miles across the lines, or to the small, three-fingered lake just to the north of them. Even to there and back meant an extra hot and more or less continuous reception from their antiaircraft, as well as the chance of encountering the enemy in much superior numbers. The latter might well be only the second team of German fighters, but who were we as yet? Except for our commander and our flight leaders, we were novices in this game, *bug riders* who had yet to bring in a winner, in the parlance of an incurable *hoss player*.

On the other hand, the German fighters, in this sector, rarely ventured any distance within our lines. Perhaps they were foxy, and figured that we might be enticed within their lines, to be despatched at their advantage, but it appeared that the only Germans who penetrated our area to any depth, during daylight, were the reconnaissance two-seaters. These tried to sneak over at the greatest altitude then possible, and especially very early in the mornings. At night of course, the Hun bombers might come over, to drop their 90-kilo bombs as far as fifty miles within our lines, but they were not our business. We did not fly at night, not having the training nor the equipment for that duty.

Looking back, it has occurred to me, that on the very moonlit nights, we might have taken off, with some chance of locating and turning back the bombers, and possibly bringing one down. On the other hand, our Spads, unlike the slow-settling Voisins used in the defense of Paris, landed very fast, at least at seventy to ninety miles and on our unlit fields, and without any airplane landing lights on the wings, there would have been many a crackup. Towards the last weeks of the war, we had one

American night-fighter squadron in action on the Argonne front. It was equipped with Sopwith Camels, and from accounts it incurred more landing casualties than victories, not having enough time to prove a reasonably successful venture. At that time, it seemed more like suicide club than a threat to enemy bombers, for the Camel, tricky enough in a daylight landing, must have been anything but easy to set down safely at night, on one of those unlit and hillocky billygoat pastures that we were often forced to use as fields, during our last and greatest battle.

After our squadron received its full complement, it would put out three patrols, one for each flight per day. The first patrol would often take off in the first pale gleam before sunrise, and one can still hear the soft voice of "Shorty" Orde, our little orderly, calling, "Lootenant, sir. It's time to get up." Poor Shorty got many an oily boot thrown at his head for doing his duty, but he always got us out of bed, and to breakfast of large, thick and rather flannel-tasting pancakes and coffee, in ample time to take off on our mission.

Our second patrol might be in the late morning, and for our group, one squadron or other would always fly a last patrol of the day, so timed as to end its mission just after sunset. So with each of the four squadrons of our group, flying three patrols a day, we were able to maintain a continuous patrol of our lines, by two flights at a time, for every hour of daylight on our sector. These two flights were usually divided into the high patrol, flying between twelve and eighteen thousand feet, and the low patrol, from six thousand down to skimming the treetops. In this manner, our quiet sector was effectively covered.

Our particular flight's patrol for the day, over, we were part of the time off duty, and for the rest of the time on the *alert*, ready and waiting in the operation tent, and with our planes warmed up on the flight line. During this time, a call might come, if some enemy photo plane had evaded our patrol, and had sneaked across for a picture. Then, there would be a rush and a scramble to take off after the nervy so-and-so, but Heinie was generally so high that he was well across his own lines and far away, before we could gain his altitude. As to climb, the Spad could readily reach ten thousand feet in ten minutes, and about eighteen thousand in a little over twenty. However in that time, Fritz could complete his picture taking, and be back at his own field, drinking beer and reporting to his commander. Once in a while, Heinie would be so intent on watching us climb from below, that he forgot what might be swooping down from above. Then there would be a burst of staccato gun fire, a falling trail of smoke and flame, and one less German.

Off duty in the hot midsummer, late afternoons, we sometimes went swimming in the nearby Moselle River. It had a fairly strong current and many eddies, but it did not seem dangerous. We swam back and forth in its warmish waters, and I can still see Hobey Baker, his muscles rippling under his broad and golden brown shoulders, with the undulations of a leopard, cleaving the water like a torpedo. Then one morning, a pilot's body was found floating in the river.

He was of our group but not of our squadron, and we had known and liked him, and had called him Germany, because his last name was of German extraction. He was genial and easy going, and we greatly regretted what was thought a sad accident. Later, we heard rumors that it was more likely a case of suicide. It was said that "Germany" had been secretly communicating with the enemy; that he had been under some mysterious pressure to spy for them. Our counterintelligence had become aware of this, and Germany had sensed he was about to be arrested. We never heard more about it, but it more or less ended our swimming.

Our 1st Flight's initial experience with the enemy did not produce very satisfactory results, but it gave us some needed lessons, and much to talk over. We were at about fourteen thousand feet and slightly over the lines, somewhere in the vicinity of Pont a Mousson, and we had been flying along, noticing the front line, observation balloons far below, more or less admiring the yellow of the wide mustard fields, and the other colors of the great map before our eyes, and not too nervous over the barrage of German archies, that was our usual greeting in this neighborhood. *Cruumph, cruumph—CRA-AACK!* they would go, showing surrounding big black balls with cores of red fire, but a miss was as good as a mile, even if they bracketed us with fairly close bursts, shook us up pretty roughly now and then, or when an occasional shell fragment would sail through one's wing fabric, with a sound like a *whut*. A few of their shots might be in the form of tracer shells, that left a long trail of smoke like a ship's main hawser dangling after them. Coming with great speed, they might arc over or under us before exploding, making one think of colossal worms or great boa constrictors, reaching and probing into the sky for us, while standing with their tail tips on the ground. These tracers were not often fired, but they were fascinating to see, and one forgot that they could also be dangerous.

Very occasionally, perhaps with one close or direct hit out of several thousand rounds fired, the German archies would bring down a plane, and some of their better batteries, such as one at Arnaville, not far north of Pont a Mousson, were far more accurate than the average. The misfortune of being brought down happened to a pilot named Emerson, a friend of Harvard days. He was flying for an observation squadron when they opened up on him, and he made the great, but understandable mistake of seeking refuge in a cumulus cloud. This gave the Boche gunners his altitude, and they filled the cloud with high explosive, from which he dropped a blazing wreckage.

Taking some evasive action from German archies, we suddenly noticed the yellowish-whitish puffs of French antiaircraft shells mushrooming into the sky at some distance ahead. Knowing this signified a German plane, we made for it, and the guns on both sides now ceased their fire, lest they hit their own, and to allow the frustrated, sweating gunners, almost three miles below, to relax, to sit on their German hams or French *derrieres*, to gaze above, to cheer, or jeer, or grunt wisely at the diversion, like the mob at the arena enjoys the grand parade of the toreadors, and the appearance of the bull. Unfortunately this time, the bull got a draw, for the picadors got in the way of the matador, and the banderillos, of which I was one, ran and hopped about all over the ring, but accomplished nothing.

The bull turned out to be a German Rumpler, a two-place silvery fish of a reconnaissance plane returning from a photo mission. Hobey Baker wagged his wings, giving the signal for attack, then drove on the now alarmed enemy, who was some thousand feet below. Hobey got in one short burst, and he might well have followed and finished the wildly twisting and turning

Rumpler, except that we, the rest of his flight, instead of coolly watching for a good opening, to attack from some other angle, and also guarding from any possible enemy attack from above, all dove excitedly, getting in each other's way, and interfering with Hobey. In this higgledy-piggledy confusion, the German dove away as fast as he could, and our last glimpse caught the Rumpler very far below, almost on the carpet, and like a Ferdinand all but sniffing the bright yellow mustard flowers of the fields, as he skedaddled for home and safety. However, he had left a slight memento. There was a long, white, splintered gouge in one of Hobey's yellow struts, the path of a thirty-caliber bullet, from the rear gunner's Parabellum machine gun.

Of course, there was a remote possibility that the Rumpler had been seriously hit, and had finally crashed in a forced landing. We debated this, but although Lieutenant Sidney Gross, our general handyman, made a special trip to the French battery and the ground troops of that area, and asking many questions, used his most suggestive psychological powers of persuasion, including plying them with the best of cognac, he could get no evidence of our confirmation from any witness. In this case, the Rumpler most probably escaped, with no more than a few holes in his fabric, and a rather airsick rear gunner. However, we had good reason to believe that our squadron got this same fellow, not long later.

Chapter 23

CHAMPAGNE AMID THE RUBBLE

Lieutenant Earl Richards, one of our pilots, having some talent as an artist, had skillfully drawn the insignia for our squadron, on which we had decided, after discussing various ideas. Our emblem was Death, in the guise of a grim skeleton running down the foe, and swinging a big scythe. A metal stencil was cut for this, and it was to be painted on the fuselage of each Spad, for the double purpose of distinguishing our 13th Squadron from other squadrons, and to add to our general *esprit de corps*, in being marked with a distinctive emblem. Other squadrons had their respective emblems, one of the first and most famous being the 94th's *Hat In The Ring*. This was the beginning of this form of heraldry in our infant air corps, although it was not new on the front. The French may have started the idea. Certainly the emblem of their famous escadrille, *Les Cigones*, the Storks, the squadron of Guynemer, had long been familiar to all flyers. The Germans, likewise, had their insignias, but in that war, most were the work of individuals belonging to the outfit in question, and were, to my mind, more appropriate, if more unprofessional in technique, than the usual Disneyish and rather cutie-pie insignia on our warplanes in World War II.

We now had our own coat of arms, but there was a more or less unwritten law, that no fighter squadron should paint its emblem on its planes until the squadron had officially accounted for a minimum of five enemy airplanes. Now, by the middle of August, we had four official victories to our credit, and we had been anxiously hoping for the qualifying fifth for over a week, but with no results that could be confirmed as certain. There had been either no Boche to shoot down, or else we could not get close to them, for they seemed to be staying well within their own lines, or they were very cunning and evasive. As to the latter, there was one predawn visitor, who was especially exasperating, and seemingly beyond catching. This German was taking pictures with impunity, and figuratively thumbing his supercilious Prussian nose at the entire 2nd Pursuit Group. This was not to be tolerated, and our own commanding officer decided to put an end to it.

Captain Biddle rose when even the French chickens were sound asleep, and well before the sun had risen, he was some nineteen thousand feet above our field, waiting and watching for the expected visitor. Perhaps a half hour later in the first rosy streak of dawn, he noticed the white puffs of French antiaircraft shells greeting an enemy plane, and he spotted a tiny telltale silhouette, sharp and black against the reddening east. This was the quarry, the Hun early bird out to get his worm, in the shape of pictures of Allied installations, signs of troop movements, and other data of interest to German intelligence. This Boche was playing it right; a sneak across at high altitude, before anyone else was up, a series of snaps with his camera, then hi-ho and home again, *mit nein schweinhund Americans shooding der bullets from der behind. Ach, Mein Gott! It vas so easy.*

However in war, as in other games of chance, most men have only so much good fortune, for the powers who may smile on mortals and grant them small or great success, in the end become bored with them, as they became bored with even mighty Ceasar, and destiny's garbage can is always quite handy. Then the fates have only to find a suitable agent.

In this minor case, it was as if some celestial adviser, perhaps the wise shade of Benjamin Franklin had said, "What we need is no more than a good Philadelphia lawyer, to settle this little business. And gentlemen, we have just the man needed, and right handy."

If this happened, and what thrice anointed with holy oil of a Ph.D., even of Harvard or a Berkeley Bear, can prove otherwise, Captain Biddle did not fail them. With the skill and experience gained from the Stork Escadrille and four victories to his credit, our commanding officer maneuvered his Spad into the right position, and then fell, like a ton of bricks, on the big, black, unsuspecting Rumpler. Attacking from the blind angle under the tail, in the classical manner, he killed the gunner-observer with his first burst, on which the German pilot turned his head in wild surprise, and headed downwards for home. From this he was soon discouraged, for Captain Biddle gave him a couple of warning bursts, first on one side, then on the other, and it was so evident that he had the Rumpler at his mercy that the German pilot decided to surrender. In slow spirals he came down and landed not far from the city of Toul and well within our lines. This was the fifth victory for our squadron, and also the fifth victory for Captain Biddle, making him an ace, and of this *coup* one of our sergeants, a chief mechanic, said to me, "Well, that's the kind of a commanding officer for men to have, by heck!" and he crossed his legs, for emphasis, in a sideways kick, like a way-down-east farmer of New England.

A few hours later, we went to Toul to inspect the Rumpler, which had been brought there by the French, and set up in a city square, where it had been quickly souvenir-stripped, in spite of guards to protect it. We stopped close by, and a young French lieutenant walked up to us, and said, "*Regardez.* You see that plane. I brought it down, last night, myself." He then regarded us with his alleged exploit, while we listened and let him run on, until he finally stopped.

Then Captain Biddle very quietly said, "What you say, *mon lieutenant*, is very strange, because I shot that Rumpler down myself, at five o'clock this morning." The imposter quickly left, while the gathered crowd laughed at him.

Captain Biddle having made the select company of aces, and our 13th Squadron having won the right to wear its war emblem, this called for a little celebration in the form of a banquet, but in a more civilized setting than our bare mess hall. That same night, we held it at the Stanislas Hotel in Nancy, which was less than some ten miles distant. Our staff car, a Cadillac touring model, and a light Fiat truck brought all of us pilots and ground officers to the beautiful and famous Place Stanislas, where our elegant hotel was located.

There was, on the second floor front of the Hotel Stanislas, a very special room for banquets of the *grands choux*, the big cabbages, as the maitre d'hotel designated the local nabobs, civic fat cats, rich and prominent poohbahs of the countryside, or visiting VIPs who might be there for some occasion or other. This room was rather cozy than large, but the walls were creamy white, inlaid with fluted arabesques of gold, and there was a chandelier of pendant crystals, and rich velvet curtains of purple to veil the light from the great French windows that opened on a balcony. It was the type of room in which Louis XV, the royal lecher supreme, might have supped stark naked with his latest mistress, but it was here that we big cabbages, pilots and gentlemen, including our own ground officers, gathered to eat, drink and make merry, and to honor our commanding officer, who had honored us in his latest victory.

There was soup of course, and the usual tasty French concoctions, all so smothered under sauces, that absolute identification was something for only a Brillat-Savarin to determine, and there were cocktails and champagne—gallons of it! The corks popped, and a great silver bowl went round and round, from hand to hand, and lip to lip, while the golden liquid electricity seeped into our blood and imagination, like the nectar of Zeus and Hera must have reacted in some cloud-wrapped roaring feast of the Olympians, ten thousand feet above the snorting chariot horses of the Thessalian plains. This made us feel like Alexander at a great victory feast. He would have known! Senators, tycoons, eminent scientists and savants, all you middle-aged fat cats of America, do you know what it is to feel like a front-line pilot, and young?

Round and round went the celestial silver bowl, and we sang:

Mademoiselle from Armentieres,
Parlez-vous;
Mademoiselle from Armentieres,
Parlez-vous;

Mademoiselle from Armentieres
Peddled herself for souvenirs,
Rinky-dinky, parlez-vous.

And also:

K-K-K-Katy, bee-yoo-tiful Katy,
You're the girl we all adore,
And when the moonlight shines over the pigpen,
We'll meet you by our cowshed door.

And likewise:

Keep your head down, Fritzie boy,
Keep your head down, Fritzie boy,
Way last night,

In the pale moonlight,

We saw you,
We saw you—
You were mending your broken wire,

When we opened up with rapid fire,
If you want to see your father in the Fatherland,
Keep your head down, FRITZIE BOY!

Besides such songs and more, we had stories and tales, so satirical and droll that they would have made a Rabelais roll on the golden floor, to the amazement of the angels, but the most memorable was when Red Stiles arose, facing us, and gravely asked, "Why am I like a stagecoach?"—a question with an answer, that might be, most appropriately, given from the speaker's rostrum of many a congress in this world, where so many pompous dullards, together with a few bigots and plain rascals, are in seats of power.

Then suddenly in the midst of this, there came the long drawn siren's howl of the alert, and soon after, the deep growling, harmonic double beats of the nearing bombers, as they followed the dusty white roads, and clearly saw the city, its every street and building a pattern of light and shadow, but all sharply etched and distinct, like a huge cameo under the full moon sky. At this, we heard the alarmed scurry of feet in the outside hallway, and our waiter, his face drawn and ashen gray with fear, begged to be excused to hide in the cellar, but NO!

We locked the door, pocketed the key, and made the cringing minion serve the rest of the dinner, while the almost bottomless silver bowl went round and round, amidst remarks and roars of laughter, that could not be drowned out by the continuous roar and rattle of untold machine guns, blazing and frantically fired by Frenchmen, from rooftops and enplacements all about. In a mad way, all this sounded like a kind of music to our ears, just as the clash of spears and swords, the shouts and screams, and the galloping hooves of war horses outside the thick palace walls may have sounded to the wine-high roisterers at Belshazzar's Feast.

The first bomb fell with a crash, and our waiter cried out in alarm, but "Garçon! Open up another magnum," we howled at him. The heavens now sounded like a hum of giant bees, and then across a street, not sixty feet away, four stories crashed in rubble, as a huge torpedo exploded with an ear-bursting roar. Windows flew into splintering fragments and glass daggers, street cobblestones flew through the air, and the city was ablaze in a dozen places, but in our banquet hall, the crystal chandelier only swayed a bit, and someone remarked, "Well, fellows. That sounded like a pretty good one."

There now came a lull in the raid, and we hustled out into the street, to see a kind of Gotterdammerung of huge fires and blazing buildings, on all sides of us. A prim MP, solemn as a funeral director, now came out of an abri and said, "All of you, sirs, take shelter. This air raid is not yet over."

To this answered Jim McAteer, a pilot from Arkansas, where they are used to tornados, river floods, hailstones as big as baseballs, and other things that either make a farmer curse God and quit, or become a calm and philosophical fellow, "An air raid, did you say? Why, man dear, why should I give a tiny damn? Can't you see I'm wearing my tin hat?"

The raiders were now about to return, but our car and our truck were intact, and away we went, through streets littered with bricks, gaping holes, and tangled telephone wires, and out into the open fields on our way to our barracks. The late night wind blew warm and moist in our faces, and in a few more hours, we would be up again on patrol. However, we had had a pleasant interlude. It had been far from a dull dinner.

Chapter 24

ROUTINE LIFE IN A QUIET SECTOR

During August, the war had seemingly, to us, been going on since time began, and our days of peace, and our old American way of life had become like a vague and half-forgotten dream. War had become the normal way of life, a life with a full expectation of an early and inevitable death, but a life with its daily routine, its chores and duties, its fun, its satisfactions and disappointments, just as in any kind of life and business. A patrol over the lines had become no more than a businessman's day at the office, or a sales call in peacetime, and the war might well go on forever. This was the general feeling, and it was reflected in the ironical reference to their prospects, by the enlisted men, with their biting slogan, "Join the army. A dollar a day. A million days, a million dollars!" and also by their cynical song concerning sergeants, generals, and such:

Oh, if you want to know where the sergeants are,
I know where they are, I know where they are,
If you want to know where the sergeants are,
I know where they are,
Down in the deep dug out!

I saw them, I saw them,
Down in the deep dug out,
Way down in the deep DUG OUT!

Oh if you want to know where the generals are,
I know where they are, I know where they are,
If you want to know where the generals are,
I know where they are,
Back in the S.O.S.

I saw them, I saw them,
Back in the S.O.S.,
Way back IN THE S.O.S.!

As for us pilots, rather cynical too in certain matters, we read the casualty lists in the *Stars and Stripes*, and it seemed as if only privates and lieutenants were doing the dying. "Oh, here's actually a colonel," someone might say, after glancing over the latest grim column of names. "Yeah, I saw that," someone else would reply. "But pshaw! The bastard's only severely wounded." And so it went, for the front had become our way of life, and although it might have its depressing moments, no other way of life, for us, was considered thinkable.

During the course of that July and much of August, a pilot's job in our 2nd Pursuit Group was not arduous. What with being temporarily grounded, for a routine overhauling of his plane's engine, and engines had to be completely overhauled after forty to sixty hours of operation, with immediate replacements seldom available, most pilots did not average more than five missions a week, a total of some eleven to twelve hours of combat flying, and seldom over fifty hours, in a month of patrolling missions. Off-duty time was spent in eating and sleeping, playing baseball with other squadrons, swimming in the river, bicycling to Toul, and perhaps visiting some other, nearby field, such as the one at Gondrevil-Sur-Moselle, which was the location of the Salmson-equipped 91st Photo-Reconnaissance Squadron. This squadron had for its emblem a Knight Chasing The Devil, taken from the editorial masthead of the old, original *Life* magazine, and among its pilots were George C. Kenney, our future air commander-in-chief in the Pacific, and Moss Gilbert, who was another old friend from prep school days. Seeing the latter was a bit of the old school tie and that sort of bosh, but it was sometimes a great relief to talk about old times, and not just the events of the present.

The rest of our time, when not patrolling, was spent on alert duty in the operations tent, where Sergeant Waller heated water for our coffee over a blow torch, and Hobey Baker might read and regale us with choice chapters from *Dere Mable*. This was the army's funny book of that war, and it was spun from the ribald imagination of Edward Streeter, a classmate at college and later, author of *The Father of the Bride*, who completely refuted the general belief that no banker ever sees anything to laugh at except, and with a true satanical, rising crescendo of an insane cackle, while foreclosing on some poor widow's mortgage.

Sitting around in the tent, during the hours we were on alert duty, we sometimes passed the time with various loose discussions, such as war aims, what we were fighting for, politics, religion, and similar subjects known as bull, all pretty vague in our minds. As to why and what we were fighting for, I do not think that most of us, being pretty young, really knew. We knew that the French knew, since it was obvious they had to kick the Germans out of France, and the British had a good reason, since if France collapsed, England and the Empire stood a good chance of being next. To the Frenchman and the Britisher, the war was to defend his homeland, institutions, family, freedom and all that, and his fighting was not only a duty, it made sense. But why were we fighting? The answer to that, few of us reflected on. With most of us, we were flying and fighting, because our country had gone to war, and right or wrong, it was our country, just like Stephen Decatur had said on a long ago occasion. On top of that, this mixing of war and aviation was a marvelous adventure for a young American to undertake.

That was pretty close to it, for in spite of the talk and the writings to the contrary, by a lot of eminent names in high places, very few of us ever believed that the United States had been, or was now, in the slightest danger from Germany, just so long as there were three thousand miles of ocean, and our navy was reasonably prepared. Of course, President Wilson had proclaimed that we were going to war, *to make the world safe for democracy*, but that was a pretty abstract reason to begin with, and it never did pack the emotional punch of *saving the holy sepulcher from the infidels*, which sparked the Crusades. Besides, to me, and a lot of us from north of the Mason-Dixon line, this democracy stuff had considerable dubiousness connected with it. I had been born and raised in a hotbed of Republicanism, and democracy seemed to have some guilt by association with Democrats, who mostly lived in outlandish parts of Boston, bounced rocks off the noggins of *Black Republicans and Enemies of his Holiness* who might visit there by mistake, and who, if good policemen and excellent prize fighters, were not otherwise quite respectable. Of course, this was pure bias which, incidentally, in some guise or other, is found in all men, even the most blatant, bleeding heart liberals, but outside of that, most of us thought that our country's participation in the war was pretty much like a romantic deed of medieval knight errantry, like going to the rescue of a damsel imprisoned by an ogre, when she was no close relative, she had no money, and there was no good reason for the trouble and expense, except that one wanted to bust the big bum's beezer, and the hell with it! Perhaps this is all wrong, but one doubts that American soldiers, in that war, ever had the emotional drive of the Athenian hoplites at Marathon, the British seamen at the repulse of the Spanish Armada, or the Union army at Gettysburg. Those gallant warriors were fighting, literally for home and mother—mother, not Mom and the rest of that baloney!—while we seemed to be engaged for a purely abstract ideal, although since we had signed up for the team, it was up to us to give it a real old college try, and cross the goal line, no matter what the consequences.

Religion also might be discussed, as a natural. Our particular group of flyers ranged all the way from the coldest roast cut of Boston, high church Episcopalianism to the much warmer atmosphere of the American Catholic Church, but although we all believed in some form of God, we had the vaguest of ideas about Him, except that He was, somehow on our side, and would take care of us. Of course, the Germans considered that He was on their side, and since the Bible says that man is made in the image of God—the converse to this, which must follow that argument, is hardly complimentary to the Deity, if one really reflects on all the implications—the Germans had made God in their own image. They called Him *Gott.*

Gott was everywhere. He was not only in heaven and on earth, but He was on all their spike helmets, and the brass belt buckles of their uniforms. These were all inscribed with a *Gott Mit Uns*, at which the British jeered, as they made the obvious pun across the intervening, narrow no-man's-land, but which put it down in writing to the Germans, that Gott and the Kaiser were in close partnership, although who was the senior member of the firm was not quite sure.

Unlike William Blake's etching of the Supreme Being, in the form of an old gentleman in a night shirt, with a long flowing, white beard and benign hands, floating lazily like a cloud in the sky, Gott was much more of a toughie. He was big and decidedly hefty, and He was garbed like something out of Wagnerian grand opera, helmet with wings, shirt of steel mail, spear, sword, and a hammer like a hard rock miner's doublejack, to really browbeat the opposition. Outside of that, he had a voice like a Bull of Bashan, and Signor Gatti-Casazza, then head of the New York Met, would have probably given Gott his walking papers, for bellowing off-key and ruining the performance. That was Graff Von Gott, or at least, that is the way that American and British cartoonists depicted Him.

As for our side, the French had *le bon Dieu*, who was very *bon*, but if in the true French image, also pretty economical. We liked and admired the French, but we did think that they could squeeze a franc with a grip unbelievable, and that compared to them the Scots were lavish, and the Jews as profligate as drunken sailors. The British had their own Church of England version, the Right Honorable, Sir Almighty God M.P., Who had kept a stiff upper lip and would see the empire through, and who was in all ways the epitome of good form and high purpose, although occasionally a bit stupid. On the other hand, we Americans, coming as everybody knew from *God's Own Country*, must have really had God on our side. *Gawd Almighty*, as he was democratically referred to by those who knew him best, was a lot of things—clever inventer, dynamic salesman, Wall Street wizard, and mighty good in all sports, a real he-man, one hundred percent American type Jehovah, with the real American look, whatever that is. The only trouble was, that the *Lawd*, to use one of his other appellations, did not seem to know the time o' day about international matters, and He never could learn, according to some critics. Of course, all the above manifestations were but caricatures of the chief tribal deity of the various nations engaged, as depicted in *Punch*, *Life*, *La Vie Parisienne*, and such, for a visualization of the ultimate supreme power and creator of the universe was and remains, as impossible as visualizing the fourth dimension, although higher mathematics and post-Newtonian physics seem to point the way that both exist. However, we pilots had too many other things to worry about, to worry about how God might look, and on our front, chaplains seemed as rare as white blackbirds, and a friend, a Jewish pilot told me, with a laugh, that he had been in France a whole year, but had never seen a rabbi.

In spite of the relative inaction of our Toul sector, during that

July and the first half of August, our squadron had managed to account for some seven or eight victories over the enemy, and had not lost any of our planes in combat. Of course, there had been some close calls for most of us, and not a few bullet holes and shell fragment tears to be patched into wing and fuselage fabric, after many a mission, but no pilot had been even nicked, nor any of our planes forced down during that period. To be sure, most of our victories had been over the two-place Rumpler reconnaissance planes, which were considered somewhat *cold meat*, since they were usually unescorted, and we always had the advantage of speed, the choice of time and place to engage, and usually superior numbers. It was true that an incautious approach to attack might end badly, since they had good gunners and excellent Spandau and Parabellum machine guns, but these were useless in the blind angle, and a close burst from there generally doomed them. The Rumplers' chief safety lay in keeping a sharp lookout, especially above, and hightailing for Bochiedom when we were still a good ways off. We also had a few brushes with the few enemy fighters that appeared in this somnolent sector. Most of these were the somewhat outdated Pfalz and Albatross scouts, but there were very few of the superior Fokkers. It was a maiden encounter with some of the latter that put me in my first really close quarters.

I had been flying tail-man-high, a sort of rear guard, rover position in our six-plane patrol, when emerging from the top regions of a huge cumulus cloud, I lost contact with my flight, and was alone. Looking around to find them, I became aware of a big black Rumpler not far ahead and about one thousand feet below, in a most favorable position for me to attack. Also, he did not seem to see me, but flew in a straight and level manner, as if no danger were threatening. This was an open invitation to go down and shoot.

Without a moment's reflection that this Rumpler might not be so easy as he looked, and neglecting to look in back and above, I started down on him. Then, the blue sky was suddenly threaded with filmy white traceries, things that resembled golden oranges flashed and streaked past my plane, there were sounds like *wha-wha-wha-wha*, and I turned my head to see the goggled, owl-eyed, smoke blackened, triumph-grinning face of a Hun pilot nosing down, and not much more than fifty feet behind my tail. Here was Death all in black leather, Dracula in a helmet ready to pounce, and not far behind and also diving for the kill, where three other Fokkers.

Most aerial combat, since everything happens so quickly, leaves, at best, a blurred and, probably somewhat inaccurate recollection, but I do remember jerking around, much as some show-off rider might jerk around the head of his saddle horse, and sharply peaking up to spray a burst at this attacker, causing him to swerve, and zoom away for a moment. Then my engine seemed to labor, my all but vertically nosed up Spad went soft in the thin, sixteen-thousand-foot air, and I was in a spin, straight down with full motor. Down I spun, since it seemed now the only thing to do, and dead below, the tiny ruined steeple of the village church at Flirey stood like a little rotten tooth at the hub of a turning map. Then, for some unknown reason, the enemy suddenly left me, and aware for the first time of my roaring and wildly vibrating engine, I throttled it. I came out of the spin and dive at ten thousand feet, and on landing at our field, it was found that the flying wires had been stretched several inches from the strains of the dive, and that my wings had come very close to leaving me. However, the whole business had been a good lesson.

This Rumpler had been a deliberate trap, set and baited for unwary attackers, while its escort of Fokkers lay in wait, well above and hidden by the rays of the sun. It was an old, well-known and classic trick, and I had only been a bit more lucky than many another green man sucked into it. A few days later, Charley Drew had a similar encounter, perhaps with these same fellows, but he escaped in a much more brilliant manner. Attacked by two Fokkers from above, one bullet smashed his mirror, and another snipped off the top button center of his helmet, as neatly as if done by his mother's sewing scissors. At this Charley, normally a quiet and gentle fellow, got so raging mad that he swore to get them both. This he did, and won the DSC for doing it.

There was one odd thing about my adventure. In the course of the spin, with the Fokkers' tracer bullets still crisscrossing around me, I had felt so certain of death that all fear departed, and a feeling of anticipation and also great curiosity replaced it. Once safe again, I had a strange feeling of disappointment, for it seemed as if I had experienced a glimpse of something unknown but not fearsome, like a fleeting peek, through a slightly drawn curtain, into a new but highly interesting world. If this is death, it is but a new adventure of the soul, a crossing of the barrier that encloses our five senses, into a fourth or fifth, or other dimensional world or worlds. All this possibility seems to be hinted at in the highest mathematics, which appear to be unfolding a new and greater theology, as it advances in its concepts.

Concerning the relative capabilities of the Spad 13 Model and the Fokker D-7, the best German fighter up to the Armistice, there have been many opinions by more qualified flyers, but it has seemed to me that the Fokker gave its pilot a wider angle of vision, especially dead ahead, and that it had a quicker turning maneuverability than the Spad, while the latter had a trifle more speed, had a somewhat higher ceiling of climb, and was of much more rugged construction to withstand the most testing strains in the maneuvers of combat. As to the latter, one American flyer was officially credited with two victories, because on sharply pulling up from a very steep dive, where two Fokkers had been chasing and shooting at his rear, his Spad kept its rather necessary wings, while the pursuing Fokkers, following suit, snapped theirs off, and that was the end of them, thus proving the old adage, of more than one way to skin a cat.

As to climb, our first flight once encountered an equal patrol of Fokkers. We were both flying in the same direction, parallel to the front lines, and at the same altitude. The day being clear and without clouds, we saw each other at the same time, and there was no chance of a surprise attack. There soon followed a climbing match, each side trying to outclimb the other, with the hopes of finally holding the advantage for attack. Up and up we jacked each other, until the air felt thin and wobbly, and it seemed impossible to climb any higher without falling into a spin. However, we just managed to squeeze a little more altitude out of our straining engines, and to get a few hundred feet above the Fokkers. At this, we turned on them, and drove them like a herd of deer chased by dogs, for a good fifteen miles into German territory, and down to a low altitude, where increasingly hot fire from the ground, and likely attack from far superior numbers, alerted to our presence, made us abandon the pursuit with uncertain results from it. On this encounter, our altimeters registered an extreme top of close to twenty-two thousand feet, which must have been, from all accounts, close to a record for combat altitude in that war.

There is no question, but that we had climbed our Spads about as high as they could go, but that was high enough to outclimb the Fokkers. Doing this, we had experienced no discomfort, nor any apparent impairment of faculties from the altitude, although we had breathed the thin air as it was, and without benefit of any auxiliary oxygen. It had been pretty cold in those open cockpits, however, and several of us landed with frostbitten cheek bones and noses.

Although our 13th Squadron had not yet lost any planes in combat, our 2nd Pursuit Group had suffered a few losses, and one of them of a very brilliant pilot. This was Lieutenant David Putnam of the 139th Squadron, who had previously flown with the French, and had a confirmed total of at least ten victories to his credit. He flew a Spad, painted bright red like a fire engine, as if to invite the enemy to meet him, and he delighted in ranging far across the lines, and often alone. Then one morning, he did not return. Surprised by a far greater number, he had been shot down and killed, although his sole companion managed to escape. We also had some casualties, but these had come from bombing.

We had been frequently bombed on clear nights, but with no more ill results than a few crater holes in our field, which were readily and rapidly filled in, and did little to hinder our operations. Then one moonlight night, a ninety-kilo bomb made a direct hit on one of our enlisted men's barracks, seriously wounding two fine, valuable men, expert mechanics. Fortunately, this bomb, on coming through the red tile roof, had exploded on striking a stout steel girder of the roof's construction, and its jagged fragments, flying upwards, missed the probable killing of some twenty men sleeping beneath it.

The countryside around our locality was honeycombed with empty, concrete-lined trenches, dugouts, tunneled hillsides that ended in vast caverns for the storage of ammunition, which had been prepared by the French or their troops to fall back on, in case of any major enemy drive in that sector. Therefore, after the bomb hit our barrack, almost everyone, except Lieutenant Brewer, who seemed to fear death much less than missing his incurable and mighty dull habit of nine o'clock sacktime, took to seeking the safety of some French abri on raid nights, or else to strolling down the road a bit until the fireworks were over.

The latter was sometimes a bit like leaving the frying pan to jump into the fire. Charley Drew and I tried it one night, but the Germans in their Gothas—"an unusually dumb bunch of Krauts," as Charley later summed up their mentalities—mistook the half-mile distant crossroad where we stood, for the crossroad where our squadron was located, and dumped their entire load on us. Naturally, we had not expected this compliment to our importance, but we did hear the warning whistles of the bombs in time to fall flat in the roadside gutter. Then the heavens lit up, clods of earth rained all around us, and the earth trembled as in an earthquake.

"Shake hands with living dead men," we greeted our companions at breakfast, for a daylight inspection of our crossroad had revealed eight craters, grouped around and all very close to the spot where even our front teeth still marked the dust, and these craters were a good twenty feet across, and some fifteen feet deep in the soil of the farmland. It had been a magnificent display of force, but somewhat a waste of good ammunition, our friends reflected, for two rather inexperienced front-line flyers were hardly that much of a military objecive. Our adventure did prove one thing. The German bombers depended on the reflection of the white, dusty roads to pinpoint their targets. Except on the brightest nights, they could not make out buildings.

Chapter 25

THE BATTLE OF ST. MIHIEL

Ours had indeed been a typical, so-called quiet sector for many months, but towards the latter part of August, there were many signs that something new was up. In the daytime, the roads were empty as usual, but at night along the dusty, poplar-lined highway that bounded our field, there were plenty of sounds and dimly seen sights to arouse any man's curiosity. With the dark, there would now come a never ending, shuffling, scraping tread of untold feet, the grind and creak of steel-hooped wheels on a hard surface, the hangle of harness chains, the snorts of straining horses, and the slow, plodding clop-clop of iron shod hooves. Added to this would come the passing, infernal clanking of a tank, the occasional loud bray of a mule, and the sight of an endless file of dark columns, revealing the shadowy outlines of guns, the dim silhouettes of innumerable, slow moving caissons, trucks, wagons, staff cars, ambulances, motorcycle sidecars, and above all and everything, men, men, men; men hiking, scuffling up the dust with their heavy booted feet, cursing softly, muttering low; fifty thousand men during all of one night, over two hundred thousand during the next few, perhaps half a million men in a week or more; men, horses, cannons, vehicles moving up, moving up, moving north, moving without a gleam of light, even the red spark of a cigarette in the dark night, moving up to occupy those same lines that had been so lightly garrisoned until now.

Something was now surely on, and even to the dullest minds, perhaps even to the long, lean simpleton who waited on us at mess, it was plain that a big pot was being filled, that a hot fire was being prepared, and that some very big dish, seasoned with some very hot sauce, was being cooked up for the consumption of the enemy. Apparently the Boches were also becoming aware that something extraordinary was afoot, for their planes became much more numerous, and their fighters bolder. Concerning all this, one evening after mess, Captain Biddle spoke to us.

"Gentlemen," he said, "we've had a pleasant time these past two months or so. We've gotten to know each other well; we've had some fine Boche-hunts, and knocked some down; we've had fun with baseball games, and dances with the Red Cross girls in Toul. All that's been fine, but it's all over now. The show starts very soon, and it will mean two to three missions a day for every man of you, and most probably no more easy meat in the form of unprotected Rumplers. Some very tough Germans have, or will soon arrive, and you'll find plenty of trouble over the lines. From now on, there will be no leaves, but plenty of long and trying hours, and you must, above all, always remember to stay with your flight, and to keep good watch above and in back, if you want to stay alive. All of you are to be ready, and down at the flight line, at dawn tomorrow. That is all, and now let us have a little song."

It had been our regular custom to drink wine or beer each evening, after supper in our mess hall, and to listen to Cy Presley, one of our pilots, tickle the ivories of an ancient and battered piano, and bang out all sorts of our favorite songs. Cy had once been a student of theology, but he had quit that to become a steeplejack, explaining that it was nearer to God than a pulpit, and he was tall and slim, as befitting his former occupation, and with great hands, that could easily span an octave and two keys besides. He could play any sort of an instrument, banjo, trumpet, piano, flute, sonorous organ, twanging jew's-harp, and once we all but petitioned Captain Biddle not to let him cross the lines, lest he be killed and his music with him. He was not only a pilot and one of us, but he was also our harpist, jester, minstrel, our equivalent of TV after dinner, in those days when even radio did not exist. He now struck the keys, and we gathered around and sang:

> Today is Monday;
> Monday, bullets,
> Oh you dirty Germans, we wish the same to you!

And in the same vein, on through every day of the week, where the last verse was:

> Today is Sunday;
> Monday, bullets,

Tuesday, archies,
Wednesday, bombers,
Thursday, Fokkers,
Friday, onions,
Saturday, hospital,
Sunday, graveyard,
Oh, you dirty Germans, we wish the same to you!

The onions, mentioned in the verse, were not edible, but were our name for a kind of orange gleaming, incendiary chain shot, perhaps fired from a mortar, which the Germans threw at us, when we were at low altitude in the vicinity of their captive observation balloons. They would come up in a string of some half dozen or so, but I never heard of their hitting any of us. We had other songs too, such as "Tipperary," and that ribald song of the British infantry, which began with a "I don't want to j'ine the aaarmy, I don't want to go to war, Gor blime!" and so forth, with many unprintable but much to the point reasons for not joining the army, especially the *po're bloody hinfantree*, which had known war, if any service ever had. Several various songs over, we all rose for the last one:

As we sit 'neath the sounding rafters,
The walls around are drear,
And the echo aloft of our laughter
Makes it seem if the dead were here.

Forgot by the land that bore us,
Betrayed by this land, we find,
That our bravest have gone on before us,
And now we are left here, behind.

So, stand by your glasses steady,
This world is a world of lies,
We have drunk to the dead, all ready,
Here's a health to the next man who dies!

This song, not very accurately quoted from a poem by Rudyard Kipling, and said to have been inspired by the fate of some hopelessly cutoff British garrison, during the great Indian

Mutiny, had become our favorite to end an evening session, since it seemed to fit the atmosphere and the mood. Many, in that bleak mess hall of ours, were going to die before long, but the next morning dawned stormy, with hard driving rain, and strong winds, up to fifty miles an hour or more in the harder gusts. Ordinarily on such a day, there would have been no flying, but 1st Army intelligence was very anxious for a late report as to what the Germans were up to, and two of our pilots, Dick Este and Harry Freeman, were assigned to fly a special reconnaissance. Flying very low under the black nimbus and the ragged, racing scud of the gale, they crossed the lines at an altitude of fifty to three hundred feet, and barely skimmed the summit of Mont Sec, which the Germans had converted into a heavily fortified anchor for the west of our sector.

So flying, they covered our entire length of front and well into enemy held territory, but they saw little or nothing on the all but deserted and rain soaked roads, and the seemingly almost vacant network of German trenches. Over Mont Sec, they did see two Germans, both carrying pails, who gaped upwards with stares of amazement on their rain-glistening peasant faces, as our two Spads, coming to them suddenly from nowhere, roared over their heads, almost brushing the treetops.

That was about all there was to see and report, but it was significant. The Germans were not, that day, bringing in troops to reinforce the sector, nor were they evacuating the area to shorten their lines. They were all in dugouts or shelters of some kind, and they were either ready and determined to resist a drive, or they were not yet expecting any great attack. Whatever the Germans thought that day, that same night our guns started roaring without letup, and the entire horizon north of our field was like an aurora, ablaze with light. This was the crashing overture for the show. The curtain was about to go up, and *Black Jack*, our impresario, was about to present to the Allied world, his first great performance, the Battle of St. Mihiel.

The opening day of the attack on the great salient of St. Mihiel was dark and misty to drizzling, with swirling gusts and fierce blasts of damp wind that scattered the dead leaves, and bent and swayed the quivering tops of the long columns of roadside poplars. Overhead, the ragged scud of clouds was less than a thousand feet, and all of us, all three flights, went up and over the lines, with instructions to watch and ground-strafe the roads leading north from the front, especially the ones towards Thiacourt, about ten miles over. Already, we had heard that penetration by our ground troops had progressed well beyond the initial objectives; that the obtusely angled German salient, where the River Meuse swept past the town of St. Mihiel, was being pushed at this hinge, and straightened out; that Mont Sec, for years the formidable bastion of the German defense line in this sector, had been evacuated. Our first big drive was going very well, and it seemed that the Boches had either been taken by surprise, or that they had not been able to afford the troops for needed reinforcements.

Our flight flew low, from a few hundred to a thousand feet over the rain-drenched woods, the bleak and muddy fields, the little ruined villages such as Flirey and Seicheprey, and across the four-mile wide, cratered and barbwired desert zone of dugouts and trenches. Much of the German side of this had been blasted to pieces by our concentrated artillery fire and, except for mopping-up parties of our own troops, it was now a mere maze of lifeless warrens. Beyond this, in a world of brown mud and gray sodden fields, larger and smaller groups in olive drab uniforms, topped by our tin hats, popped in and out like gophers from their holes, and from under the covering slope of some slight hill, or from the hiding border of a wood, the mouths of field artillery guns winked and blinked when they fired like, the little red eyes of angry ferrets.

From our altitude of only a few hundred feet, all below looked so tiny, that it did not seem to be a real battle going on. There were small, round, black puffs from bursting shells, the red wink and gas rings from gun muzzles, and crawling, wallowing trucks, well scattered, plodding bodies of troops, horses tugging light guns, but everything in miniature. It was a war of tiny toys, inch-high lead soldiers, not men of stature, flesh and blood playing their parts on this rain-sodden, drab relief map, as we swept over it. We were like boys viewing a battle of bugs and beetles, and we felt without danger, in a world apart from it.

Then near Beaumont, and still some distance from the vague and constantly shifting front lines, a sound like the ick-click-click of clacking typewriters could be heard over the roar and beat of our engines and propellers, thin smoke trails crisscrossed about our flight, and something pinged on my wing fabric, as more of the clicking bullets flew past. This was rifle and machine gun fire from the ground, from our own troops, who had not been sufficiently instructed to distinguish between Allied and enemy airplanes, and who in some cases seemed to care very little. In fact, until the war's end, the general idea of many of our American infantry units, was to fire first at any low-flying plane, and to ask questions afterwards. Part of this attitude came from an unreasoning, but somewhat understandable hatred of all planes, aroused by having been bombed and strafed from the air by the enemy, and part of it stemmed from the confusion concerning our wing markings and national insignia.

Back in the United States, our planes had always been marked with a large, white, five-pointed star near the wing tips, one very similar to today's. In France, we had discarded this star, on some theory that it might be confused with the black crosses of the German planes, and that as a consequence, Americans might be attacked by British and French flyers. How any pilot—a young man with the best of eyes, and not the bifocaled, pince-nezed orbs of some deep thinker in Washington—could ever mistake a white star for a black cross, seems utterly improbable, but the idea prevailed, and our wing tip insignia had been changed to conform with those of our allies, in yet another design of three concentric circles. In our case, the outer circle was red, with an inner circle of blue, and a white center. The French and the British had the same colors and circles, but in differing order, and the Italians and the Belgians had circles with their respective national colors.

Circles for all of us Allies was all right with us pilots, but the doughboys, the foot GIs of that war, did not understand the markings. "No star on that buzzard," they would say, seeing us at a low altitude. "Shoot the no-good sonofabitch down," some officer would command, who should have known better, and itching fingers would crook by the dozens. Fortunately for us, few infantry men had had much practice on leading on such fast-moving targets, and veteran duck hunters were few in each company. None of our planes were ever shot down in this way, at least officially or to our knowledge, but our planes were occasionally hit, and the stupid business could be pretty irritating to a flyer.

On this mission, we saw few German troops to shoot at on the roads. Temporarily, our advance had come to a halt, and the Boches, except those dead or taken prisoner in the first hours of the drive, were no longer retreating, but had dug in and taken new positions. We did scatter a few groups with swooping bursts of fire, and someone went low on a staff car, chipping the paint off its body, and so raking it that the low, open car swerved into a ditch, tossing out five peak-capped officers, who rolled in the mud as we flashed overhead. Then the mists thickened to a grey soup, the rain in our faces stung harder, the black clouds pressed still lower, and we returned to our base, sometimes flying at such low altitudes that we were forced to zoom the roadside trees, in the manner of steeplechasers over fences, and causing some chance-encountered American infantry to lie flat or duck, on seeing us suddenly come swooping out of the murk, only a few feet above their heads. Just before reaching our field, my oil pressure gauge dropped sharply, and I was barely able to effect a safe landing. For that day, our other patrols had more or less similar reports as to the situation, although the rain caused some motor failure and forced landings, fortunately on our side of the vague front lines. For us so far, there had been no air victories, but also no losses.

The second day of St. Mihiel had more sunshine and a higher cloud level, but I was temporarily grounded. My engine had to be taken out for a complete overhaul, and there was no available replacement. That day, seemingly endless columns of horribly dirty, unshaven German and Austrian prisoners—over fifteen thousand, we heard—were marched and herded past our field, with a thin, but very hardboiled, single file of our infantry, at ten yard intervals on both sides of them.

Here were the glorious representatives of the master race—the *Herren Volk*—the partners of Gott, the splendid descendants of Barbarossa, being drive like cattle to the pens that awaited them. They no longer looked like part of the Kaiser's army. They looked like a ragtag collection of hooligans, and even in the open air, one could smell them. Once, one of them broke ranks to squat by the roadside and relieve himself. A short, thickset doughboy, his tin hat at a cocky angle, gave him a prod with his bayonet. "Get a move on, Hindenberg," he said. "We ain't got time for your comforts."

In contrast to the dejected herd of prisoners, the atmosphere of our field and the skies above was electrifying. Scores of motors were purring on the flight line, then roaring like lions into life, as they warmed up, flights were taking off, flights were landing from the battle, while above there seemed to be an almost continuous procession of flights, and even full squadrons from other fields—French, British, and ours—sweeping across the skies, appearing then disappearing behind cloud wisps, their combined motors sounding like swarms of angry bees, as they headed for the lines, to strafe, to bomb, and to combat with the German air power. The heavens sounded like a great, rushing torrent of wind, and the air was charged with an intense excitement and a kind of wild joy, greater emotionally but similar to the gathering of the crowds, and the sudden, fast running appearance of the team, before some great football game.

Planes kept landing, pilots hopped out, and reports came with them. For one, there was "Texas" Tobin, a pilot of our group, although not of our squadron. His eyes were great black circles from the blown back smoke of his own guns, and he told how he had dove upon and strafed a train full of German troops, so raking the locomotive that it had stopped in a great cloud of escaping steam, his bullets had sent great splinters flying from the wooden cars, and he had returned to strafe the men who poured out of them. Many of these had fired back, and he had over a dozen holes in his wings and a splintered strut for his repair crew.

Another was "Little Gene" Jones of the 103rd Squadron. His flight had encountered an artillery column on the road and, through tight lips, he spit out words about horses wildly running and jumping fences, of guns hitting boulders to bound high and overturn, of gray uniforms scrambling for cover, and of tangled masses of men, horses and guns, surprised and in great confusion. His plane too had suffered, and there was work for his crew of mechanics, but all this was typical.

All that day, the reports kept coming in. There were new German squadrons, which had been transferred from other fronts, and these were filled with expert and veteran fighters. No longer were the Huns being met in small flights of three to six planes, but in layer on layer of flights, piling up like huge and threatening thunder clouds, and giving battle at all altitudes. There were shoals of the usual, round-nosed Albatross, and the Pfalz, which somewhat resembled Niewports, but there were also a great many Fokkers, formidable fighters with square-cornered, coffinlike fuselages, and projecting snouts like sharks. One group of these had their nose tips painted bright red. Richtofen's Flying Circus had arrived.

The Red Baron was dead, but the Circus was as formidable as ever. Among its winged wolf pack, there was Udet in command with sixty planes to his credit, Lothar the Killer, the brother of the Baron, Lowenhardt with fifty-three to his score, and Wuesthoff, Rheinhardt, Sergeant Thom, and one, Herman Goering. This one was then young and slim, but in contrast to the gentlemanly Richtofen, his face was hard and brutal, in keeping with the obese Nero creature he would some day become, as one of the three satanic lords of the hellish realm called Nazi Germany. None of these deadly fighters had less than a score of victories over Allied flyers to his credit, and the Circus had many more lesser aces. At its peak, the Circus may well have been the greatest collection of fighting flyers ever united in one squadron. On this day of its first appearance on our sector, one of our pilots, Lieutenant Converse, did not return from our last patrol. We had been surprised by seven Fokkers, who had come diving out of the sun, and although two of the enemy had been accounted for, we had suffered our first casualty.

The third day, still having no plane to fly, I accompanied one of our ground officers, the witty Lieutenant Sidney Gross, who was bent on obtaining confirmation from our ground troops of our two victories of the previous day. Over shell-torn and muddy roads, whose borders were constantly marked, almost like a line of telegraph poles, by the gas-swollen bodies and mute, sky-pointing hind legs of slain horses, our staff car slowly churned and wallowed its way to the little town of Thiacourt, a short time before an important depot of the enemy. A bare half mile beyond this town was our furthest outpost, and although fighting on the ground had lulled, the town was under intermittent shellfire.

On that day however, there did not seem to be much danger from this sporadic action. Like children tossing a tennis ball over a fence at each other, if one sent a shell at the Germans, they tossed one back, but otherwise, they only fired at regular stated intervals, and according to the clock. This was the methodical Teuton way, with everything in its place and a regular time for everything, but from a baseball point of view, it was no way to win ball games. It was as if a pitcher had no change of pace nor variety of pitches, and always the same curve and speed would fool and strike out few batters. They killed a wandering artillery mule in front of my shelter, while I was in the ruined main square of the town, but the poor brute had carried no wristwatch. From the tunneled entrance of the dugout, I saw him hit. It was like a jaywalking pedestrian crossing the highway against the traffic light. In a moment more, it would have turned green, and there would have been fifteen minutes of certain safety.

Although I had had a relatively peaceful and relaxing day visiting the ground troops, our squadron had severely suffered. Twelve of our planes had taken off, and in twin formations, one flight above and slightly behind the other, they were flying a protective mission, as guards for the 96th Day Bombardment Squadron, and the objectives were the German back depots, and the rail terminals from Metz to Thionville, the last a score of miles beyond our furthest advance. Twelve Spads and fifteen Breguet bombers seemed a strong combination, and quite safe from enemy attacks in most cases. However, the Circus was a horse of another color.

Wha-wha-wha! From above and out of the sun, thunderbolts, in the form of white-tailed, crimson Fokkers fell upon them, the smoky trails of tracer bullets crisscrossed all around, and before the attack could be finally beaten off, four of our Spads were seen going down, one to crash in flames near a wood. The returning mission landed when it was almost dark, but even up until midnight when hope was finally abandoned, the devoted members of the ground crews waited on the field, with flares all ready, hoping against hope for the return of their pilots.

That night at supper, we all edged up much closer to Captain Biddle, at the head of the table. We did not know the ultimate fate of Charley Drew, who lost his right arm that day, nor that of

Buck Freeman, Alton "Little Steve" Brody, and Converse, but there was no doubt as to poor George Kull. He was dead in the hot flames of his Spad, named Helen Air, and no more again would ever take his countess friend to tea and cakes at Paris Rumplemeyers, as he had once delighted in. The next day, Robert "Red" Stiles, of the immortal stagecoach story, was shot down and killed by the Circus, and although I had been with him at Harvard, I was not with him in that fight, since I still had no engine in my plane.

Inside the next few days, the drive was over, the salient had been straightened out, and the objectives, for the time being, had been fully obtained. The air war had also slackened, and we had no more losses in that sector. However, although our 1st Army had scored an impressive victory, and we had confirmed some fine kills over the enemy fighters, we felt sad and depressed. There were the mute and empty seats at the table, from which had come so many jokes and laughs a short time before. We had lost almost a third of our pilots, and the missing had all been friends of long standing.

Chapter 26

THE FINAL DAYS OF THE WAR

Like a long dormant volcano coming suddenly to life, spewing death and destruction during an intense eruption, then quieting down and resuming its former sleep, our old Toul sector had become even more placid and inactive than previous to the St. Mihiel drive. The brilliant Hun Circus had departed, our victorious 1st Army was, under the direction of a certain Colonel George Marshall, effecting a remarkably secret transfer to a new sector, while leaving the green troops of the newly organized 2nd Army to hold their former lines, and our last air patrols had little more to report than would follow a stroll through fields and bosky dells, on any Sunday afternoon, back home on the farm. However, since we were no longer a novice pursuit group, we were soon shifted to a coming active front, leaving our old areas and hunting jungle to the newly activated 4th Pursuit Group, in which two of our former flight leaders, Hobey Baker and Maury Jones, had been given squadron commands.

On September 23, our entire 2nd Pursuit Group moved to Belrain, a strictly pastoral locality, some eight miles north of Bar le Duc, and not a very nice place as Major Spatz remarked of it. Major Spatz, our future four-star general, then in charge of flying training at Issoudun, had been attached to our 13th Squadron, to obtain some firsthand experience in combat flying. He was with us for several weeks, and he disregarded his rank to follow experienced, flight leading lieutenants, but in his brief sojourn on the lines, he gave a very good account of himself as a combat flyer. Major Spatz, while in general charge of flying at Issoudun, could on occasion show a grim sense of humor. Once, Lieutenant —then cadet—Leighton Brewer was called before him for some minor infraction, late to reveille or similar. "Do you realize what, in wartime, could be the penalty for your lack of discipline?" said Major Spatz. "No, sir," said Brewer. "Death!" said Major Spatz and eyed him grimly.

Belrain had lately been but a flattish hilltop pasture for dairy cows, and it was no better a landing field than that, although it had been transformed into a Spad airdrome, through the erection of canvas hangars, and the usual shacks for barracks and mess halls. Below this glorified meadow, rolling and boggyish in places, and widely trapped for the unwary pedestrian, with the still pungent droppings of its former Holsteins or other bovine inhabitants—"Thank God, cows can't fly!" was the standard joke of that field—was Erize La Brulee, a hamlet of the most primitive sort, where there was nothing but the sourest of *vin ordinaire* at what passed for an estaminet, and where Madame, who owned it, had great beefy red hands, and a most probable history of having never taken a bath since the morn of her wedding day. Belrain was rustic France in its rudest guise, but it was our base during most of the great and final drive, called the Battle of the Meuse-Argonne, and for that it is remembered. We had been there but three days, when on September 26, some four thousand or so of our cannon opened with a roar, and the great battle started. From then on, we flew as many daily missions as was humanly possible, or as the condition of our planes and engines, and the replacement availability of both pilots and equipment allowed for maximum operations.

One well recalls Belrain and a certain day in October, one of those typical days for any pilot in our group, or in the 1st or 3rd Pursuit Groups, during the many weeks of our last and greatest battle. One remembers leaving the barrack in the cold raw darkness that comes before the very first light, and stumbling along a dim and narrow path, where ice-encrusted mud crackled and sucked underfoot, and where prim clusters of trees, gaunt and melancholy mourners of fall, dripped and brushed cold wet branches across one's face, and one recalls the first glimpse of our mess hall, a shadowy hut, whose one small window gave out a feeble radiance into the autumn chill and gloom.

However, once inside the creaking door, the oil lamp was softly shining over our breakfast table, and there was Captain Biddle, calm as a philosopher in a book-stacked study, giving out some new information in his brief and quiet way, Dick Este cocking an ear, while he rubbed his hands together before our cherry-red glowing stove, Frank Hays discussing some point with Murray Guthrie, and Gerry Stivers, "Big Steve" Brodie, Laddie Brewer and others of our squadron, all nervously tense in speech and manner, seated around, with one or two holding old letters for one more rereading, although they well knew their contents by heart. And as usual, there was Slim our mess attendant, an Ichabod Crane, southern mountaineer, with a body like a weed, and the mind of a nine-year-old, who would be shuffling about as he passed the eggs, or awkwardly filled our cups from the pot of steaming coffee.

"Slim," I had once asked him, "who are we fighting? Who are our enemies?"

"Sir," said Slim, "Ah really don't know, but Ah think we're fighting the French."

"Right for once, Slim," said Charley Drew. "And now, Slim. Bring on some nice, fresh, real hot coffee, and quick! Or I'll shoot you down."

Breakfast over, we put on our fur-lined helmets and oil-stained leather jackets, and went out to look into the faint white glimmer of a still morning. All about was mist, shadow, the raw cold of autumn, and that penetrating damp chill that emanates from cold rivers in the fall. Peaceful? Yes, in a way it was, back here so many miles from the lines, but the stamped-down mud was now quivering beneath our boots, and our ears were filled with a low, never ending roar and mutter, like the crash of long swells on a distant reef at night. A look toward the north! There it was, across the whole horizon, a continuous flash and dance of lurid red and silver, a solid wall of fire—Foch's orchestra, as someone had called it, playing the dance of death. But now the vague outlines of our hangars loomed ahead, and out on the flight line, one could hear the soft purrings of our engines warming up.

"Meet over the village, a thousand meters. You two fly five and six. If we go down on the Boches, you both stay up and guard our rear. Okay? Well, let's go," said our leader. For an instant, we watched his Spad gather speed over the half-frozen, tufty ground, then take the air with a jump, and a steep, sharp, spiral rush.

In turn, the others took off, while for a few moments, I continued the final checking of my plane. It had been the usual routine; first the boss of the eight-foot wooden propeller, and from there working aft, testing the tension of each wire, checking every cottar pin.

"Line her up good?" I ran my thumb and forefinger down a

flying wire, feeling for little pricking ends of possibly broken strands.

"Sure, Lieutenant," my crew chief said, as he sighted down a leading edge. "We raised this wing,"—he shook it, testing the strut—"about an inch. She won't drag, now."

"Ailerons?"

"New control wires in last night. Also the rudder and elevator. Everything is right. The gang worked most all night, sir."

"Thanks, Sergeant. You're all doing a swell job, and don't think that all of us don't know it."

The sergeant grinned. "You'll have no worry from that engine. She'll turn a good twenty-one hundred, easily."

Then, *Coupe!—Contact!* A downward sweep on the propeller, and the motor roared to life; a taxiing turn, a gathering rush, and the withered field, with its upturned faces, lay below. Then the stiff wings bit into the icy firmness of the dawn's air, the dark vapors gave way to a pale yellow light, and the hamlet was a hub, three thousand feet below, around which we wheeled and wheeled to find our alloted place in flight. Soon we were all a part of a broad V, a tightly knit, stepped up wedge of six Spads, on a long and steady climb towards the north, and a quickening sky.

Eighteen thousand feet, and the cold brilliancy of a sun-dazzled Greenland ice cap; around, about, above, below, the sense of freedom of the upper air, the austere beauty of terrific heights; below, close to four empty miles, the somber, ever reaching plain of earth. Now scanning the mosaic pattern so far below, I tried to fix our flight's position on my roller map.

Ah! There lay Souilly Field, marked by its huge white cross, the tiny, narrow gauged railroad, wandering close to it, and the long dark woods of the Argonne, with the River Aire marking its eastern flanks, until that stream turned in a great bend to the west, at the famed gap at Grand Pre. Far beneath our flight, and seemingly almost on the ground, although they could not have been less than six thousand feet, scattered woolly clouds dotted the background of the shadowy earth, and the dank morning mists still hung white in the long and narrow valleys of the Meuse. It looked as if our flight were floating on the surface of a boundless sea of glass, at whose bottom, far away in another world, lay the front lines, a broad brown belt studded with tiny red sparks, the flashing mouths of many thousand guns.

I now glanced at my companions, noting their position and manner of flight. Red, blue, yellow, and brown, our close formation droned its steady way. In this vast and utterly isolated altitude, our planes seemed unreal, more like something from the brush and imagination of a mystically minded artist, than real objects of canvas, wood, aluminum and steel, and somehow they made me think of great dragon flies, such as had once existed eons past to rule the insect world. Sometimes a scalloped flipper would move a trifle, but the detachment of these heights, the apparent lack of any motion, and above all the rhythmic hum of many motors gave a dreamlike feeling of unreality. It was as if we were not so much men as disembodied spirits, not active partakers in a living drama, but rather dispassionate observers of a play.

Onward we held our never changing course, brilliantly colored fish in an ice cold, crystalline sea, but as yet there had been no other signs of life. Now aware that the sun had well risen, I craned my neck to scan the sky above, and rolled my Spad to look below, but all I saw was the blue sky, flecked with cirrus at a still greater height, and a pellucid ocean, at whose depth spread the motley patchwork of the earth.

Again I scrutinized the depths, seeking some telltale glint of sun on varnish, a mirror's flash, or any sign that might betray an airplane camouflaged against the carpet beneath, but all there was to see were green woods and brown fields, the black and jagged stumps of tiny ruined towns, the blazing pyres of many hamlets, and roundabout a sort of never-never land, like white and ghastly craters on the moon. A grey-green anaconda snake, the River Meuse, coiled in and out this scene of desolation.

Once or twice I fired my guns, lest the cold freeze the oil of the mechanisms, and again I carefully noted the dial readings on the instrument panel. A glance at the clock. There was only an hour before we would have to return, but as yet there had not been the slightest sign of danger in the skies. Below and far removed from us, tiny beings fought, suffered, and died, but up here one was like an Olympian, an immortal, for the great battle, the actions of the earthbound marionettes seemed to have no bearing on us. We were real. They were but tiny puppets in a show.

Intoxicated by the feel of power from my Spad, by the color

and vastness of the scene, and by the cold air, which tingled the blood like frosted champagne, I sang and shouted, cursed and challenged the absent foe, and once tried to wave to my companions, but the gale almost tore the leather gauntlet from my wrist. However, the others seemed to catch the same exultant mood, for our tight formation opened up, until each plane was a good hundred feet distant from its neighbor, and each man waltzed his ship, with a slow heave and nose, and a roll to the left and right, like porpoises cavorting. Then the sun flashed and glinted on the varnish of the yellow struts, and the bright hues of the drum-taut canvas, and it seemed as if the stiff wings were sprouting from one's own shoulder blades, as the ship became the body, the man, the soul, in one living thing.

"Cr-rumph!" Four black disks hung in the middle distance, conjured as if by magic out of empty air. They slowly dissolved in shreds of smoke, while our flight held its straight course down the lines.

"Cr-rumph! Cr-rumph!" Four much larger disks, lurid in the center with red fire, bracketed us on four sides. "CRR-AAACK!" Something ripped the wing above my head, part of the contents of the small, reserve fuel tank whipped back into my face, and my plane plunged in eddies, like a young horse bucking on a frosty morning. All dreams and reveries were gone now. I watched our leader for a signal.

Another salvo shook our formation, blotting out some planes from sight with black, and acrid smoke, but our leader merely turned and grinned, then wagged his ailerons deliberately. Then on the sharp and sudden turn, our wing tips pointed to the zenith and to the nadir, and I could feel the pressure of my body crack the light cane seat. In reverse direction, our flight resumed its steady way; a few more *rafales*, and we were out of range, but the spell was broken. Now intently on the alert, we were scanning the sky for danger, peering through the lattice of our fingers into the glare of the sun, but seeing nothing, not a speck.

Out of the sun they came, like the diving charge of the fabled Norse valkyries on their winged horses, and just as deadly. Globes of dazzling orange flickered and streaked before our startled eyes, the hacking *wha-ha-aha-ang* of Spandau guns clanged like sounding bronze in our ears, and there they were: blood-red wings with bodies of gold; balanced rudders marked like chess-boards; black crosses on wing tips, coming like a hurricane from some great dive; Fokkers! They were all amongst us.

And now began a hurly-burly of the air. Above in the blue, below in the naked depths, around about, and in and out, long white streamers of smoky gossamer crossed and recrossed, floated and dissolved. These were the trails of tracer bullets which, like shuttles of incredible speed, wove the warp and woof of aerial combat. The sky hung in festoons of filmy traceries, through which planes wheeled and turned, dove and fired, appeared and vanished, all in an instant. All was a vast confusion, and as I twisted in and out the milling ships, my ears were filled with roaring engines, whistling wires, and crowning all, the ringing monotone, that harsh metallic laughter that guns seem to give out when under the great vault of the sky, miles above the sound-muffling carpet of the earth, they sound and resound in bursting spurts of fire.

All contact with comrades was quickly lost, but a few hundred feet below, a long snouted body, marked with black crosses, reared straight up on its tail to loose a conelike spray of bullets at me, close enough but ineffectual. It then fell off on a wing, and I dove to get it. I have never measured the speed of a Spad's steep dive. Perhaps three hundred miles an hour is a conservative estimate, but I remember nosing almost straight down, with the full power of two hundred and twenty galloping horses urging me faster and faster, until the wires screamed like mountain lions, the tachometer registered twenty-seven hundred revolutions of the engine, and everything shook and shivered, as when in some tide-ripped channel among the Cape Cod shoals, a heavy vessel grounds upon the ribbed and yellow sands.

The hurricane sucked around the corner of my tiny windshield, tearing the helmet from my head, the cold air seeped beneath the rubber rims of my goggles, filling my eyes with tears, but I could still see the back of a leather-clad head, through the crossed circle of my ring sight, and hear above the shrieking of the wires, the double staccato of my own guns, as the diverging cone of tracer bullets seemed to envelope the enemy. Then through the blown back smoke, a head turned in alarm, and the

Hun flipped with a roll under my wing, and seemed to vanish, completely disappearing from further knowledge.

Shaking with excitement, I gradually nosed up the Spad, fearing the built up pressure on the wings, whose canvas quivered and thundered like a drum, and then climbed upwards in steep circles. There was nothing, only empty skies. The rush, the frenzy, the mad melee of the fierce encounter had ended; the flashing whirligigs of spitting fire and smoke were gone; both friend and foe, quick and possible dead were somewhere vanished in this vast cold ocean of air. Reaching our former altitude, I cruised along, searching for the others, wondering about their fate.

I may have flown for ten minutes in this fashion, seeking my companions, even vainly calling their names. The sun, now well risen, shone with a cold and brilliant beam on the great vista below. In the hard autumn light, the white and slender ribbon of every road, the purple shadow of each fosse showed clear and distinct; the intricate networks of trenches, with their tiny, scalloped patterns, seemed intaglios upon an ochre background; the ruined steeples stood like little rotten teeth.

Over the ravished forests, the pitted desert fields, the blasted withered country northwards of Verdun, a whispy, black and greenish smoke rolled and drifted, but in the narrow valleys further south, lingering white mists gaped open, then closed upon themselves, when some great, railroad gun belched and thundered. Amidst this huge scene, I was alone. No friends, no enemies, it seemed an immense and lifeless void. Now for the first time, a strange dread swept over me. The loneliness, and a horror of something unknown, like the panic of a man lost in a wilderness, assailed and greatly depressed my spirit.

The air war was more than dangerous, and all our squadrons suffered great losses, but unlike ground warfare, which from all accounts was a grizzly business of filth and mud, of men drowning in the slime of shell craters, being buried alive in caved in dugouts and trenches, or wounded, crushed like insects under the treads of tanks, or dying of thirst while caught in the barb wire, the air war had dignity for the contestants, and great beauty for the participating beholders. The air war would have inspired a Homer, for essentially the flashing and colorful Spads and Fokkers, swirling about each other in the celestial blue, were one with Achilles of the glancing helm, and his great shield forged by Vulcan, with the horses of Diomedes, the feats of Trojan Hector, and all the personal element, and the beauty and grandeur of war found in the *Iliad*. In the ground war, the ideal of the individual, the gentleman, the aristocratic concept of the warrior had become an impossibility. Ground warfare had so degenerated under the impact of modern weapons, that each side tried to handle its opponent as a farmer would try to destroy a swarm of locusts, and the individual soldier had become little more than vermin, to be exterminated in any manner. In the air of World War I, war was still glorious and worthy of poetry. It was truly big game hunting, but unlike the modern safari and such—too often little more than stupid murder of magnificent and fast vanishing species of animals—both sides were in the dual role of the hunters and the hunted, and both sides were equally armed.

As is well known, our last great battle began on September 26, and from that date until November 11 and the Armistice, every pilot in our group flew as many as three missions a day, and seldom less than two, unless grounded for engine repairs or replacement. We flew at all levels, and on all manner of missions: regular patrols of five to a dozen planes; escorts for bomber or photo-reconnaissance planes; ground strafing of troops; balloon attacks; special missions of various sorts.

On some of our missions, we carried two small bombs that were attached to the fuselage about under the cockpit. These weapons were about twelve kilos each, and they were to be used against concentrated bodies of troops, railroad trains, parked vehicles, and light enemy installations, such as hangars and barracks. As I recall, they were not very popular weapons, since the added weight of some fifty pounds handicapped a Spad's performance, especially at the highest altitudes, and there was, in addition, a vague feeling that they were just as liable to blow one up, as to cause trouble for the enemy. When we had to carry the two vulgar little eggs, we were apt to get rid of them as quickly as possible after crossing the front lines, and on the first target that seemed at all legitimate, for they could be of too much handicap in a meeting with a Fokker.

Sometimes one of our bombs, on being released, might get caught and retained by the landing gear, and unless noticed and shaken loose by some violent maneuver, the results could be disastrous on landing. Fortunately, this did not happen to any of our squadron, but it almost did to Lieutenant Jack Seerly, one of our best pilots. Returning to Souilly Field, where our group had transferred its base during the last week before the Armistice, he playfully dove on headquarters to pull sharply up when about three hundred feet above the enclosure of the little seat of administration. Unknown to him, a released bomb had caught in his undercarriage, and this dislodged it.

It fell with a great bang right in front of headquarters, wrecking a parked staff car, and creating a near panic among our *city hall* gang, who thought that the Germans had come over, and who scurried yelling out of the building, like eunuchs out of a sacked Turkish palace, in the words of one satirical observer. Besides these two bombs, one might instead carry a traylike device of forty-eight grenades, equipped with vanes and contact plungers to drop on troop columns, by the trayfull. To most of us, they seemed less effective than our two machine guns, and few pilots ever used them.

In our squadron, we also had one Spad equipped with a 37-mm cannon, which built into the body of the engine, enabled it to fire through the boss of the propeller. With this cannon, four shells were carried; one already in the breech, and three reloaders, racked in the cockpit by the pilot's left knee. When the cannon fired, the light Spad seemed almost jerked to a stop, and the recoil of the breech seemed uncomfortably close to one's vitals. It was an unpopular weapon, for there was a feeling it might land in one's lap if fired, and its extra weight impaired the plane's performance. As one recalls, it never got too much chance to prove its effectiveness in combat, but had the war gone on another six months, many planes with cannon would have probably seen action.

We had one other innovation, a kind of make-it-yourself forerunner of armor. Lieutenant Brewer conceived the idea of inserting a round, cast iron stove lid under his seat cushion, as protection from a dreaded blow from below. This piece would have never stopped a bullet striking at a sharp angle, but it might have deflected an antiaircraft shell fragment, especially if somewhat spent. In our squadron's history, there is no record of its ever having sounded the gong, while proving its combat effectiveness, but it did add some mental relief from fear of a fate worse than death, and Brewer's *posterior protector* became a popular combat accessory. As to other arms, many pilots carried a pistol, in case of a forced landing in enemy grounds, and a few of us also carried gas masks, in case of such a happening. At this, many laughed, but gas was constantly used in that war, and a shot-down pilot, landing otherwise unhurt in the area of shell fire, would have felt rather naked without one.

Of all our many Argonne missions, three are especially recalled, one being a dramatic and tragic loss to our squadron. On this occasion, Lieutenant Guyon Armstrong was leading a rather low patrol, when he was directly hit by a shell, in full view of everyone. It might have been, but it was not enemy antiaircraft, we think, but rather a chance encounter with one of our own six-inch shells, whose trajectories our patrol was passing through. On previous missions, many of us had felt the close passage of these big shells, as our planes had bounced in the turbulence of their wakes, but this one hit, and we lost a very fine patrol leader. About this time, we also lost Gerry Stivers, and Clarence A. "Big Steve" Brodie, both shot down in combat.

On low patrols, anywhere from six thousand feet to down just over the carpet, there was, in addition to considerable fire from the ground, and ever present attack from above, a hazzard from a chance fouling with the anchoring cable of some observation balloons, either ours or theirs. These gasbags, somewhat resembling elephants in outline, roughly paralleled the front lines, at intervals of several miles, and about three miles to the rear of the no-man's-land. They could be dived on and shot down in flames with incendiary bullets, but on alarm their mobile, ground winches could wind them down with amazing speed, and they were protected by nests of antiaircraft machine guns, that could be very effective at low altitudes. However, the greater danger to a balloon attacker came from above. At a low altitude and intent on his highly inflamable target, a lone *balloon buster*—a lone, sneak attack was generally the most effective, since the crew at the winch and the balloon observers might not have warning of nearing danger—was a sitting duck to any Fokkers, that taking advantage of some clouds or the bright sun, may have hovered unseen above, and many a pursuit pilot perished in this manner.

Regarding our observation balloon service, it was organized into companies of about one hundred and fifty men, and around a half-dozen officers, with two gasbags apiece, one being a reserve piece of equipment. The observing officers in the basket were generally two, and the balloon, if the cloud stratum were not too low, generally rode to anchor at around three thousand feet, although sometimes considerably higher, even up to six thousand feet in a few instances, according to our observation. From their vantage point, the balloon observers, by telephone, regulated artillery fire, located enemy targets, and reported on all activities they could see. The two observers had no personal means of repelling an attack, but they did have very effective parachutes, in case their balloon caught fire. We lost a good many balloons to enemy action, in our three major battles, but only one observer was killed, when most unluckily the burning gasbag settled over him as he parachuted earthwards. In addition, two of our observers were carried into German territory and prison camp, when their balloon cable parted in a strong wind. Such accidents to the cable happened to others, and there was some story of a French balloon, torn from its moorings in a gale, that bounded and hopped over a great part of France, with the observers, unable to use their parachutes, in great danger before it was finally secured.

From enemy shell fire or attack planes, our service lost nearly forty balloons during our three major battles, but our balloon, ground machine gunners did bring down two attacking Fokkers within our own lines, and they may have seriously hit others who managed to get to their own lines. Towards the war's end, these balloon-protecting machine-gunners were getting pretty good, as they had had plenty of live marks to practice on.

During the Argonne battle, the Germans had one big advantage over us, on attacking balloons. As our troops advanced towards Sedan, our airfields were forced to be based further and further from the front lines, since nearer territory was too pitted with shell craters for landing fields. On the other hand, the Huns were retreating over unfought country, and their air fields could be based much closer to the lines, sometimes as much as five minutes or more of flying time, from their air field to the line of our balloons. These few minutes, little as they may seem, gave the Germans a very precious time allowance, just before night and complete darkness set in to render landing too hazardous for us to attempt, since in that brief leeway, they could attack our balloons with little fear of attack from our own aviation. During the last few minutes of twilight, they were often able to shoot down our balloons, while we could no longer linger. They were also able to use this time advantage to strafe our front lines and outposts, and this strafing by enemy planes, with none of our planes coming to the rescue, was misunderstood by our ground troops, who often swore and made bitter remarks about their own American flyers. Even some generals, who should have known the true facts, were pretty insulting, although not officially.

Concerning attacked balloon observers, they generally escaped by parachutes, and although a few may have been gunned down as they floated, it seldom happened, for most pilots of those days would never press an attack on a dangling and helpless parachutist, on the grounds that, war or not, it was a most unsportsmanlike business. As to parachutes, we did not have them, for two reasons. One, the gasbag parachutes were not designed for the cockpits of our planes; two, most of us pilots and airplane observers wanted no parachutes, considering such devices to escape the consequences of losing one's plane in combat, not in keeping with the ethics of flying warriors and gentlemen. This battle etiquette, like ancient Sparta's of returning with one's shield, or lying dead on it, sounds ridiculous today, but so do most of the ideals of a bygone chivalry. For the observer, this proud foolishness was even more so, for even untouched, he was a *gone 'coon*, if his pilot was killed, or the plane ruined while airborne. It took a brave man to be an observer in those days, especially with a day bombing squadron.

As for chance fouling of balloon cables by an airplane, on clear and not too windy days there was little danger, but when clouds hung low and perhaps, for the time, enveloped a balloon, it was easy to miss seeing a slender cable. Also, even if the balloon were seen, but a strong wind was blowing, a pilot might not realize that the cable was extended at a great angle from ground to air, instead of rising perpendicularly to the floating gasbag. From such causes, planes were lost by fouling cables, although to none in our service that I heard of. However, there were many close calls, and I once swept by, not a wing's span from a cable whose balloon was hidden by a bank of clouds.

Our first use of captive observation balloons were round gasbags in the Civil War, and in the service of the Union army. For some reason, they were little exploited, but more use might have handicapped General Lee from so pulling the wool over the eyes of many Union commanders, such as at the Battle of Antietam. They were of great value in World War I, but advanced techniques have made them useless, and World War II did not use them. Like the sailing warship, and the cavalry, they are gone for good, but although the other, obsolete arms have been depicted in songs, poems, and stories, the public knows next to nothing about our once-efficient, brave and valuable balloon service.

Another memorable mission was a great bombing sortie in October. On this occasion, all our available bombers, Libertys and Breguets, from the 96th, 20th, 11th, and the 166th Day Bombardment squadrons, some forty-odd in all, and escorted by around one hundred Spads, from our three pursuit groups, flew in World War I's greatest aerial armada to strike the concentration points of any German counterattacks, their reserves coming up, and the roads and railroads supplying them. That day, our bombers flew from around ten to twelve thousand feet, and we flew over them, layer over layer, squadrons and flights at increasing altitudes, up to almost twenty thousand feet.

Our squadron, and especially our particular flight flew at the tip top of the whole show, and I, as tail-man-high, rode at the apex of the pyramid, a mighty safe position, save from engine breakdown, which seldom happened. It was a clear day and a most magnificent spectacle, as some eighty or so, 250-pound bombs fell and the earth, as ground witnesses reported, seemed to rise in huge fountains. This effort, puny though it sounds by modern standards of destruction, did seem to have been fairly effective, and to have caused some consternation and confusion to our ground enemy, and it did cause the Fokkers to attack with fury and desperation. However, they were outnumbered and beaten off, with some eleven of them shot down, and no losses, of bombers or Spads, on our side. This alone was enough to make the sortie a great success, and this, at last, was day bombing as it should be, with ample escort for a strong force of bombers, and not the small, unprotected, and too often, all but suicidal missions that had resulted in such great losses to our day bomber squadrons.

Although I missed it, we flew a patrol during the last few days before the Armistice, which seemed to point out that the Germans were running short of even half trained, replacement pilots, and were being forced to use those of the greenest sort. Our six-man patrol met seven Fokkers, and shot all down but one, without any loss on our side. Our patrol reported that it was just like shooting down a bunch of sheep, for the Fokkers flew right under them, and did not know what to do on being attacked. This was far different from our former encounters with the old and formidable Circus, but by this time the German air force was also running short of high-test gasoline, of rubber (then used as shock absorbers on the landing wheel axles), and of other spare parts for their planes, in addition to experienced pilots.

When the Armistice finally came, the 13th Squadron had suffered a total loss of thirteen pilots, from an original roster of twenty-one. Of this total, five were killed in action, one was shot down, losing an arm and being taken prisoner, six others were shot down and taken prisoner, and one was all but killed in a crash. Although these casualties were not inconsequential, for only four months of flying combat missions, they were much less than than those suffered by several other squadrons, such as our day bombers. On many of these missions, our bombers might use up all their ammunition in fighting off a Fokker attack, only to be attacked by another swarm of black-crossed hornets as they ran for our lines. On such occasions, and they were too many, the lucky survivors of our day bombers told of throwing the empty cartridge drums at diving Fokkers, since that gesture was all they could do. The four squadrons of the 1st Pursuit Group had considerably heavier losses, but they were in action months before we were, and at Chateau-Thierry, they were both outnumbered by the enemy, and up against the Circus and other much more experienced pilots.

It was down there around Chateau-Thierry that many, among them Quentin Roosevelt, were shot down, and a pursuit pilot had, at best, about three weeks of life as expectation. Our 2nd Pursuit Group, and our 3rd Pursuit Group, both not in action at Chateau-Thierry, but on the then quiet Toul Sector, had had it comparatively easy on the casualty lists. On the other hand, in the Argonne, which was our "Chateau-Thierry," our two groups suffered more than the more veteran 1st. In combat flying, *experience* was the most important arm and armor of a pilot, but too many did not live long enough to acquire it.

On the credit side, we had received confirmation for 28 victories, and several of us were given the DSC, and most deservedly. I rated no medals, there then being no minor decorations, for flying some minimum number of combat missions, as in World War II, but when the war ended, I had engaged in about eighty, two-hour missions over enemy lines. I would say that this was about the average for the survivors of our original bunch, that started in July on the Toul front, and our own squadron had completed a total of about three hundred patrols or other missions, which was probably typical for an American pursuit squadron, for the same length of stay on the front. All in all as that war went, our squadron had not had it too tough, nor too easy. For the length of time in action, the job had been about normal.

Officially at the Armistice, we had forty-five squadrons, and close to nine hundred planes, on front-line duty with our 1st and 2nd Armies, but a great many, if not the majority of these squadrons, arrived too late to experience much action with the 1st Army, and those with the new 2nd Army, on the old, quiet sector to the east of the Meuse River, saw very little of any consequence. The brunt of the American air effort had been carried by little more than twenty-five squadrons all told, including pursuit, bombardment, photo-reconnaissance, and observation units, with a total effective force of probably no more than three hundred planes on any given day, and far less on many occasions. Ours had been but a small percentage of the total Allied air power, but it was rapidly growing at the end, and the Germans knew this and saw it with dismay. In all, we lost 289 planes, with their pilots and gunner-observers, in combat, but there were probably many more where the planes alone, but not the crews, were put out of business. At any rate, we lost a good sixty percent of the crews that saw any considerable action, and of these a good half were killed in action, and a few in crashes.

As to total American victories, we were officially credited with 781 confirmations, but a great many of us who flew over the lines in those battles doubt that we ever so surpassed the Germans, and we think that the total was far, far less. For this we have several reasons, the main one being that the average well-trained German pilot, flying his excellent Fokker pursuit plane, was no setup for anyone, even an ace of reputation, and he was just as good as most of us. As to any confirming of our probable or possible victories, they were very difficult to fully ascertain, since the great majority of our air fights took place well over the front lines, and the wrecks of the majority of claimed German planes could not be located, even after the Armistice. In fact, less than one hundred were absolutely confirmed, either by capture or inspection of the wreckage. As to all this, German records would have shed much light, but for some reason, they seem to have been destroyed, although one should think that subsequent interviews with veteran members of the German air force would have brought out a pretty accurate version of their official losses.

With regards to individual scores, there seems, at least in many cases, to have been a great deal of reduplication, where more than one, and sometimes as many as five pilots shared in a victory over a single enemy, but each one was given full credit for a kill, since everyone had taken a shot at some plane, and it was impossible to know whose burst had really scored. More than one of our rated aces has privately admitted that he was only really sure of a certain minimum number of victories, in one case as little as one, but that to his surprise he had been credited with a good many more, in cases where he had merely reported that he had fired his guns at some enemy who had then disappeared somewhere, but had not actually been seen to catch fire or to crash. All this is pretty understandable, if one has ever witnessed, as a participant, the great suddenness and utter confusion of many aerial combats, such as between Spads and Fokkers. On the other hand, the outcome of a deliberate attack, on a lone German photo-reconnaissance plane, was generally known without the slightest question, and the same with an attack on a balloon. These are just opinions, but in connection I quote below excerpts from a recent letter of a World War I veteran pilot, and later a famous, air force general:

November 4, 1959

Dear Stu:

. . . . In regards to our claims of German victories, I certainly agree with you. During the show in the Pacific, where we synchronised pilots watches and used camera gun pictures, also timed with watches for confirmation, we normally took off about 40% of the pilots' claims. After the war was over, investigation of the Jap records showed that we were still about 5% too high. Maybe some of the guys we reported shot down and crashing, crawled out of the wreck and had to be shot down again. The official figures of our losing 289 planes in combat is way low—it probably means that many planes in which we lost the crew as well. I was shot down twice and the planes lost, but I'll bet these were not included in the 289.

My guess is that we got a few more German pilots, then they got of ours. If we lost 289, I'd say they lost about 300. I think our reporting error was greater than I encountered in the Pacific. As far as airplane losses were concerned, our margin may have been greater, as toward the war's end, the Heinies had some parachutes. As to the number of squadrons on the front at the end of the war, again I agree with you. Not only were there a lot of them that saw no action, but the older squadrons were filled up to strength towards the end, to make an impression somewhere. The 91st, my outfit, by the 15th of November, had 24 full crews, of which only 10 had any combat experience. Finally, that Hun was a toughie. As late as November 5th, I know he was still an aggressive eager beaver, whose squadron still had 12 Fokker D 7s in it, and in spite of losing, a couple chased me back as far as our own balloon lines. I seem to remember that American air losses, during the time we were on the front, ran to about 60% of those who crossed the lines.

Best of luck etc.

Sincerely
George C. Kenney
General George C. Kenney, USAF Ret.

With regards to confirmations of claimed victories, we do not seem to have been as strict as the British, and our looser policy seems to have come from much higher up, even back in Washington, where something good was needed to offset the failure of our airplane production program. In any war, national pride demands that our side dish out more damage to the enemy than we receive from them, and how one reads history depends on whose side has written the book. From the days of extreme antiquity, extravagant claims are the norm, one of the most notable being the one about a certain Samson, who was credited with "slaying 1000 Philistines with the jawbone of an ass." What the *bad guys*, on the other side, said to this, we do not know from any records to date, but they probably retorted, that the most durable jawbone must have really belonged to the head of the then Israelite War Department.

The Armistice brought a mixed feeling to many pilots. On the one hand, we survivors were mighty glad to have won, and above all to be alive and healthy. On the other hand, our job was over, and all long preparation, hard work, and dearly bought experience were no longer needed. It was as if one had studied to become a doctor, and just as one had begun to really know something, all disease had vanished from the earth, and one had suddenly become an anachronism, an unwanted drug on the market. We were mighty glad, and yet we were sorry, for our own American air machine had just begun to roll into high gear, and we had become a veteran part of it.

Speaking of the treatment of prisoners of war by the Germans, one heard various accounts. It was said that Russian common soldiers were badly treated and more or less starved. As for American flyers shot down and captured, treatment seems to have been as correct as possible, under the circumstances that the

Germans were very short of food and other necessities. I quote from a letter of a member of the 13th Squadron, who was a POW, shot down during the battle of St. Mihiel:

> Now as to my experiences during WW1 as a POW. As I look back on it, I received fairly decent treatment. Of course we did not get enough to eat, and were fed almost entirely by the Red Cross from Switzerland. The barracks were fairly comfortable, but were getting quite cold about the time of the Armistice. There is one thing that I do remember—the morning I was taken prisoner when my motor quit, I landed very near a dugout in the trenches, and they stripped me of my watch, Sam Browne belt, a few other personal things, and all the French money I had. About a month later and many many miles inside Germany, I received an envelope with absolutely everything in it, except the Sam Browne belt. I think our boys who were privates got an entirely different kind of treatment, as they had to do some manual labor and eat the prisoners' food, which was pretty tough. Practically all the officers were in a camp at Villigan.
>
> Harry B. Freeman
> 1st Lieutenant, 13th Squadron, 2nd Pursuit Group, AEF

Chapter 27

ARMISTICE, AND BEYOND

The Armistice came at precisely eleven o'clock of the morning of November 11, 1918, almost two weeks and four months after our 13th Squadron had begun combat flying in the Toul sector. Although its coming had been rumored for several days, most of us had been a bit sceptical until the previous evening. Now on the morning of that day, every pilot in our air force knew the exact time when the last gun could, or might be fired with malice aforethought to hit the other fellow, and on this last morning patrol, every pilot kept his fingers crossed, muttered prayers, and did not seek out any unnecessary trouble or last minute glory over the lines, for to have been shot down at 10:45, not to mention 10:59 and 59 seconds A.M., just when the white-whiskered, venerable and illustrious dean of the Royal Greenwich Observatory was about to say, "HA!" and drop the big black Time Ball for the ending, would have made for a very stupid finish. Apparently, the Germans felt the same way, and if a flight of Spads had met a flight of Fokkers, I think that helmets might have been lifted in polite and formal greetings, but that no bullets would have been exchanged, except by utter madmen. However, our squadron had no encounters on that memorable morning.

Like after the final whistle to a victorious football game, the Armistice was celebrated in Paris, and all over France, in ways many times related, but even those festivities did not make for more jollity than Thanksgiving Day at the old Lafayette, now our 103rd Pursuit Squadron, whose party at Foucaucourt, for some reason or other, I attended. Here the good cheer and attending enthusiasm reached such a high pitch that almost everyone started dancing, Cossack style, ballet entrechats, Indian war dances and such, until for lack of an exciting partner, Lieutenant Percy Pyne, formerly in his Issoudun cadet days known as the King of the Kaypees, or Grand Exalted Potato Peeler, came marching in, clad in a great coonskin coat—in that war, they were fashionable in the air corps—and announcing that he was about to pick up the big, red hot, pot bellied stove, to waltz with it. Fortunately, he was in the nick of time dissuaded, but it was an interesting proposition, not to be forgotten. Shortly after, I was once more at Colombey Les Belles, there to await orders to be shipped back to the U.S.A.

By this time, Colombey Les Belles had really become Colombey Les Bums. It was still an air depot, but it was also an overnight stopping place for the countless trucks and convoys that were now servicing our 2nd Army, and those troops destined for occupation duties on the Rhine. Consequently, the base was always filled with hundreds of transients, the great majority, legitimates on duty, but also including many, army *Wandering Willies*, and other drifters. Not a few of these were pitiful unfortunates, such as Russian soldiers, made leaderless, homeless and payless, due to the revolution and the new Communist government. These poor devils had no place to go, and seldom enough to eat. Many of them drifted from one of our army posts to another, sleeping in sheds and being fed by our cooks, in return for help around the kitchens.

However, other drifters had no such excuse. These might be AWOLs or even outright deserters from all armies, with some glib tale to account for their appearance, and among these were some American hoodlums and other drafted criminals, and also some former French Apaches. These last were especially vicious types, and there were tales of more than one murder at Colombey. These generally happened after the huge, evening crap games, played by the transient truckers, after which some observant thugs would follow and waylay a big winner on some dark and lonely path to his barrack. All this was eventually put down, but not until General Pershing had taken vigorous steps to round up the army riffraff, to raise the general morale of all, and above all to check the great letdown in discipline that had arisen in many units, once the war was over.

Although there was a natural letdown in ambition, the air corps units that I observed never became as slack in conduct and duties, as did some other units of the AEF. In our squadron, there were no AWOLs, and never any trouble. However in our 13th Squadron, and this was also true of the entire air corps, the enlisted men were not only mostly volunteers, who had not awaited any draft, but were also far above the army's general average, both in intelligence and education. Many of our enlisted men were high-grade officer material, and more than one, and probably several, would have been trained and commissioned, if the war had continued. Our men had worked very hard, very efficiently, and for very long hours during the months of the fighting, and on several occasions, our air crews had worked for forty-eight continuous hours, so that the planes would be readied for combat. They were like a rock to rely on, and the pilots well knew it, and the same of course can be said for the ground officers who directed them.

During that late autumn and early winter after the Armistice, Colombey was a gloomy, rainsoaked hole, and still more depressing when the dreaded Spanish flu arrived, to take its great toll from the barracks. Not unlike the Black Death of the Middle Ages, a friend would be gay, strong and well one day, and three days later he would dead. He would be lying stiff and blue in his cot in the morning, drowned during the night by the choking mucus in his lungs. The plague itself did not kill, but it softened one up for the following pneumonia, which like that disease caught by mountaineers at high altitudes, was especially deadly. Most of these deaths might have been avoided, had the patient stayed in bed a week longer, but they felt all right, got up, and were dead the next day in many cases.

The plague was partial to the younger men, and it was the fate of several pilot friends, who had survived months of combat. They died like flies at the end of summer, and the harried doctors seemed to know nothing. Fortunately, our outfit lost only one man, poor "Shorty" Orde, he who had been our faithful orderly during the fighting. Until the flu abated, Colombey seemed like some pest-ridden camp of the Dark Ages. It was bad, but one heard far worse tales of many Atlantic crossings. It was reported that, on many a transport, scores of bodies were consigned to the deep, on every day of the long crossing. The war having ended, the Second Horseman of the Apocalypse had taken over. In the United States alone, he accounted for around one half million victims.

About this time, I heard that Hobey Baker had been killed. He had received his orders to return to the U.S.A., and he had taken off in his Spad for a final hop, when the engine failed, and a fatal crash ensued. This was very sad news to his many friends, but a great hockey stadium was erected and named for him at Princeton University, which was befitting one of our nation's greatest all-around athletes, and finest of true sportsmen.

During these dull and grim days, a fad for walking sticks arose. Everyone, from colonels down to privates who aspired to be in fashion had to have some sort of a fancy stick with which to smack his legs, or to twirl and flourish with graceful nonchalance while promenading around the purlieus. Everywhere, one could hear the swish and swosh of swagger sticks, and never before had so many Fancy Dans appeared together in one man's army. Naturally where there is a demand, there follows a supply, and those clever with tools were soon in business. Any sort of wood could make some sort of a stick, but the most desirable ones were turned from the laminated blades of damaged and discarded Spad propellers. These props were made from alternate strips of hard woods, featuring oak and mahoghany, and a slim cane fashioned from such presented the appearance of a giant, yellow and maroon, candy stick. These were *de rigueur*, and commanded a good dollar from the maker. Then the demand exceeded the supply, for there were not enough discarded propellers. Raw material had to be sought elsewhere, if free enterprise were not to wither at the base.

In the midst of this crisis, an innocent Frenchman, flying a brand-new Spad, ran out of gas in the region near Colombey, and made a forced but safe and undamaged landing. Leaving his plane in an isolated but open and level stretch of countryside, he made his way to our field, where he presented credentials, explained his predicament, and sought our kind offices as an ally. This was naturally granted, a meal was provided for the gentleman, and a truck, carrying an ample supply of high test gasoline, was despatched to the site of the Spad's landing. Approached from its tail, it looked all right, the truck halted, the two enlisted men began to unload the containers, and then I heard a kind of sound that seemed only possible within the confines of an insane asylum, being among the most dreadful screams ever uttered by human voice.

I rushed around, thinking a murder was taking place, and near the front end of the Spad, was the Frenchman, shaking and pointing. *"Espece d'espece, d'espece! SACRE NOM DE DIEU EN CIEL! SAINTE VIERGE MARIE, et SACRE JESU! Jamais, jamais, jamais! Mais, regardez la, Monsieur Lieutenant!"*

Following the Frenchman's quivering finger, I gazed at the Spad. All looked all right, except a certain detail concerning the propeller. This seemed quite foreshortened, and a good bit on the stubby side. In fact, it lacked the usual, two slender and graceful blades. They had been neatly sawed off, and only two stumps projected from the boss, like the stubby handles of an earthenware demijohn. It was difficult to keep from laughing, although my new French friend seemed on the verge of apoplexy. Naturally, all this brought about an investigation of the vandalism, there was a court martial, and a couple of new faces appeared for a long time within the barbed wire stockade of the guardhouse. The Frenchman's loss was replaced from our stock of Spad propellers, and the incident was smoothed over. Shortly after, new, striped swagger sticks appeared for eager buyers.

In order to keep mentally well, I flew as often as possible. Many of the Colombey planes were Liberty DH-4s, the loathed, so-called *Flaming Coffins* of some of our bombardment squadrons, although better liked and more successful with some of our observation units, where lack of a five hundred pound bomb load did not handicap their performance in the air. These planes were at Colombey in great surplus, and awaiting the coming day, when they would all be burnt up, in a gigantic, multimillion-dollar bonfire, since no one could think of anything else to do with them. In that war, like in our second great war, the taxpayer was the forgotten man, for the military authorities could not dream up a use for anything expensive, except as a weapon for war. War being over, the easy way to get rid of something surplus and no longer needed was to burn it, heave it over a cliff, or to sink it in the deep, blue sea, and so clear the books of it. Of course, if the discarded items had been articulate, had commanded votes, and could have put the old, political heater on Congress, this would not have happened, any more than to our hugely, war expanded, and forever after, much overstaffed bureaucracy. Some day when pigs fly, and the Russians pay back their eleven-billion-dollar debt to good old, gullible Uncle Sam, those suckers supreme, the long suffering

American taxpayers are going to hold a huge *auto-da-fe* of surplus government bureaucrats—come the happy day of that kind of revolution!

There were also some Salmson planes on the field, and I took one up, with a newly arrived transportation corps second lieutenant as passenger, and with the idea of flying over the country around Metz, to view the old lines once more, and our former, air combat areas beyond them. It would be a sort of busman's holiday outing, except for my passenger, who had never been up in an airplane in his life. This small shave-tail was very young and very curious, and before the war, he had never seen an ocean, the Ziegfeld Follies, a dry Martini, and about a thousand other things that I then took for granted as having been seen by everybody not too utterly poor, of voting age, and sound in mind and limb.

Little Goldie Bars, as a sour and cynical old major dubbed him, had seen the birds and the bees, the rippling wheat fields, and the wide open spaces of Kansas, but prior to joining the army, he had never even smoked a cigarette, for prewar Kansas had been a super-moral region, and there even to smoke a *coffin nail* marked a man as depraved, and not to be trusted with a God-fearing farmer's wife or daughter. Now my new friend was an officer, and he wanted to smoke cigarettes all the time, and to dip his beak, not into the pure running brooks of pure Kansas, but into the red wine of France, and he wanted to fly in an airplane, and much higher than an "elephant's eye." So, I took up this innocent.

We took off, reached Metz, which was some fifty miles to the north, flew low to observe the city and its surrounding ring of forts, for it had been a most formidable bastion of the Germans, and then started back, after regaining some altitude. Then, ten miles or so west of Metz, and not more than three thousand feet above the rugged terrain, my engine, which had all the time been ticking along like a fine Swiss watch, began to sputter and miss, and show all the signs of failure.

Below, was a countryside of steep, forested ridges and narrow valleys, and the nearest airfield, the abandoned German base at Mars La Tour, was too far away, but there was a flat, cleared hilltop, whose long meadow was marked out with a huge red cross, signifying a hospital site, and not to be bombed according to the rules of civilized warfare. This location seemed the only possible haven. Hoping for the best, I nosed down for it. Gliding down, I once turned my head, and yelled back at my passenger, "Brace yourself. We've got to land. It may be rough."

He nodded. His lips were tight set, and his face was white, and for him, a greenhorn on his very first flight, it must have been a tense moment. Once and not so very long ago, he had been a farmer's son, who had never seen a hill, and had thought of the tall corn as high. Now like Icarus of the sun-melted wings, he was in for a dubious landing.

"Hang on, tighten your belt!" I yelled again. "It may not be too bad, after all."

My engine now gave one last poop and quit, the stick was dead, but it looked as if my glide might just reach the open field, which was bordered by a narrow road, and which now revealed itself to be covered with many upright wands, like slender telephone poles. Over these, like a maze of spider webs, wires were strung, all radiating from some central location. All this did not look like too good a place to land, but there was no alternative.

With a last swoosh, my Salmson swept low over the country road, its landing wheels touched the stubbly, coarse grass of the meadow, and then it was rolling and humpety-bumping over the rough and rolling surface, with its broad stretching wings snapping numerous slender poles, as if they had been so many matchsticks. Finally trailing and festooned with a tangle of light wires, its run ended, with neither of us injured, and not much damage, except to the much dented, leading edges of the wings. We now climbed out, and set forth to explore and determine our whereabouts. This just seemed to be the middle of nowhere, but we followed the converging line of poles for some distance, until we came to a long, low, white stone building, topped with a cupola, and all the marks of a former military hospital.

Within were long narrow halls or rooms, whose bare stone floors were a confused litter of straw pallets, bloodstained, soiled and discarded bandages, empty drug bottles, and other evidence of its former but recent use. German doctors, nurses, and patients had all gone, but they had not been gone very long, for there was still the mixture of the smell of blood and hospital odors in the silent wards, pieces of not too stale bread on tables, cups filled with the dregs of some sort of poor substitute for coffee, and a great litter of personal articles, soldiers' letters from home, pictures of wives and children, and many other signs of a recent and apparently hasty departure. This great building was very empty and still, and outside, under the grey and lowering autumn sky, it seemed just as still and utterly empty.

In the entire neighboring countryside, there seemed to be no people, for the rural inhabitants had gone during the fighting, and had not yet moved back, the Germans had evacuated and marched back to the Rhine, perhaps with flowers stuck in their rifle muzzles as reported, and the troops of our 2nd Army had not yet advanced far enough over the heavily shell-cratered roads and across the wrecked, and very possibly booby-trapped bridges, to occupy this region. Now, the atmosphere of this entire area seemed weird, being so silent and devoid of all humanity, for it was not like the usual wilderness, where there may be no signs of man, but birds flutter and cry, animals rustle about, and there may be the cheerful babble of running brooks, the tinkle of little waterfalls, the beauty of wild flowers, green and majestic trees, and the general look of rich and verdant life.

This utterly still, withered and empty countryside, where no birds were seen to fly and perch, nor any animal, even a hare, to move, inspired a feeling of awe, and almost of grue. It was as if one had wandered into some large and decayed mansion, like one of those old, long deserted and abandoned, plantation houses, such as may be found on the little visited east coast of the island of Dominica, some ancient great house of a long ago and forgotten era, now filled with bats and owls, rats, lizards, and centipedes, a decayed abode of lonely ghosts and dim memories, but still showing, amidst its silent chambers and corridors a trace of former lives and a way of living, rooms where children had played, and wives and husbands had once lived a secure and happy existence. This whole region seemed like that. It was bleak, lifeless, and abandoned; a land of pits and dark tunnels, of raw, gaping holes, of fields of brown, scanty grass, that showed the mute hoofprints and dried droppings of departed horses, the ruts of heavy caisson and cannon wheels, and over all and roundabout was a dead look, gloomy and vaguely menacing, like the atmosphere of that evil, gray plain, in whose midst the ominous Dark Tower of Browning's poem, had stood. Above all, the land seemed so terribly silent.

Being curious and with nothing better to do, we explored the entire hospital. Stairs led to the cupola, from which there was a sweeping view of the surroundings, especially towards the south. It was in this cupola that all the wires converged, and there was evidence that instruments, either telephone or telegraph transmitters and receivers, had been hastily removed from their ends. Obviously, this cupola was some sort of a central directing post, protected from our day bombers by the Red Cross sign of the hospital, a clear infraction of the rules of so-called civilized war.

We followed one set of wires to its other end. This led for a considerable distance, across fields and through bare copses, until they came to what had been gun positions. This battery had been the equivalent of our six-inch field guns, for all about were abandoned collections of tall, brass shell casings, and other telling remnants. The slopes of the nearby hillocks were honeycombed with tunnels and dugouts, which we hesitated to explore, for fear of possible boobytraps. However, I did enter one, to find the elaborate, oak-paneled and tile-floored underground suite of a full colonel—living room, office, and bedroom, this latter with a walnut double bed, neatly made up, as if the orderly, through the ingrained habits of discipline of the German army, had done his accustomed job, in spite of the fact that everyone was leaving for ever. In these luxurious (for the combat zone), quarters of this Herr Oberst, I found a half-destroyed diary of his private life, and several letters. One of these was an impassioned missive from some Frenchwoman in Metz, there being plenty of collaborators in that war, as in all wars of history, since sex is an urge bestowed by God and his primal forces, whereas patriotism, like chastity, is a virtue unknown to the untaught animal, and man has only known and valued either of them, for a very brief moment of his existence.

That night, we slept supperless, except for a chocolate bar, in a room of the deserted hospital, and in my dreams, I seemed to hear cries and groans, the heavy tread of booted feet, and to see coarse red faces, under *spitzhelms*, glowering down at us. The next morning, we were doubly cheered by clear skies and a warm sun, and by the appearance of a working section of our engineer and signal corps troops, who had been sent in advance to clear the roads and bridges, and to set up communications for the rest of our occupation, 2nd Army. Through them, we were fed and got in touch with Colombey, who sent a truck and mechanics. Our trouble had been too little gas. Someone had misunderstood, and had neglected to fill our tank before leaving.

In January, our squadron got the welcome news that we were going home, and we entrained for the port of Brest, in an American-run troop train. This journey, of not over four hundred miles, took five days and nights, there was snow all the way, and we almost froze in the unheated, third-class carriages, and the jocosely famed, *hommes quarantes, chevaux huits* freight cars. However, one could take turns riding in the cab of our engine, a real, honest-to-goodness, bass-voiced, all-American, Pacific type locomotive, instead of one of those tree-frog French contraptions, and with an ex-Pennsylvania Railroad engineer at the throttle, instead of a long moustached brigand, and so get thawed out for another few hours. Finally arriving at Brest, we marched six miles to stone cavalry barracks that dated back to Napoleon, a general who did not think it necessary to pamper soldiers. In damp, stone corridors, and surrounding, floorless tents, we stayed for forty continuous days of rain, drizzle or sleet, until the countryside was a horrid quagmire, our spirits had sunk to the lowest level, and it seemed small wonder, that most of the Bretons that one saw, appeared to be such hard drinkers.

These Breton fishermen and small farmers seemed very unlike the typical Frenchmen we had previously encountered. They did not speak their own country's language, but some barbaric tongue, called Breton or Amorican, which was some horrible form of Gaelic, or Cornish, or Welsh, and incomprehensible to us. All in all, their speech seemed more fitting for their ancient Druid ancestors, than for good Catholics. All of a week, these Bretons worked hard at pulling in their nets, or grubbing their tiny fields, but by Saturday night the old Druid blood would start boiling over, and the old fun of blood sacrifices being illegal, most of the male population got roaring drunk, staggered along the roads, singing and even tossing empty bottles at our passing trucks, and many might lie around in the highway ditches, until they were assisted home, reeling and shouting, by their sober and strangely sympathetic wives or sweethearts. It was a strange corner of France, still somewhat of a hangover from the Middle Ages, with possibly the last of the werewolves wandering its waste spaces, and in one nearby village, no one got married, except on one special day of the entire year.

Then, all the engaged couples, some already with tiny infants in their arms, got married, in one big, general ceremony, and there was dancing and drinking, hoopla, singing and feasting, and the baptizing and legitimatizing of all babies, until, as the saying goes in the Vermont dairy regions, the cows came home. All this seemed not France at all, but more like some county in wildest, westernmost Ireland, before the coming of Saint Patrick.

Finally the agony of the rains and the mud was over, we were once more deloused in the nearby army delousery, and we then embarked on the S.S. *Amerika*, a former German liner taken over by our government, and we were bound for the port of New York, in company with an artillery brigade of the 27th Division. On our big ship, the cargo had been badly stowed, or something else was askew, for the vessel had a great list to port, and had a great storm arisen on the voyage over, we might have all gone to the bottom, to sample the cold damp fare of Davy Jones's Locker. However, a special section of Providence is said to watch over drunkards, sleepwalkers, and the enterprises of the United States government, and we had continuous good weather.

As for the 27th Division, most of them spoke tongues called Bronx, Brooklyn, or similar, while our men spoke plain American, and there was little fraternization. Then one clear night, Nantucket Lightship flashed to starboard, the next morning we entered Ambrose Channel, passed Sandy Hook, nosed through the Narrows off Staten Island, and the great Statue of Liberty, which for many months I had thought never to see again, loomed into full view, and also the marvelous skyline of New York City, thrilling and dynamic, and our hearts choked to see it. Escorted by all sorts of smaller vessels, greeted by roaring whistles, we warped up to a dock, where a huge crowd waited, men, women, and children, waving flags and cheering. We too cheered and waved, and not a few may have wept and even prayed, for we were home.

Back in the U.S.A. and at Mineola once more, we were all soon discharged. Everyone hastened to get out of uniform as quickly as possible, and very few, that I knew of, gave the slightest thought of signing up for any sort of a reserve military status. What for? The Great War To Save Democracy, the Great War To End All Wars had been won by us, had it not? There would never, never be another war, at least a major one? Of course not! That was the great and solemn assurance of our great and most wise, modern Olympians, in the supreme ranks of the victorious Allied governments, and everyone believed it. It was a fact. Accordingly, in New York, the world's most stimulating city, there were parades and excitement, and lots of parties. Many of the best were small, select dinner dances at private houses, where I again encountered my *sweet friend and ladye faire* of some eighteen months previous.

"Oh, how wonderful to see you again!" she said, and she was as beautiful as ever, but there was her fiance in white tie and tails, tall and protective, and smiling as blandly as a Buddha, and actually an excellent fellow, in spite of having been a captain in the ground forces. So all that was like yesterday's newspaper, or that ticket at the track, when your front runner on the rail gets caught in the last yards, by the comer-from-behind, who can run in the stretch.

Besides the smaller private parties, there were huge Victory Balls at the great hotels, where entertainers like the Six Brown Brothers, dressed like clowns, and tootling on saxophones, snaked in and out the dancers. These were attended by a mad crush of almost everybody, except those lying in hospitals, or more quietly in the fields of France, and although some bitter British poet wrote something, that went something like "See how those dead men grin by the wall,/Watching the folk at the Victory Ball," with some other lines, descriptive of many of the dancers, war profiteers and similar fat cats and rich riff-raff and their womenkind, ". . . with a fat wet hand, on a fat wet back," and everything as sweaty as a county horseshow in July, few people read much poetry, and fewer still did much real thinking. As to the general atmosphere of back home—New York—and, I imagine many another big city, it was filled to the brim with beautiful women, with the come-hither and the devil in their eyes, but in spite of this, many of us felt sunk, and spent long afternoons in club grills, and dark, depressing bars, gloomily drinking, and listing ourselves as bona fide members of the Grand Order of The Utterly Useless Club.

About this time too, something called the Aviators' Club got going in the city. One of the prime movers was no flyer, but a sculptor, named Gutzon Borglum, a character of incredible energy, who seemed to be *ag'in the gov'ment*, and who wanted to sign up all us pilots, to overthrow the War Department, because it had so mismanaged airplane production. One doubts if any of us were too interested in all this, as we had too many personal problems of our own, and little came of it, but Borglum went on to carve out colossal heads of four of our country's presidents on the face of a mountain, two Republicans, one Democrat, and George Washington, who belonged to no party, all of which seems to put the G.O.P. one up on the party of the *pee-pul*, at least when it comes to carving out the hills eternal.

In time, our depression, since we were young and the world was an open door before us, gave way to a great talk of what were going to do, and how to get into the ground floor of something that was bound to grow rich, and how our past was all over, and best, quickly forgotten. However now and then, someone would remember France, and an ex-pilot might sing:

Maintenant, la guerre est finie,
Tous les soldats partis,
Mademoiselle's in a family way,
Elle a un Americain pickaninny.

That was just a ribald jinglet, but although none, except a very few wise men, suspected it, Mademoiselle Europe was already pregnant with the embryo of another big war in her womb, but the really wise men had little following, and the general idea was to forget the whole thing, and to let *old Yurrop stew in her own juice*, as some brutually expressed it. All over the U.S.A., there was an immense sentiment for national isolation, for a return to *normalcy*, some kind of prewar, general status, and President Wilson, the League of Nations, and a lot of Democrats were like gone 'coons up a gum tree, surrounded by hunters with houn' dawgs and shotguns. There then arrived Prohibition and bootleg liquor, womens' suffrage and bobbed-haired flappers, the Charleston and the great Banana song, a frenzied scramble to get rich, and so much mushrooming country clubs, and such a bursting of exuberant breeches all over the nation, that coming from way down deep, in the bottommost pit of Hell, no one heard the Devil's loud and scornful laughter.